Readers acclaim the first edition of

Whole Child
Whole Parent

"*I can hardly contain the joy and elation that keep welling up from within me as I read* Whole Child/Whole Parent. *It gives me a 'feeling for wholeness,' along with a sense of 'it is possible—loving is possible.'* "

"*It would be difficult to overestimate the positive influence you, through your book, have had on my life. . . . The practical advice it contains is valuable, but the spiritual insights are invaluable.*"

"*Reading* Whole Child/Whole Parent *is like having a spiritual revelation. . . . Books by Dr. Spock, John Holt and Piaget share space in my library. But not until I found your book did I realize what parenthood could mean, the spiritual depth it could attain, and the inner growth I could foster within my child and myself by being a 'loving' parent to my child.*"

"*I have been one of those for whom parenthood has been 'easy' and I think one reason is that you have helped me to see what is true about it. . . . It must have taken courage to write such a book. Watching my little girl blossom, less hindered than she might have been otherwise by my errors, I am extremely grateful to you for sharing what you have learned.*"

"*In the past few years as a mother and La Leche League leader I have read a great many books about childrearing, but never have I encountered one so calming and yet so inspiring as yours.*"

"*I want you to know that* six *years and three children later your book is the one I seek out more than any of the others. . . . In its pages I find the highest level of guidance during those times when my foggy and worn consciousness can't quite get to the truth.*"

Whole Child
Whole Parent

Books by Polly Berrien Berends

The Case of the Elevator Duck
I Heard, Said the Bird
Ladybug and Dog and the Night Walk
Vincent, What Is It?
Ladybug and Dog Tales
Who's That in the Mirror?
Whole Child/Whole Parent

Whole Child
Whole Parent

Revised Edition

Polly Berrien Berends

1817

HARPER & ROW, PUBLISHERS, New York
Cambridge, Philadelphia, San Francisco, London
Mexico City, São Paulo, Sydney

Grateful acknowledgment is made for permission to reprint the following:

Passages from *The Sailor Dog* by Margaret Wise Brown. Copyright 1953 by Western Publishing Company, Inc. Reprinted by permission.

"i am so glad." Copyright 1940 by E. E. Cummings; renewed 1968 by Marion Morehouse Cummings. Reprinted from *Complete Poems 1913–1962* by E. E. Cummings by permission of Harcourt Brace Jovanovich, Inc.

"i thank you god." Copyright 1947 by E. E. Cummings; renewed 1975 by Nancy T. Andrews. Reprinted from *Complete Poems 1913–1962* by E. E. Cummings by permission of Harcourt Brace Jovanovich, Inc.

"love is a place" from *No Thanks* by E. E. Cummings by permission of Liveright Publishing Corporation. Copyright 1935 by E. E. Cummings. Copyright © 1968 by Marion Morehouse Cummings. Copyright © 1973, 1978 by the Trustees for the E. E. Cummings Trust and George James Firmage.

Passages from *The Dhammapada* translated from the Pali by P. Lal. Copyright © 1967 by P. Lal. Reprinted by permission of Farrar, Straus & Giroux.

"Child Moon" from *Chicago Poems* by Carl Sandburg, copyright 1916 by Holt, Rinehart and Winston, Inc.; copyright 1944 by Carl Sandburg. Reprinted by permission of Harcourt Brace Jovanovich, Inc.

"Baby Toes" from *Smoke and Steel* by Carl Sandburg, copyright 1920 by Harcourt Brace Jovanovich, Inc.; copyright 1948 by Carl Sandburg. Reprinted by permission of the publisher.

"Star Wish," from *Lullabies and Night Songs* arranged by Alec Wilder, edited by William Engvick. Copyright © 1965 by Alec Wilder and William Engvick. Reprinted by permission of Harper & Row, Publishers, Inc.

Music from "Seal Lullaby" arranged by Alec Wilder from *Lullabies and Night Songs* arranged by Alec Wilder, edited by William Engvick. Copyright © 1965 by Alec Wilder and William Engvick. Reprinted by permission of Harper & Row, Publishers, Inc.

Lyrics from Rudyard Kipling's poem "Seal Lullaby" from the *Jungle Book* by Rudyard Kipling by permission of Mrs. George Bainbridge, the Macmillan Company of Canada Ltd and Macmillan London Ltd.

Passages by the author, Polly Berrien Berends, from *Growing Child Store* and *Growing Parent*. Reprinted by permission of Dunn & Hargitt, Inc.

Designer: Abigail Sturges

Library of Congress Cataloging in Publication Data

Berends, Polly Berrien.
    Whole child/whole parent.

    1. Child rearing.   2. Children—Care and hygiene.
3. Children's literature—Bibliography.   4. Parenting—
Religious aspects—Christianity.   I. Title.
HQ769.B515   1983   649'.1   81-48029
                                AACR2
ISBN 0–06–014971–X   83 84 85 86 87 10 9 8 7 6 5 4 3 2 1
ISBN 0–06–090949–8 (pbk.)   83 84 85 86 87 10 9 8 7 6 5 4 3 2 1

And he replied, "Who are my mother and my brothers?" . . .

Whoever does the will of God is my brother, and sister, and mother."
—Mark 3:34–35

TO MY BELOVED FAMILY
in fact and in truth
especially
Mary and Curtis

Contents

Acknowledgments

In addition to Thomas Hora whose important contribution to this work is discussed more fully elsewhere, I would particularly like to thank the following:

Jody Blatz, Leslie McKenzie, and Tessa Melvin for helping enormously with the writing of this book by providing when needed the kind of detachment it would have taken me months to achieve;

Sue Alexander, Midge Dunne, Susan Goldberg, JoAnn Ross, and Nina Smith for generous help with parts of the manuscript;

My husband, Jan Berends, with whom all my living and learning takes place and who never fails to have flowers blooming near my typewriter;

My sons, Jan Berrien Berends and Andrew Lukas Berends, who, without rivalry, accepted *Whole Child* as a sibling and lent me to it with extraordinary patience through long nights, weekends, and vacations;

Rowie Edelman, Sooky Kyle, and Jan and Ann Linthorst for active enthusiasm and support of this book since its first publication;

Cleta Booth, Arlene Donegan, and Beth Lewis, whose early teaching of my children taught me;

Debbi and Andy Ostrovsky for important inspiration;

Dennis Dunn and Pat Payne for giving me the opportunity of reviewing children's books, thus preparing me for this updated edition;

Ed Ball, Robert Baensch, Lyn Canfield, Paul Edelman, Jethro

Lieberman, Stan Mack, and Frank Scioscia for various kinds of counsel and assistance to this project;

My students and clients for rich instruction and good company on our mutual journey;

Readers of the first *Whole Child/Whole Parent,* whose astonishing letters and continued demand for the book have been largely responsible for giving it this new life;

Corona Machemer, editor of this edition, for seeing to the heart of the first edition and for valuable editorial direction in this fuller work;

Hugh Van Dusen and Janet Goldstein, my new editors at Harper & Row, for their warm welcome and for bringing this work to fruition (it is indeed wonderful to have fallen into such capable and caring hands);

William Monroe, copyeditor supreme, who couldn't have been kinder or more patient, and who made the change of editors mid-production seem almost natural.

"Why do elephants paint their toes red?"
"I don't know. Why?"
"So they can hide in cherry trees."
"I never saw an elephant in a cherry tree."
"See, it works!"

"How are you?"
"Perfect, thank you. I'm just traveling incognito."
"Oh? As what are you disguised?"
"I am disguised as my self."
"Don't be silly. That's no disguise. It's what you are."
"On the contrary, it must be a very good disguise, for I see that it has fooled you completely."

Introduction

*Once I had a dream. In the dream I was to receive a diploma
as a spiritual teacher or guide of some sort. There were two of
us being presented with such a certificate at the time. The other
was a man—Swamibabagururishiroshirabbisoandso. He wore
long colorful robes and had a fist full of degrees and papers.
To receive his diploma he only had to step forward and present
himself with his long titles, flowing robes, and abundant
credentials. But before me there stood an enormous mountain
of laundry. To receive my diploma I would first have to climb
over this huge heap of laundry.*

When *Whole Child/Whole Parent* was originally conceived, I had one baby and was fairly shy about speaking in overtly spiritual terms, except among fellow seekers. In my own life I was examining certain spiritual insights, looking to see how they were true in parenthood. Like any new parent I found it hard. I got stabbed by diaper pins that popped open and experimented with a theory or two that either didn't help or turned out to be distractions. But the spiritual insights validated themselves ever more clearly—and they proved to be so practical! I just couldn't imagine how parents without this spiritual viewpoint could get by at all. So, as if I didn't have my hands full enough with one baby, I conceived again: of a book, a book baby. Almost immediately our second child was also conceived, and I was doubly pregnant.

As conceived, the book was to be a sort of catalog. Based on my experience as a new parent and my past as a children's book editor, I would put together a practical book about what I wished I had known (such as which diaper pins stay closed), and what I was glad I knew and was sure other parents would appreciate (e.g., the tremendous value of books, and which books, for preschoolers). In between, I would sneak in some spiritual ideas which I knew were the only important issue, but which I didn't think many people would be interested in at first. So it would be a catalog of books and things and tips on using them, and here and there would be this smuggled truth. The publisher planned to offer by direct mail everything recommended in this "whole child catalog." There was even to be an order form at the back of the book.

It seemed such a great idea: direct mail for new parents, just when it was suddenly not easy for them to get to the store; an expert selection of books for young children; and all those smuggled nuggets of truth which I hoped some would find inviting enough to pursue further. As I write, it still seems a fine idea; it seemed fine then, too—right up until the day after I signed the contract, when the book disappeared in my mind. It was a good idea; someone could make a fortune with it; it would even be helpful; *but I could not write it that way.* Placing so much emphasis on techniques and things without discussing forthrightly the spiritual principles that led to their discovery suddenly seemed misleading, even dishonest. So despite all my careful planning the birth of *Whole Child/Whole Parent* came as a shock because, as with all babies, this baby (and how to raise it) was considerably different —and more spiritual—from what it was expected to be.

Doubts and fears notwithstanding, in due course, a book that surprised even me did get written and was successfully published. And though it was decided not to sell even the recommended books by mail, after a few years, from out of the blue, the publisher of a newsletter for parents contacted me. He had read *Whole Child/ Whole Parent* and wanted me to select and write about preschool books which he would then offer by direct mail to his subscribers. So part of the original idea came to fruition after all. And thus incidentally I was kept up to date on new children's books, so that when it was time for a revision of *Whole Child/Whole Parent,* I just happened to be ready to update the book lists with a minimum of effort. Isn't it wonderful? We all have ideas that we think are ours —and that we will put to use to serve our own purposes. Instead, over and over again, we can see that the ideas have a life of their own and that, after all, it is they that are putting us to use!

When the opportunity came for revision, I told my new editor the story of how *Whole Child/Whole Parent* had turned out to be a more spiritual book than anticipated. "And now it will be even more that way, won't it?" she said brightly. I concurred, signed the contract, but again found it surprisingly hard! It was clear that all the material originally included for the book as a catalog could be deleted, dated information removed, the book lists streamlined and updated, the rest smoothed out. Generally the book would become more spiritual and be expanded somewhat to include parents of older children. Easy. Obvious. But in practice, less clear and not easy.

Whole Child/Whole Parent was originally prepared when I had two piles of diapers in my house. Now my children are older. Now diapers and pins seem too trivial to mention, and I was inclined to leave out all the material information specific to babies. Not only can you never step into the same river twice; you are also never the same person not stepping into the not same river again. So I found myself writing an altogether new book.

But something didn't sit right about this. Many parents have written over the years to say that this spiritual book is the only truly practical book on parenthood they have ever read. Others have written that at first they read only about books, toys, and techniques—but that after six months they were interested only in the "spiritual stuff." Some have written that although their children were older, they found the principles still applied. Some even say that although they do not have children the book has been helpful in their own quest for spiritual understanding.

While I was stewing over my revise/rewrite dilemma I suddenly received a number of calls from people wanting to know when the book would be available again. It was clear that they weren't looking for anything other than the original. So it was brought home to me that while there are other books to be written, the old *Whole Child/Whole Parent* still had a job to do—one a completely new book, maybe even a better book, might not be able to do. In some ways this is a new book. It is much expanded, for in trying to spell some things out more smoothly and clearly I have had to add material to the text. I have also tried to be more inclusive of fathers and to make clearer the relevancy of these ideas to parents of older children. But the original book is here, and everything new was there by implication in the original. At the end of most chapters are sections called "Practical Information for New Parents" which include additional information particular to the parents of very young children. For the most part, parents of older children will want to skip over these sections, as they are largely concerned with equipment, toys, books, and activities for babies and very young children. No attempt has been made to cover this information for older children because they have more individual tastes and interests. Also parents of older children are by definition more experienced, and the children themselves are able to make their needs and interests known. Particular topics of special interest to parents of older children are mentioned at the beginning of each "Practical Information" section.

Rafts for Crossing

Quotations here and there in this book are intended to show the relevance of the great mystical teachings to the practical experience of child-rearing and, at the same time, to bring to light the far-reaching spiritual significance of even the meanest momentary details of our experience.

We live in such a wonderful time. Almost all the world's great teachings are available in our own language. And they all shed light on each other! It is remarkable that so many wise ones independently have seen life in so much the same way and in such radical contrast to the views of those around them. They all have insisted that freedom from preconceptions is an absolute prerequisite to any spiritual realization. They all have maintained absolutely the importance of not confusing the teacher as a redemptive person with the redemptive teaching, or even the redemptive teaching with the redemptive truth. To be loving, to be wise, to be happy —it is all the same: everything clung to has to be let go.

Pai-chang asked: "What is the ultimate end of Buddhism?"
Ma-Tsu said: "This is just where you give up your life."
—D. T. Suzuki, *Zen Buddhism*

Jesus said, "If any man would come after me, let him deny himself and take up his cross and follow me. For whoever would save his life will lose it, and whoever loses his life for my sake will find it."
—Mark 8:34–35

Buddha said: "Only he crosses the stream of life who wishes to know what is known as unknowable."
—*The Dhammapada,* trans. by P. Lal

He also said: "Monks listen to the parable of the raft. A man going on a journey sees ahead of him a vast stretch of water. There is no boat within sight, and no bridge. To escape from the dangers of this side of the bank, he builds a raft for himself out of grass, sticks, and branches. When he crosses over, he realizes how useful the raft has been to him and wonders if he should not lift it on his shoulders and take it away with him. If he did

this, would he be doing what he should do?"
"No."
"Or, when he has crossed over to safety, should he keep it back for
someone else to use, and leave it, therefore, on dry and high ground? This
is the way I have taught Dhamma (teachings), for crossing, not for
keeping. Cast aside even right states of mind, monks, let alone wrong ones,
and remember to leave the raft behind."
—*The Dhammapada,* trans. by P. Lal

The quotations in this book are but the sticks, branches, and grass which may be useful to some to build a raft for crossing over. Then the raft can be left behind. It is better not to get caught up with the raft itself and with questions about whether it is preferable to be Taoist or Christian or Buddhist. On the near bank it is easier to build a raft using everything buoyant that we can get our hands on. There is no advantage to using only maple or only pine, especially if we are eager to cross over. On the far bank no raft is needed and will impede our progress if we linger over it or try to take it along.

In fact, no one raft gets us all the way across, and in the beginning it is usual to ride on the raft of another. When you first find your way to the near shore you may meet someone who is willing to take you partway on his raft. This is your teacher. His raft is made of the finest, aged wood, driftwood gathered from up and down the river to carry himself—his life—and anyone else who wants to go along.

In my case, this master raft-builder has been Thomas Hora. My studies in psychotherapy and religion and my personal quest for peace and joy brought me to a point on the shore where he stood completing his raft. As a God-centered psychiatrist he had selected and pulled together fine and fitting planks of spiritual driftwood into a raft of spiritually based psychotherapy. It has since come to be called Metapsychiatry because it takes him and those that come aboard beyond the shores of psychotherapy into the river of spiritual truth.

From the middle of the river the students of any master can see all up and down the river those other rafts, ancient and new, which have been gathered under different lives. Some, abandoned on the far shore by seers who have left them behind, have broken up and lie floating about for us to gather into new rafts when our time comes. Out there on the river we are taught by our teacher to build small vessels of our own. *Whole Child/Whole Parent* is such a raft.

From Metapsychiatry I have received two precious staffs that I could not seem to find anywhere else. One is the idea that God is love-intelligence. The other is the idea that all life, problems included, is meaningful, and that each particular problem we confront is presenting to us the very next lesson we need. Further, Metapsychiatry has taught me how to rig these two staffs together and to stretch between them a sail (individual consciousness) to catch the wind. The first is the mast from which the sail is hung and by which the craft is oriented. The second is the boom on which the sail is anchored and by which the craft can be steered.

So there are three types of quotations in this book: age-old statements of truth from the world's greatest teachings which in juxtaposition shed light on each other; new and recent insights and teachings which reveal the relevancy of these ancient truths to our life and times and thereby stretch even further the frontiers of consciousness; and finally, as illustrations, anecdotes and quotations from the lives of individual children and parents. Included are stories from my students and friends as well as incidents from my own family life.

The timeless teaching, the timely instruction, and the daily lessons all conspire to reveal the one great fact of a wise and loving God. My gratitude for the teachings and teachers—especially my own master, colleagues, companions, students, family, husband, and children—knows no bounds.

Zen Mom

Child: Mom, how come you know so much about God?

Mother: I don't know so much. But I have been around for a while and been to many schools and studied with many teachers. There were Moses and Isaiah and Jesus and Buddha. There were many books and professors, and Dr. Hora. But besides all those I have two private Zen masters who are always teaching me and making my learning into real understanding and love. I am very, very grateful for them.

Children: Tell us! Who are they? What are their names? You never told us about them!

Mother: Their names are Jan and Andy. It is you who are my masters.

Children [laughing]: Oh, Mom! *We* teach *you?* You're joking!

Mother: No, I am not kidding. You are my two wonderful Zen masters.

Whole Child
Whole Parent

1
Wholeness

What he saw as One was One, and what he saw as not One was also One. In that he saw the unity, he was of God; in that he saw the distinctions, he was of man.
—*The Wisdom of Laotse,* trans. by Lin Yutang

I and my Father are one.
—John 10:30

Getting married and having a baby are part of our idea of fulfilling ourselves and being "whole." We expect somehow to have a fuller life experience and complete ourselves through having and raising children.

Generally we do not doubt that we can do this. These days we all prepare for childbirth, which we know we don't know much about, but there is very little preparation for what comes afterward, even though it lasts for years. Having been children ourselves, we feel ready to go. Merely by avoiding our parents' mistakes we expect to get it right.

Yet so often parenthood turns out to be a "mixed blessing." Many of us wait long years for a baby to be born, and as soon as he's born we begin wondering when he will ever grow up. So up he grows, and immediately we are pining for the days when he was just a little baby. Along the way we often let each other down. Sometimes we hurt each other. We don't live up to his expectations; he doesn't live up to ours. Yet even when our children are unhappy or the family is in conflict, we are never quite satisfied with the idea that unhappiness is "just a fact of life." Even if we could adjust to it for ourselves, we cannot accept it for our children.

Just how difficult it is to be somebody's parent is one of the best-kept secrets around—along with that other one about being somebody's spouse. We all think we're supposed to know. Children don't know. Adults know. And because children don't know, parents above all *have* to know. So whenever it hits us—maybe before or maybe not until after the child is born—the idea that we *don't know* is both frightening and inadmissible. A successful journalist recalls:

> When I got pregnant I was so happy. I was good at everything; surely I would be good at this too. But before three months were up, it began to hit me that this was going to be *very* different from all the other challenges I had faced. So I read. Three pages into Dr. Spock panic struck. For every one thing Spock told me that I hadn't known before, fifty more previously unknown hazards were revealed to besiege my confidence. To keep from crumbling altogether I had to stop reading. I stopped just before the part about Caesarian deliveries—just a short time before my child was born by Caesarian section.

Whenever the going gets rough we each feel uniquely awful. *What's the matter with me? What is the matter with my child? What am I doing wrong? Why can't I get it right?* Nobody dares to admit how tough it is—especially not if everyone else is doing fine.

Helping to keep the secret are all the books on child-rearing, full of techniques for doing it better. Implied is that it *can* be done better. If we knew how. Which, the existence of such books implies, we don't. So we read until we think we know. And then when our efforts don't work we are more convinced than ever of our inadequacy. This is pretty hard to take, since our whole purpose in becoming parents was to be "whole"—a "whole" parent having a wholesome relationship with a "whole" child.

But what "wholeness" are we seeking? Here it seems we have two or three separate beings—a parent or two, a child. What are they? What do we mean by using "whole" to describe them?

Wholeness, we are fairly sure, has something to do with love and understanding. We want to be loved and understood, to be loving and understanding. So we become parents, a circumstance in which love and understanding clearly are central issues. But then how come it's so difficult? How come hurt and confusion happen right where love and understanding were on the agenda? Is it something the matter with us? Is it something the matter with our children? With life? Or could there be something mistaken in our *idea* of what it means to be a whole parent or child? What does it mean: whole child, whole parent?

Wholeness as Completeness

If you'll be m-i-n-e mine
I'll be t-h-i-n-e thine,
And I'll l-o-v-e love you
All the t-i-m-e time . . .
—"Zulu King," traditional camp song

We tend to think of ourselves as separate beings (I, the parent—you, the child) existing in relation to each other and trying to perfect ourselves as complete, "whole" persons. Parent and child alike are believed to be *completable*, each in quest of wholeness, each to some extent *deriving its wholeness from the other.* Without realizing it, when we think of loving each other we tend to mean getting wholeness from each other.

But whether we call it love or not, there is a certain built-in contrariness to the idea of many would-be whole selves seeking personal completeness together. In breast-feeding, for example, the apparent situation is that the mother has got what the child has not. So the mother gives of her self, and the child gets. And what is the mother getting? A sense of personal completeness *and* a sense of self-sacrifice. On the one hand she thinks she is fulfilling herself and being loving, but on the other hand she may feel secretly robbed and resentful. It takes so much time—much more than she thought—it's so tiring. Must she give up her whole life for her child?

When the child becomes more "self-sufficient," it is time for weaning. Now the mother is relieved and freed, and so is the child. But (on the other hand) they both feel cheated. The mother feels less whole, less of a mother if the child is weaned; she is less of a mother if he isn't! And while the child may seem reluctant to give up nursing, underneath it may be the mother's secret clinging that prolongs the nursing and inhibits the child's growing freedom and wholeness.

Fathers also experience such conflicts. A man wants a child to complete his marriage and his picture of himself as a whole fa-ther/husband; yet he seems to lose his wife (thereby diminishing his husband self) in the process. He wants his son to be a little man; but at the same time he wants to dominate, be looked up to and obeyed.

If we—parent and child—are indeed separate personal enti-ties packaged in separate selves, each in quest of personal whole-ness, such running conflicts of self-interest are inevitable. Just as a doctor's healing work seems to depend on somebody else being sick, so our ambition to be whole parents and raise independent whole children seems to depend on their being dependent on us. Our sufficiency seems dependent on their insufficiency. Each of us in making our claim to personal wholeness is inclined to rob the other of his claim to wholeness. But where is the love in that?

Where indeed? And where the wholeness? If there is wholeness in any of us, what is this need to go around getting it from somebody else?

If you don't think that the title of this book is *Whole Parent/ Whole Child,* then you are the exception. Most people do. The implication is that *if* the parent is whole *then* the child will be whole. *If* the parent knows how to do it, *then* the child will turn out okay. But then—oh, horrible thought and worse experience!—*if* the child seems not to be whole, *then* the parent must not be whole either. The nine-month-old next door is already walking, while our eleven-month-old hasn't taken a step. The manager of the super-market reports that our seven-year-old has stolen a package of gum. From silly to serious, every difficulty suggests to us that the child is not whole, which in turn suggests that we are to blame, which in turn suggests that we are not whole parents. God forbid!

So we seek diagnoses, explanations for what's wrong with the child. If we can't take credit for our children, then at least please excuse us from the blame! *Thank goodness it's dyslexia! I thought it was my fault. I thought he was stupid, lazy.* Secretly we are almost grateful to think that there is something really the matter with him, some-thing only mechanical. So in a strange way, the very thing we started out in favor of (rearing a whole child) turns out to be something we are somehow also against.

There are all these hidden clauses—the fine print we don't see when we make this contract to have children and become parents. We act on assumptions and motives we don't know we have; we reap consequences we don't expect.

> One mother has a wonderful governess who raised her as a child and now helps with her children. The children love the governess; the governess loves and cares beautifully for the children. Any busy mother would be delighted to have such assistance and such loving care for her children. But this mother feels rejected and jealous! In her picture of her "whole" self she is the complete, perfect mother. She wants her children to love, depend on and look up to her alone, for everything. But does she really want them to be afraid to leave her side? to find no love anywhere except from her? She sees how ridiculous this is, and yet the desire is very strong. Her desire to be

the complete mother conflicts with her being a truly good mother. And she is bewildered by the fact that her children are always pulling away from her.

Are we using our children? You bet we are. But while we are not as good as we thought, we are not as bad either—only mistaken.

The Myth of Me, Inc.

The real culprit is only a misperception of the goal we all seek, a mistaken idea of wholeness: the idea of the complete me, me embodied, me *in corpus* Me, Incorporated, Me, Inc. seeing ourselves as separate selves, we aim to complete (become whole) ourselves. But each one's would-be complete me is a proposition mutually exclusive of everyone else's, and *in trying to build itself up; each Me Incorporated is always laying claim to the lives of others.*

> Even though I knew better, when my son's first tooth came through early, I was proud. I was proud of him, and I was proud of me. It was perfectly clear to me how absurd this was. Yet there it was anyway. I said to myself, "This is ridiculous. It's *his* tooth. He didn't make it; and I didn't make it. It just came." Then I called up two friends and bragged about the precocious tooth.

To Me, Inc. as parent the child is necessarily either an annex or an accomplishment. In taking credit (or blame) for our children—even for giving them life in the first place—we are really "taking the life" of our children. It is no wonder that as our children take up the lives they have supposedly been given, troubles arise.

> *Jesus said, "A man's foes will be those of his own household.*
> —Matthew 10:36
>
> *Paul said, "The good which I would, I do not, but the evil which I would not, that I do."*
> —Romans 7:19

It is no one's fault that parents and children are frequently at their worst with each other. In a way this is inevitable, since it is in our families above all that we are always at our most. In our families we are especially concerned with this business of claiming complete selfhood. But we are absolutely not to blame. Neither can we through any process of civilization or technique become *personally* (as separate selves) any better or nicer. For it is the very idea of the separate self, Me, Inc. (praiseworthy or blameworthy) which is itself a mistaken idea; it is a universally held idea from which we all suffer and which we must transcend.

Me Gets Born

> *If a man thinketh himself to be something when he is nothing he deceiveth himself.*
> —Galatians 6:3

> *Judge not according to the appearance but judge righteous judgment.*
> —John 7:24

It is in judging by our senses—by what we see, hear, and feel—that we get the impression that we exist separately from everything else. Experiencing ideas in our heads, strength in our arms, love in our hearts, life in our bodies, we infer that we *have* intelligence, strength, life—that we cause it, are it. Like the circus clown who mistakes the place where light strikes the floor for the light itself and tries to sweep it up, so do we infer that we exist on our own and that our good is something outside of ourselves. We seem to be "in here" while everything else is "out there."

But in so conceiving of ourselves as separate realities with our own intelligence, love, strength, life, we place ourselves in double jeopardy. For whatever we claim to *have* we also experience the *lack* of. The claim to personal knowledge brings with it the awareness of not knowing enough. With the belief in personal power comes the experience of powerlessness and frustration; with the belief that we have a life comes the sense of there being an end to it. With the experience of being autonomous comes the experience of fear and helplessness; with the experience of being self-sufficient, the sense of insufficiency, loneliness, fragility. And in parenthood all this is compounded, as we begin to view ourselves as responsible for yet another self.

What we call "self-consciousness" is in fact a peculiar form of semiconsciousness. In Eastern thought it is referred to as the "illusory self." In the New Testament it is represented as "life according to the flesh" (2 Corinthians 10:2). This has nothing particular to do with sex, but with the idea of being a self contained in a body: Me *in corpus*, Me, Incorporated, Me, Inc. = Me Limited (Ltd.) = Me Desperado. Me, Inc. sees having and doing (or possessing and exerting power) as the primary issues in its survival. Judgment by appearance sires Me, Inc. in every one of us. It happened to us when we were children. And as new parents we observe, even celebrate, the advent of self-consciousness as it occurs in our children.

Me Grows Up

At first, as babies, we do what we do, get what we get, and are pleased or displeased accordingly. But gradually we begin to make connections between what we feel and do, and between what we do and what happens next. We begin to view ourselves as causing thoughts and events; simultaneously we begin to be our own cause célèbre—to be self-centered, and to view all other selves as adjuncts or adversaries. Through praise and blame and push and pull, the whole world transmits its belief in the complete me to the child, pointing out to each of us that we are really something. Our senses confirm this impression. Here I am in my skin; there you are in yours. Parent selves will care for our child self until it becomes self-sufficient, whereupon we will take care of our "own" self. Thus Me, Inc. comes into its own and embarks on a long period of self-completion called growing up, gathering the strength and virtue to be personally powerful and good *in its own right.*

Me Gets Married

By the time Me, Inc. is full grown it is aware of certain limits that it cannot overcome by itself. It isn't half what it thought it would be. So a new plan is sought. Next best to self-completion—maybe even better—how about this? The addition of another self! How better to enlarge and complete the self as possessor than to annex another self ? So Me, Inc. takes a big step: Marriage. The corporate merging of two Me, Incs. Two half-selves will become one whole one. But which of the two will they both become? Ah, there's the rub! *Just whose self do you think you are anyway? I thought you were for me—mine. But I thought* YOU *were for* ME!

Me Makes a Baby

After marriage what could better establish Me, Inc. as both power and possessor than the production of—ta da!—another self. Whether we follow tradition and have children soon after we marry, or put career first and wind up hurrying to get pregnant before it's too late, we continue to associate having children with being whole persons. Two selves combine to make another self— a baby one. And surely this little one will be more manageable than that other spouse one has turned out to be! So Me, Inc. extends itself two ways—both through having and through making (doing) another self. The complete, self-sustaining self, self-proprietor and self-producer in business for itself. If only all the other selves, spouse and child included, didn't have the same idea, maybe it would work.

Ta Da!

At one year old he always came so fresh from his nap—all new and warm and flushed—smiling, bright and lovable with cherry red lips and fatfolds over his wrists. Still leaning too far forward, he toddled forth pell-mell to see what was next. We thought his entry so spectacularly cute that one day somebody jovially announced it with a cry of *ta da!* It was even cuter when he took to saying *ta da!* himself. We liked it that he thought of himself as a good thing worth a little fanfare. But when he was in his high chair and couldn't leap into the room himself, he would hurl other things— spoon, food, cup, dish—across the room, gleefully crying *ta da!* and waiting for everyone to be pleased. For a time there we were all leaping about; because whenever he said *ta da!* we knew something was going to get thrown. It was harmless, humorous, inevitable, but looking back we can see—he came from his sleep to see what's what, and we said to him, *"You* are what's what." One confusion leads to another.

Unmistakable confusion is one of the surest and greatest benefits of parenthood. Built into the idea of having a baby is the idea of losing it. Built into the idea of making a baby is the possibility of wrecking it. But as confusion and anguish mount we begin to ask questions. Initially we may chalk up all problems to poor technique, lack of equipment, bad luck, or each other's shortcomings. But underneath a secret sense of personal failure grows which we struggle in vain to conquer and conceal. After coming at the thing from every direction we are forced to question our premise. At least our ears prick up when this is suggested. Something in us whispers in relief, *You mean I'm not the only one? You mean it's only a mistake? I thought I was supposed to know better.* Once confusion is recognized and embraced as confusion there comes a possibility of better understanding. And this is where the laughter and the joy of being a parent return again and again.

Wholeness as Oneness

Sooner or later, defeated and frustrated by all attempts to achieve wholeness as completeness, we are ready to welcome a different idea—the idea of wholeness as oneness.

Like waves on water, leaves on trees, beams from the sun, islands on the earth, everything including ourselves and our children can be viewed two ways. Superficially they appear to be separate, isolated, vulnerable, complete things. But looking deeper we find a oneness between each appearance and its underlying source of being: the island is really one with the earth, the leaf with the tree. Every aspect of the whole expresses the whole in unique ways, and the relationship of each to all others is harmoniously governed by the underlying reality with which each is one.

For us then *the quest for wholeness becomes not to acquire, not to accomplish, not to complete our selves—but rather to discover what it is with which we are one so that we can go ahead and be one with it.* Parenthood is neither the having of children, nor something we do to children. Parenthood is a time when we are pushed to discover the nature of the whole and our oneness with it. It is a time when both our mistaken ideas about who we are and truer ones are brought to light. There is so much that is beautiful and good to wake up to. Our children drive us toward this awakening. We begin ignorantly with what seem to be two or more separate selves having and doing to each other and trying to get wholeness from each other; but life forces us to look deeper for the fundamental reality from which we derive our uniqueness and which alone can harmoniously govern us in relation to each other. So we say *Whole Child/Whole Parent* instead of *Whole Parent/Whole Child* to indicate that our wholeness already exists and is not something to be given or forced upon or gotten or taken from each other in the future—but rather, now upon now, awakened to.

So we come to see that Me, Inc.'s objective of wholeness as self-completion is no target, but a fundamental mistake. Can an island exist apart from the land, or the beam from the sun, or the leaf from the tree? No more do we exist or love or know apart from whatever it is that we belong to. Does one island get its life from another? Does one sunbeam manage another? No more do we cause or control each other. Our efforts backfire not because we are bad or inept, but because they are contrary to the truth.

No one can learn this from reading a book. Instead it is a lesson to be lived out. When problems come up it is not that we are at fault; it is only that some false idea is being proved false. Well hooray for that! Proving what isn't is part of discovering what is! Parenthood is a rich, uncompromising time in which even our problems can be appreciated as revelations once we learn to see them for what they are. Every step of the way everything points out to us either what is true or what isn't. Clarification of what isn't tends to be painful and embarrassing. The revelation of what is— beautiful, liberating, a joy. Both occur together. Realizing just this fact eases everything and sets us to laughing and loving. Our children help us much more than we help them, playing out the distinction between what is so and what isn't before us in clear broad gestures.

> On entering the sixth grade the boy suddenly found his world and freedom sizably enlarged. He became aware of all kinds of new possibilities for himself. He made marrowbone soup, baked wonderful cookies, took a first aid course, and treated his brother's injury.

Through it all there showed in fits and starts both the true and the false. On the one hand he felt this tremendous sense of possibility and freedom based on some underlying force and burgeoning up as the fulfillment of potential. This was expressed as joy, assurance, generosity, gratitude, and huge bursts of goodness and love. He whistled constantly and sometimes even in the middle of a "boring" task, he would burst out, "Do you know how happy I am?" He was grateful. But there were other moments when he took credit and felt powerful and important. This expressed itself as overexcitement, anxiety, demandingness, competitiveness, envy, bossing, jealousy and boasting. Sometimes it was infuriating, but sometimes amusing and touching. When we liked his cookies, he might say, "Aren't I great?" Already uncomfortable, he would put his hand over his mouth and say, "Oops, I was only joking." But still, sometimes he had to say that he was great. Ta da!

Like wheat and tares these two ideas grow up together. Sometimes we march in all heavy-footed, trying to yank out the weeds, trampling the wheat, and only breaking off the tops of the weeds and sowing their seeds. Other times we stand back. Then we see that the wheat is strong and true and that the weeds will die out as the wheat grows. In this beholding we understand ever more clearly our own confusion. We even notice that whatever is governing us is also governing our children. They are only less covert. Their behavior is like a windsock indicating the direction of our own attention. As the years go by we find ourselves telling them less and learning more from them. We also see that they learn better from our learning than they ever did from our telling.

Love and Intelligence: At Odds

Our hearts are restless until we find our rest in thee.
—St. Augustine

With what fundamental reality are we one? When we feel separate what is it we feel separate from? At the root of all our yearnings —to marry, to have children, careers, friends, possessions—we can recognize two primary urges: the desire for love (which is synonymous with goodness) and for intelligence (which is synonymous with order). In all our strivings to be whole, it is always love and intelligence we seek: to express, to be met by, to dwell in, to find at the heart of life and self. Wanting this for ourselves we have children; having children we want it for them.

The Desire

Parent and child alike seek love and intelligence. From the beginning we recognize these urges in our children, who, fed, bathed, cared for, and exhausted, nevertheless will not sleep unless genuine love is present, who even in taking apart everything they can get their hands on are looking for some knowable and reliable underlying order—security.

As women we not only want homes (love), but also careers (intelligence). As men we not only want careers, but lately also feel we are missing out if we are not sharing, caring, loving parents as well. We who stay with the children rightly want it understood that this is intelligent as well as loving "work." We who "go to work" are equally concerned to find love as well as achievement.

As parents the quest for love and intelligence shows up in the demand for both love and authority. All child-rearing theories emphasize parental love or authority or the striking of a balance as the key to raising whole, happy children. On the side of "love" are freedom, permissiveness, gentleness, generosity, cooperation; on the "intelligent" side, discipline, firmness, security, independence. We all agree that both are necessary; we all try—and nobody tries harder than parents—to express both. But we find no amount of effort and no theory sufficient to actually endow us with the love we need to be loving or the knowledge needed to approach our children with anything even faintly resembling authority.

The Experience

The child ran from one parent to the other. "May I go? May I do such and such?" she would ask. There was never a simple yes or no —but always a negotiation. "It's up to your mother," her father would say. "It's up to your father," her mother would say. "He says it's up to you," said the child to her mother. "She says it's up to you," she said to her father. She quickly learned to wheel and deal.

"It's all right with her if it's all right with you. It's all right with him if it's all right with you. So, please?" Each parent wanted to be both nice and right, both loving and intelligent. Neither wanted to be blamed. So finally an answer that was no answer came. "Well (sigh), dear (sigh), you do what you like; but you know what we really want you to do." So the "choice," such as it was, ultimately fell upon the child. And no matter what the question was, the choice was always the same: guilt or resentment. "Why *are* you pouting so?" they'd ask. "You know we said you were free to choose." Everyone wondered why the child seemed unhappy. No one wondered more than she. "What's wrong with me?" she puzzled. "Why am I not nice?"

So often what's loving and what's intelligent seem to conflict. There are always tradeoffs. To be "nice" turns out to be not nice; to be "right" turns out to be wrong. We want to be nice *and* smart, taken care of *and* respected. Where love is called for, we are short-tempered or apathetic; where authority is required, we feel frustrated or uncertain. Strangely, our "love" is met with rejection, indifference, ingratitude, resentment. Strangely, our careful, "intelligent" plans are beset with chaos and rebellion.

Yet we are fundamentally unable to abandon our conviction that both love and intelligence are absolutely necessary. Something in us recognizes that both are vital, essential, part of our very nature. We know we are not mistaken in our restless seeking for both love and intelligence.

The Meaning

It is only the belief in Me, Inc. that divorces love from intelligence. It is only in conceiving of ourselves as separate that love and intelligence become separated from each other as well, divided into such tradeoffs as nice but dumb, shrewd but cold, masculine/feminine, work/pleasure, weak/strong and in parenthood strict/permissive, gentle/firm, loving but wishy washy. Me, Incorporated *on its own* can only conceive of love and intelligence as something to be done and had, to, from, for, by, and against others. In each of us Me, Inc. necessarily functions *on its own behalf*, perverting love into exploitation, corrupting intelligence into a struggle for power.

On the night of their wedding anniversary it was traditional for a certain couple to have a private, elegant dinner together. One year at the wife's suggestion they planned to go out, and the wife made reservations at their favorite restaurant. But to surprise his wife the husband secretly arranged to provide a gourmet dinner catered at home and canceled the reservations. They were both surprised. The dinner was perfect but the evening was not. She was disappointed by his surprise; he was surprised by her disappointment. The next year again they planned to go out, and the husband made reservations. But this year the wife secretly prepared her husband's favorite dinner at home and canceled the reservations. Again, for both, surprise and disappointment. Each was outgiving the other. They were taking giving from each other.

Like this couple, often in trying to express ourselves as both loving and intelligent persons we prevent genuine love and intelligence from finding expression. There is self-expression and Self expression, the expression of the complete Me, Inc. and the expression of the underlying One. Whenever we are unhappy together we can expect to find self-expression—with Me, Inc. in the act of self-promotion at others' expense, a charade often acted out under the guise of love. And whenever harmony occurs, we can be sure that that self (Me, Inc.) has been lost in the discovery of its oneness with the underlying whole.

He who loseth his life for my sake, shall find it.
—Matthew 10:39

Before Abraham was, I am.
—John 8:58

Love and Intelligence: At One

It was one of those days. I had something important to get done. Yet from the time the children came home from school until 9:30 P.M. there arose one conflicting demand after another. The music practice that needed supervision, the bike with a flat that had to be retrieved, the uniform that had to be purchased before the meeting, the dinner that had to be eaten early to get to the meeting on time, the second sitting that resulted thereby, the ungrateful complaints because everything was so rushed and chaotic. By bedtime mother/saint was rapidly turning into witch/martyr. Over and over I muttered to myself: *"Why do I always have to be the one . . . ?"* At 9:30 when I went to tuck my son in bed and saw his laundry on the floor, I did a number. It began with tsks, sighs, and humphs, and ended with a speech full of phrases like *after all I had done, how could he,* and *the least he could do . . .* I concluded irrelevantly by asking just what it was he thought I was for anyway? As if that was anything he was ever meant to consider.

He stood before me with tears of outrage. "Can I say something?" he said, spluttering.

"Of course," I answered, already sorry.

"I know I should have put my clothes away," he said, "but the way you said that was so . . . so . . . *self-saying!"*

It was suddenly clear. *Self-saying.* He had hit the nail on the head. All evening all that I had set about to do was really *self-saying* —to express me as a competent, intelligent, personally good, loving, wise, hard-working, successful, creditable, admirable, appreciable, complete self. Ta da! It all came together—and fell apart—in my absurd little speech. The coincidence of thought and experience was unmistakable. Also clear was its perversity. As I wished to show myself to be good, nice, loving, here was an exposé of the hidden self-seeking nature of that love and how it inevitably yielded only anger and hurt. As I sought to appear intelligent and wise, here was an exposé of the actual stupidity of my "wisdom." What I had done and how I felt and what I wanted was no true basis for the picking up of dirty clothes. On the contrary, the more I would make myself the issue in picking up the laundry, the more it would be suicide for my son to comply. So my self-righteous demand for order was in effect producing chaos. Was that stupid? Or what? Then what was the true basis—the real issue in the tidy disposal of dirty laundry? Now there was a good question. Order, peace, freedom, purity—I could feel myself subside as the value of these spiritual qualities washed over me. Did I really wish to become loving and wise? Did I really wish for love and wisdom to be expressed as goodness and order in my life and in our home? Then I would have to behold these qualities in consciousness. Only then would they be placed in charge and allowed to take shape in our lives.

Once more I saw that there was much to be understood. But I was filled with gratitude that one way and another what I needed to see *was being made clear.* The speed with which the atmosphere could change amazed me. My son and I were laughing now. Relief and love filled us. It was all so good, this life of ours together. How loved I felt knowing that the truth I couldn't grasp refused to desert me. How relieved I was to think that it would never abandon my child either. How beautiful was the way we were being brought along together.

Before we marry and have children we may never have asked the question *what is love?* We continue to operate on Me, Inc.'s ignorant assumptions until our experiences as spouse and parent bring us up short and begin to expose the fact that our idea of love is exploitative and bankrupt. Love is not a sentiment or a feeling. It is not something we have to give or can get from each other. It is not a fair trade. Love is a way of knowing, a mode of perceiving, a way of seeing. Ultimately it is *the* way of seeing. Anything less than love is not knowledge; it is opinion or belief, and it is always mistaken. Love is the accurate perception of the nature of the truth of being and our oneness with it. Love is intelligence. Intelligence is love.

As impossible as it is for separate selves to be loving to each other, it is impossible for love not to take place once we recognize our oneness with our fundamental source and force of being, which is itself love-intelligence and to which the name God is given.

> *In the beginning was the Word, and the Word was with God and the Word was God . . . and the Word became flesh and dwelt among us . . . full of grace and truth.*
> —John 1:1, 14

> *Love-intelligence is the basic attribute of God, the most fundamental aspect of divine reality. It becomes manifest every time we let it.*
> —Thomas Hora, *Existential Metapsychiatry*

Water is the truth about a wave. Everything else—its shape and size, its place in space, its duration in time, its force and speed —have nothing to do with the lasting truth of its being. In its wetness it is one with all water. Dryness or firmness is the truth about land. Similarly in its solidity an island, which appears to be floating, is one with all land. Superficially each wave is separate and largely surrounded by air. But the underlying truth is that each is entirely supported by the water from which it came, of which it is made.

As water is to wave, as land is to island, so consciousness is to us. Consciousness is the truth about us. It is our definitive characteristic: to be aware, conscious. In consciousness we are one with all consciousness. Consciousness is seeing; it is the awareness of whatever truly is. Because the substance of truth is idea and the substance of an idea is spirit, all true consciousness is spiritual.

> *He is before all things, and by Him all things consist.*
> —Colossians 1:17

As ideas, *baby, child, teenager* are all limited, just as *wave* is a limited representation of the idea of water. They all imply incompleteness, weakness, dependency, unconsciousness. But the truth of the child's being is whole. Essentially he cannot be half-true any more than a wave can be half-water. Therefore perfect consciousness is the truth of the child's being. Everything else, anything less, no matter how convincing it seems at the moment, is transitory and untrue. Whatever passes away is insubstantial. True substance is that which can be substantiated. True love is substantiating. Love takes place when we distinguish between the substantial and the insubstantial, the true and the untrue, allowing the untrue to fall away into nothingness.

The Waking of the Seeing Being

> *There is a Hindu myth about the Self or God of the universe who sees life as a form of play. But since the Self is what there is and all there is and thus has no one separate to play with, he plays the cosmic game of hide-and-seek with himself. He takes on roles and masks of individual people such as you and I and thus becomes involved in exciting and terrifying adventures, all the time forgetting who he really is. Eventually, however, the Self awakens from his many dreams and fantasies and remembers his true identity, the one and eternal Self of the cosmos who is never born and never dies.*
> —R. H. Blyth, in *Games Zen Masters Play*,
> selected and edited by Robert Sohl and Audrey Carr

To grow from babyhood to maturity is not a matter of changing from baby to adult, but a revelation, a coming to light of what is already so. It is not a matter of the baby becoming what she wasn't

or isn't, but rather of becoming what she is: a conscious consciousness, a Seeing Being.

Truth is what *is*. *Is* is now. *Is* is always now. *Was* isn't. *Will be*
isn't. Only truth always *is*. Anything that passes away is not truth.
Only that which always *is* is truth. All the helplessness and limitation that define a baby as a baby will pass away. The only quality
of the new baby that will remain is consciousness. All of the foibles
that define us as persons will pass away; the only quality that will
remain is consciousness. None of us is or ever really was Me,
Incorporated; we *are* Seeing Beings.

This is no less true for us as parents than for our children. If
anything it is more the case with the parent than with the child. As
we repeatedly encounter the fact that we are not perfect parents, we
feel discouraged. Again and again we have to face the fact that we
cannot by any personal, willful effort be perfect parents and raise
perfect children. We may try to cultivate indifference and settle for
less. Give up. Compromise. Be realistic. But the choice is not
between being perfect or imperfect parents. The choice in parenthood, as in everything else, is between acting for our selves or being
here for the sake of spiritual realization; for seeing what is.

So learning (waking, coming to) rather than accomplishing is
the issue in parenthood. Whether we understand this before our
children are born is not so important. Whenever it happens it
liberates us. Thus the point at which we are most discouraged or
ashamed or despairing may be the turning point where the love we
could not do and the wisdom we could not acquire begin to take
over.

To bring forth love, which is idea(1), is a matter of realization.
Love is not done. Wisdom is not had. But if we understand the
essential idea—what being is—we become *at once* its expression.
When we understand (see) what is we are (be) loving. When we
love we are wise. True knowing is loving. True loving is knowing.
God translates itself through our seeing into being.

The Clown and the Light

The clown notices the spot of light upon the stage floor. He deems
it beautiful and desirable. He is right. The light is good and it is

necessary to his life and happiness. He should, *must* have it. But here his understanding fails him, for he does not understand what he sees. The light spot seems pretty, warm, shapely maybe, a thing he wants. Or maybe he wants it to shine on him. So he tries to scoop it up—perhaps to stuff in his pocket or hold for a hand-warmer, or make himself more noticeable. So he crashes around on the stage with pan and broom, trying to sweep or scoop it up, falling all over the place, hurting himself, acting a perfect, blind fool. But in the end, perhaps after falling off the stage and through a drum in the orchestra pit, he despairs. And, in our story at least, he drops his hands to his side and looks up sadly only to find the light streaming into his face. He looks around—light is everywhere. He sees by it, and is guided by it and can move around freely and safely. What has happened here? The clown and the light are one. They were always one. The light illumines; the clown sees. The illumining and the seeing are one. The spot of light on the ground was not the light; but it did signify the light. The clown in his seeing also signifies the light. What he was trying to get was all the time what he was: a seeing being.

Son, thou art ever with me, all that I have is thine.
—Luke 15:31

Parenthood is just the world's most intensive course in love. We are not parents merely to give or get love, but to discover love as the fundamental fact of life and the truth of our being and thus bring it into expression. And so, parents and children—children all —we embark on this journey together. It is a far different journey from what we may have thought—through the twilight zone from the myth of Me, Inc. to the realization of the seeing being. Even though we still struggle, it helps to know this. Like one who wakes having turned around beneath the covers, we grapple ignorantly in the darkness beneath a blanket of ignorance—sometimes frustrated, often afraid—while all the time the perfect light of day is streaming through the window. Suddenly, stretching, blinking, we find ourselves in the light aware of only the good in ourselves, in each other, and all around us. In love.

The path of the righteous is as the light of dawn
that shineth ever brighter unto a perfect day.
—Proverbs 4:18

In his later years, when India had become electric with his message and kings themselves were bowing before him, people came to him even as they were to come to Jesus asking what he was. How many people have provoked this question: not "Who are you?" with respect to name, origin, or ancestry, but "What are you?—what order of being do you belong to, what species do you represent?" Not Caesar, certainly. Not Napoleon, nor even Socrates. Only two, Jesus and Buddha. When the people carried their puzzlement to the Buddha himself, the answer he gave provided a handle for his entire message.

"Are you a god?" they asked. "No." "An angel?" "No." "A saint?" "No." "Then what are you?"

Buddha answered, "I am awake." His answer became his title, for this is what Buddha means. In the Sanskrit root budh *denotes both to wake up and to know. Buddha, then, means the "Enlightened One" or the "Awakened One." While the rest of the world was wrapped in the womb of sleep, dreaming a dream known as the waking life of mortal men, one man roused himself. Buddhism begins with a man who shook off the daze, the doze, the dreamlike inchoateness of ordinary awareness. It begins with a man who woke up.*
—Huston Smith, *The Religions of Man*

Hui-Neng said, "If you come for the faith, stop all thy hankerings. Think not of good, think not of evil, but see what at this moment thy own original face doth look like, which thou hast even prior to thy own birth."
—D. T. Suzuki, *Zen Buddhism*

Buddha said, "Be a lamp to your self, be like an island. Struggle hard, be wise. Cleansed of weakness, you will find freedom from birth and old age.
—*The Dhammapada,* trans. by P. Lal

Jesus said, "You must be born again."
—John 3:7

2
Spirit

Meister Eckhart said, "The seed of God is in us. Given an intelligent and hard-working farmer and a diligent field hand, it will thrive and grow up to God, whose seed it is; and accordingly its fruits will be God-nature. Pear seeds grow into pear trees, nut seeds into nut trees, and God seed into God."
—*Meister Eckhart,* trans. by R. B. Blakney

In the beginning was the Word.
—John 1:1

Getting the Idea

Parenthood is surely among the most beautiful of all phases of human existence. But it is good to know just what we are looking forward to when a baby is on the way. It is easy enough to feature ourselves charmed by the gurgling, smiling infant or the earnest child bursting with sweet questions, and certainly that is all part of the wonderful way it is. But how many times do you picture yourself vaulting the table and saying evenly, "Oh no, darling, you'll have to drink your milk before you can get the macaroni out of the bottom of the glass." My list of things I never pictured myself saying when I pictured myself as a parent has grown over the years. "Please, don't put any more pennies in the pizza dough." "Please do stop licking the sofa." Or, in a busy parking lot, "No, you mustn't untie my wraparound skirt while I am tying your shoes." At how many ten-minute intervals in how many nocturnal hours will you get up cheerfully when your not quite housebroken toddler crawls into bed with you, pulls off his diaper, and announces brightly, "I have to pee"?

A sense of humor helps a lot, but there is only one way to look forward to all this with realistically happy anticipation, and that is to have a pretty clear idea of what's in it for us.

Spiritual realization is the whole point. It is the driving force, heart's desire, and lifelong task of both parent and child. It is the whole purpose of our being together, and the only workable way. But to say that parenthood, childhood, the quest for wholeness is a spiritual quest does not make it otherworldly. Truth is either supremely practical or it isn't truth. In fact the practical is just where the true gains specific expression. It is only when we see how truth is relevant, how it applies to or is revealed in our most mundane experiences, that any kind of realization can be said to have taken place. Sometimes we start with a principle and then see it expressed in the ordinary. More often it is our practical problems that drive us toward truth.

Suddenly we have a baby who poops and cries, and we are trying to calm, clean up, and pin things together all at once. Then, as fast as we learn to cope—so soon—it is hard to recall why diapers ever seemed so important. The frontiers change, and now perhaps we have a teenager we can't reach. But even if we are no longer new or expectant parents, conception is a good place to begin. Even when our children are older, we can still remember the marvel of conceiving and bearing a child. What a big event it was, is. But who did we think we were? Who, what, do we think we are? What is conceived at the time of conception? At whatever point we are it is good to consider this, because this is where it all starts.

Conception

Mostly it is said that we *get* pregnant, *give* birth, and *have* babies. But if getting, giving, and having are all we understand of this process, both we and our children will surely be quite miserable. Having children doesn't turn us into parents. It just makes us busy. It takes becoming fatherly, motherly, parently to make us parents. Conception begins when we first conceive of the idea of becoming parents. Now we are responsible for learning what this means and redefining ourselves accordingly. We can use *at least* nine months! A good question to start with is: What's so great about a baby coming? What's so great about becoming a parent? A lot of us have children before considering these things. But it's better to give the idea a little thought as soon as it occurs to us, as soon as we conceive.

Parenthood Is for the Parent

Even during the early so-dependent years, our children's dependency on us is actually fairly superficial. We say the child in the womb is completely dependent on his mother, but he is not depending on her to mother him—she is merely the environment within which he is taking place. As long as this environment is adequate his progress toward birth goes on, regardless of whether the mother knows much about motherhood or children. She isn't doing the child: she is housing it.

After birth, it is only slightly different (although our experience is vastly different). Childhood, too, seems a temporary condition to be outgrown, and it is given to our children themselves to hunger and thirst after whatever they need to help them do this. As parents we are still only the environment—though now a more obviously mental and spiritual one than a physical one—and the caretakers of this environment.

In short, we do not mold, make, raise, bring up, our children at all. We can help or hinder, but our basic responsibility is mostly custodial.

So who needs whom? Of course the child needs the parent, and we are all too aware of the damage wrought by ignorant, irresponsible, or overzealous parenting. But a less obvious and yet existentially vital fact is that most of us need our children. Some may learn the arts of motherliness and fatherliness without children, but most of us get a big push from our children toward the discovery of these qualities—qualities absolutely necessary to our fulfillment and of more lasting value than most childhood lessons. We learn them for the sake of our children, but they benefit us most of all. Once we have learned to be truly motherly and fatherly we will be forever happier. The gain is not the having of children; it is the discovery of love and how to be loving.

> *Each man to himself, and each woman to herself, such is the word of the*
> *past and present, and the word of immortality;*
> *No one can acquire for another—not one!*
> *No one can grow for another—not one!*
>
> *The song is to the singer, and comes back most to him;*
> *The teaching is to the teacher, and comes back most to him;*
> *The murder is to the murderer, and comes back most to him;*
> *The theft is to the thief, and comes back most to him;*
> *The love is to the lover, and comes back most to him;*
> *The gift is to the giver, and comes back most to him—it cannot fail;*
> *The oration is to the orator, the acting is to the actor and actress, not to*
> *the audience;*
> *And no man understands any greatness or goodness but his own, or the*
> *indication of his own.*
> —Walt Whitman, "A Song of the Rolling Earth (A Carol of
> Words)"

If Tao (the Way) could be made a present, everybody would have presented it to his parents. If Tao could be told about, everybody would have spoken to his brothers about it. If Tao could be inherited, everybody would have bequeathed it to his children and grandchildren. But no one could do it.

Pregnancy

If it is primarily the idea of parenthood that is conceived at the time of conception, then pregnancy is not merely the time when a child develops in the mother's womb; even more it is a time for the concept of parenthood to develop in the parents' consciousness. So mother and father are both pregnant—with seeds of parenthood. It is certainly advisable to make use of the nine months of pregnancy to prepare not only for the child but also for parenthood. But even if we do not have children, once we have conceived of the idea of being loving, parently, we are pregnant; and we remain pregnant until realization has taken place. In this sense we may conceive and remain pregnant long after our children are born.

When as individuals or couples we are pregnant there are necessary preparations to be made, techniques to learn, information to be gathered. But it is a mistake to prepare only for delivery, and to think only of things to get and do for the child. We need to look deeper for the underlying issues in the lives of both parent and child. At least we can become aware that they are there.

The Necessary and the Essential

There is so much to think about, so much to buy, so much to read, so many books on childbirth and child-rearing. It's easy to go overboard and drown in confusion. How can we tell what's important, and what isn't? It helps to make a distinction between necessities and essentials.

Esse means to be. We are *esse*ntially seeing beings. Therefore our harmonious being—every aspect of it, even the most mundane —follows from our seeing what is. We now have a principle of discernment: *we do whatever is necessary while keeping sight of the essential.* If we are approaching life as seeing beings, then no matter what confronts us we approach it—not from the standpoint of good and bad, right or wrong, or even how or how not to, but *what is* and *what isn't*.

On the simplest level this means merely orienting ourselves according to issues. For example, we could ask *what are the issues in pinning a diaper?* The pin is a temporary necessity; but what is essential in a diaper pin? Once that question is conceived it can be asked and answered: safety, ease in putting on and off, security of the connection. Now you can recognize a good pin when you see one, which is a whole lot easier than buying an assortment of faulty pins and learning by painful experience what the issues are and which kind of pin works.

Considering the deeper, essential issues of being helps to put things in perspective and to orient us toward what is really important, really necessary, what has to do with the essence of our real being. Simultaneously it enables us to deal with all the temporary but time-consuming trivia of parenthood with maximum intelligence and much less fuss. The idea(l), the essential, the true, the real, never begins and never ends. It is spiritual. So in any situation, even while doing whatever is momentarily required, it is helpful to keep sight of that which is of lasting significance. This makes momentary difficulties more clearly momentary than difficult. It prevents us from overblowing small things and going off on tangents and wild goose chases. And it keeps us on course, in quest of the fullest possible realization of our essential spiritual being—ours and our children's.

When our diapering days are over, the diapers and pins, which were so necessary and seemed almost to take command of our lives for a time, quickly become too trivial to speak of. But to us as parents there is something essential taking place in our involvement with the trivial. The necessary and the essential touch. As we lay our pleasures and customary life aside to get up in the night for our babies we are repeatedly pushed toward the discovery of what is essential—and what isn't. We move back and forth from the necessary to the essential, from the Word to the Word made flesh, from seeing to being, from the basic idea to its "practical" expression. Diapers, pins, maternity clothes, cribs—for new parents these are a starting point from which to take off. For others—parents of older children, or any of us whether parents or not—the basic principles remain the same. There will always be necessities, and they will always be points where the essential is to be discerned and expressed.

Getting Ready

While trying on maternity clothes or while bending down to tie your round wife's unreachable shoes, consider what parenthood is. What in essence is a parent? Not how it should act or how it will feel, but *what is it?* Not what is happening to its body or its sex life, but *what does it mean?* What is going on in the long run? Is this a career change and from now on you will be a gynecologist or an obstetrician or a natologist or a neonatologist or a child psychologist or a pediatrician? Oh, a parent! Well, then, what is that? One who fosters the growth of the child? O.K. But then what is the child *in essence?*

When she has outgrown being a fetus she becomes a child, and you will be busier than you can imagine with her bare necessities, but all the time she will be outgrowing childhood. What will she be then? What is it about the child from the very beginning that becomes ever more evident rather than less so all her life? You experience this essence as vitality when she kicks inside your belly, pressing against limits. When she is born she will look at you, and you will see this essence peering out at you. Where did it really come from? What is it? How are you going to feed and nurture that Seeing Being?

> *Unto us a child is born*
> *Unto us a son is given*
> *Not out of us*
> *   by us*
> *   from us.*
>
> *Not we are going to make*
> *   we are going to have*
> *   we are going to get or produce*
>
> *But unto us a child is* **is**
> *   is born*

The discerning shopper. While buying things for the forthcoming baby, waiting for service—even just while brushing your teeth—practice being parently to a child of God. Apart from hugging, cuddling, nursing, burping, diapering, *what is parentliness?* Behold everyone as a child, a good child. Everyone is someone's good child—at least at the outset. The good parent keeps sight of that essential goodness and is always inviting it forth and paving its way. Learn to regard and pay silent respect to the good, lovable, aware child in everyone, *especially* when it is not at all apparent. Disassociate all seeming imperfection, foibles, bad traits from the essential reality of each individual—yourself included. Whatever isn't perfect is only ignorant.

> *Forgive them, Lord, for they know not what they do.*
> —Luke 23:34

Buy a bathtub or figure out some bathing arrangement in which she can get clean as necessary and *become aware* of her one-ness with love. Set up a diaper-changing station at which you will change her dirty diapers a thousand times while a thousand times sighing or a thousand times marveling at and welcoming forth her essential purity, goodness, perfection, and *amazing conscious-ness.* Get a highchair where you will clean up a thousand spills while a thousand times fuming or a thousand times acknowledging that it is love and intelligence that feeds you both and does all the work. Buy a baby seat for when you need to put him down and from which he can *see what is* going on. Make, buy a few toys, a mobile, a music box, a soft light. All the better to taste, chew, touch, hear, *and see* with, my dear.

Set up a crib or other sleeping arrangement to put the baby's body in so he may get the sleep he needs. That's the necessity. But what is going on essentially? Here you and your child will have to learn that life goes on even when you are apart. Here you both discover and find met your need for peace. Go on from here. This perspective will help you make a good choice regarding crib or bed, and to avoid the bedtime struggle many experience—or to live through it gratefully.

Closet Cleaning

*. . . the most important factors in the life of their children are not the
school, the television set, the playmates, or the neighborhood, but what the
parents cherish, what they hate and what they fear.*
—Thomas Hora, *Existential Metapsychiatry*

Before the baby comes and you get too busy, get rid of all the old
clothes in your closet—the ones you've been saving in case they
might come back into style. Get rid of all the old junk in the
basement and garage—the things you were going to fix up to make
do, but meanwhile have replaced with something better. Do the
same with worthless old-fashioned or fashionable ideas in your
head. At least drag them out and look at them. What are my
preconceptions? What are my mental pictures of my child and
myself as a parent? What are my worries? What is the basis for these
ideas? Where did they come from? God? Society? My parents? Have
they any validity? Or are they just troublesome assumptions?

Wishballs, Follies, and Wishing Prods

You may or may not throw out your old football when you clean
your closet. It makes no difference. But watch for wishful fantasies.
Notice how these productions feature yourself: Metrogoldwyn Me,
Inc. the Madonna, Metrogoldwyn Me, Inc. the good old Dad. Metrogoldwyn Us the up-to-date ecologically minded liberated unisex-
ual family. What if your daughter isn't interested in playing with
dolls? Worse still, what if she is? What if your son wants a doll?
What if he doesn't? During pregnancy a football is neither a necessary nor an essential preparatory purchase. So when your wife says,
"We're pregnant," if your first urge is to run out and buy a football, *question that.* The idea that you and your (if it is a) son or (if
it isn't) daughter will be companions is fine. But the thought that
this should take the shape of a football might be something to kick
out of your secret closet.

*Because he thinks that he "knows best" many a parent not only dictates
the way his child's message is to be delivered, but even the message itself.
All of which leads to confusion, discouragement and finally to failure.*

Instead, the parent should ever encourage the good in his child, patiently removing every obstacle in its way, remembering that each one's message comes from God—is divine; and that his child's true self, like his own, is from eternity—two rays of divine light of exactly the same value, but pointing in different directions.
—Nora Holm, *The Runner's Bible*

Things That Go Bump in the Day

Fears are thoughts about what shouldn't be. We fear for our children. We don't want anything unpleasant to happen to them. But, we say, we have to be "realistic." Some unacceptable, dread fears we find too awful to think about, but there are others that we consider more or less acceptable. Acceptable fears are small ones which seem to be inevitable. We expect "our share" of these to come true, and so we prepare for them with ointment, vitamins, and a good healthy attitude. We are confident that we can deal with them as they come—preventing some, coping with others.

The list of acceptable fears includes colic, diaper rash, cradle cap, teething, reactions to injections, the need to suck, getting buckteeth from sucking, spoiling, food allergies, attachment to bottle or breast or security blanket, and before long the terrible twos and sibling rivalry. Most we accepted so long ago that we do not even question them or recognize them as beliefs. We call them "facts of life." Moreover, we are constantly being bombarded with fresh suggestions and an endless variety of embellishments on the old. An advertisement for a skin preparation begins, "When your baby gets a diaper rash . . ." *When,* it says. Not *if,* but *when!*

So these are fears made acceptable. There are so many that we could just get eaten up by fear. They cannot simply be ignored, avoided, denied, or thrown out of our mental closets. But we can question them. They are questionable! For instance, while almost nobody escapes all these problems, hardly anybody is afflicted with them all either. And there isn't anything on the list that everyone experiences. Isn't that amazing? Evidently, while some discomforts are usual, none is an absolute necessity. So then it is at least theoretically possible for babies to grow up without suffering any of the discomforts we have always taken for granted. How about that?

Fears are thoughts about what should not happen in the future. As such, like wishes, they are fantasies. They haven't happened yet, so in a way they aren't real. Yet here we are one way or another preoccupied with them. During pregnancy we need to examine our preoccupations. At least we can haul them out of the recesses of our mental closet and look them over, asking some of the same questions that we ask of our old clothes. Are they becoming? Do they befit us? On closer inspection, will they hold up or are they falling apart and ready to be shed? If they are falling apart or unbecoming and we still treasure them, what is it that we are really valuing? Does Me, Inc. have some vested interest in these ideas? Are they costumes for Metrogoldwyn Me—the hero? the brain? the good kid? the brave and strong?

Dwelling Place for a Seeing Being

. . . In his ship Scuppers had a little room. In his room Scuppers had a hook for his hat and a hook for his rope and a hook for his spyglass and a place for his shoes and a bunk for his bed to put himself in.

At night Scuppers threw the anchor into the sea and he went down to his little room.

He put his hat on the hook for his hat, and his rope on the hook for his rope, and his spyglass on the hook for his spyglass, and he put his shoes under the bed, and got into his bed, which was a bunk, and went to sleep.
—Margaret Wise Brown, *The Sailor Dog*

As long as we are pregnant, our children live within the confines of our physical bodies. We are never more intimately connected than at this time, yet scarcely ever again will we have so little knowledge of each other. At the birth of our child, suddenly and at long last, we will confront each other, an overwhelming experience that defies description. Fathers are likely to be almost more overcome by this than mothers as, for the first time, the child "becomes a reality."

Yet no matter how dramatic the experience of child-bearing seems, from the child's side the move from womb to room will not be as tremendous as we are inclined to think. The child remains what she has always been, a perfect, unique idea—spiritually whole, unending, unbeginning. On a material plane, where she is an immature being seeking maturity or the realization of this ideal selfhood, the move from womb to lap is not so huge either.

> *Keizan said: "Birth cannot alter the mind, embodiment cannot transmute Original Nature. Though the essential and the physical bodies have changed, mind is as it has always been."*
> —*Zen Poems, Prayers, Sermons, Anecdotes, Interviews,* trans. and ed. by Stryk and Ikemoto

In the womb or out, the very young child lives almost entirely within the limits of his parents' consciousness. He is capable of realizing very little as yet; he has not become conscious of his idea(l) nature. As his parents we are only just approaching this possibility ourselves. In metapsychiatry *experience* is reserved to mean that which comes to us through the senses. The very young child is subject only to *experiences* and *encounters* (see page 101) through experience; and his experience is almost totally governed by the ignorant beliefs or enlightened awareness of his parents. He lives as much in us after he is born as he did while still in the womb. We are his environment as long as he is a child.

Therefore as we prepare a room or corner for the coming baby, it is appropriate to seek the highest possible awareness of the idea(l) individual and its idea(l) dwelling place, and then to consider how the qualities of this idea(l) dwelling place might be translated into terms the child can appreciate. What ideal qualities do we wish him to encounter, to be surrounded by? What will best serve him on his path toward realizing his ideal selfhood? Disregarding the newborn's apparent weakness and limitation and considering only his ideal, spiritual selfhood (call it potential if you prefer), it becomes obvious that the proper environment includes peace, beauty, order, simplicity, joy, and love.

Without this perspective it is easy to get the impression that a baby is something to be taught and entertained through constant sensory bombardment—the more the better—and to give too little thought to what message is being brought to the child through his senses. There is just this idea that the more stimulation the better. A few hours of children's television advertising or a stroll through a few stores can lead to tremendous expenditures of time, money, and effort in decorating our children's rooms in a way that quickly proves inefficient, unsafe, inconvenient, monotonous, unpleasant, and impossible to keep orderly. Covered with cute, busy things, the walls crowd in; the floors are dangerously cluttered with toys and parts of toys; the bed is a sort of padded cell, littered with things that he only pitches over the side. His bedroom, which should be where he finds peace enough to sleep, becomes a restless place where nobody likes to be.

But by keeping his essential, spiritual nature and needs in mind, we find all the guidance necessary to prepare a room where he can truly be at home. There is no need for specific suggestions: if we cultivate an awareness of peace, beauty, order, and love they will be reflected in the decoration, furniture, and arrangement of the child's nook or room. The important thing is to *address everything in the room to the ideal child, not only to the material one,* to keep in mind the spiritual or essential issue behind each aspect of the room and its furnishings:

- *Floor*: security, ground of being, freedom. Make sure it remains unhazardous, uncluttered, spacious in appearance.
- *Walls*: security, protection, privacy, but again also freedom. Do not let them become confining, oppressive, or overly cluttered.
- *Light fixtures, windows, curtains*: light, illumination, seeing, understanding. Choose things that help him to see beyond his room, not always things that merely catch his eyes and capture his attention. There are so many cute things available that it is easy to wind up with an overly busy and confining room in which the view from the window is almost the last thing the child will discover.
- *Toys*: fulfillment, unfolding consciousness. As with lights and windows, it is the function of toys to lead children beyond themselves, not merely to entertain.
- *Bed*: peace, stillness, letting go. It is not a cage or a playpen or a learning or achievement center.
- *Arrangement*: simplicity, order, efficiency, unity.
- *Decor*: beauty—again, toward seeing beyond.

Such a room will be joyful, not merely exciting (and therefore not soon boring); it is after all a place of privacy and rest. It will be cheerful and pleasing, but not overly stimulating or startling.

It will emphasize becoming rather than having, seeing rather than sights, understanding rather than doing. And love—how does a room reflect love? It cannot be pinpointed. It is the overall result of a consciousness of true goodness—the goodness of the child and the goodness of life as they are met in us, the parents, tonight.

In the end, of course, the room is nowhere; the child is not brought peace or love or security or beauty or vision by the room at all. It is in our consciousness where he encounters these realities. Much stronger than the messages that come through his senses is his immediate spiritual awareness of whatever is governing our consciousness. Whatever we are aware of he encounters. So once we achieve the kind of awareness that can reflect itself in the preparation of a lovely room, the room is less important. It never really was, except as an exercise for us. Our children can go anywhere, sleep on anything, do with nothing, and still be happy and grow beautifully if their earthly dwelling place, the mind of the parent, is love-filled.

Name and Identification

As our baby's arrival draws closer we begin to think more and more about the baby per se. We need to buy clothes—but for a boy or a girl? At first they are just babies—boygirls and girlboys—anyway.

Let's not worry about raising boys to be boys and girls to be girls, just whole, individual, unique children. The ideal man/woman is as gentle as a woman and as strong as a man. As a father you are now called on to develop some of your feminine qualities. As a mother you will find this baby requiring of you some traditionally masculine ones. Differences between boys and girls can be acknowledged and appreciated; but they do not have to be taught. In the long run they have to be transcended anyway. To emphasize group or sex membership is less a means of identifying uniqueness than of stereotyping sameness. Positive and negative group identifications dull the child's sense of uniqueness and worth. Let's see how God will be, what shape God takes as this child. Let's see.

When I was preparing for our second child's birth I sat down one day, propped open the bible on my bushel belly and opened to the passage that speaks of not hiding one's light under a bushel. It reminded me to think of the baby as a point of divine light, rather than a body. It reminded me to think of the birth as a revelation rather than an expulsion. For a boy we had selected Andrew as a name because of its gentle sound. Finding this passage in the book of Luke, which itself means light, we now added Luke. Andrew (sturdy, steadfast, stout) Luke (light). The next day our whopping son was effortlessly brought to light. And indeed he has proven to be a sturdy, steadfast light.

Let your light so shine that men may see your good works and glorify your father which is in heaven.
—Matthew 5:16

As the birth draws near you will hear about pushing. Even when the time comes and you are pushing, meditate on the idea of letting. Letting to be born. Letting sleep. Letting be. Letting mature. Letting be revealed.

This little tiny light of mine,
I'm gonna let it shine.
This little tiny light of mine
I'm gonna let it shine.
Let it shine, let it shine, let it shine.

Hide it under a bushel? No!
I'm gonna let it shine.
Hide it under a bushel? No!
I'm gonna let it shine.
Let it shine, let it shine, let it shine.
—Negro spiritual

In him was life, and the life was the light of men. The light shines in the darkness, and the darkness has not overcome it. . . . The true light that enlightens every man was coming into the world. He was in the world, and the world was made through him, yet the world knew him not. He came to his own home, and his own people received him not. But to all who received him, who believed in his name, he gave power to become children of God; who were born, not of blood, nor of the will of the flesh, nor of the will of man, but of God.
—John 1:4–5, 9–13

Hearken to me all which are borne by me from the belly, which are carried from the womb; and even to your old age I am he; and even to hoar hairs will I carry you; I have made and I will bear; even I will carry and will deliver you.
—Isaiah 46:3–4

What is it that sires and conceives and delivers and is expressed in us? What is it that husbands and wives? What sisters and brothers and mothers and fathers us and our children? What is our essential nature? What are we here to realize?

Special Delivery: Parentbirth

Traditionally childbirth has been thought to be a more or less painful experience for the mother to endure with more or less grace depending on the degree to which she was fearful, brave, or lucky. With anesthetics came the possibility of doing away with the experience of pain altogether. For several decades nearly every woman in this country who could afford it slept through the event of childbirth, waking only in time to be introduced to her baby by a doctor or nurse. Fathers were more or less out of it. The mother was pregnant; the mother would give birth.

Recently the idea of staying awake and having both parents present throughout labor and delivery has been gaining favor, partly on the ground that it is better for the child, partly because of a growing desire not to miss the wonderful event. With this change in attitude numerous techniques have been developed for avoiding pain while staying awake, for dealing with pain if it occurs, and for being a cooperative participant in the baby's delivery. For some, pain-accompanied tensions based on fear of the childbirth process are alleviated simply by being told what's going on or by having their husbands present. Breathing and relaxing skills seem to help others pass more comfortably through labor and delivery.

Regardless of delivery techniques there are (and always have been) some for whom the moments of childbirth pass harmoniously and with surprising ease, and many for whom they seem difficult and dreadful.

It is generally believed that these differences can be explained by medical science. But no theory has turned up yet that applies consistently enough to be counted true. Many advocates of conscious childbirth techniques believe that the answer lies in the parent's skill in executing them (both mentally and bodily). But results are spotty when it comes to the record of easy versus difficult births. Some of the best-prepared mothers have the worst labors; some of the least prepared breeze through with no complications.

Choosing to be alert and awake during the moments of childbirth is surely a positive trend. It is certainly better to view birth as a healthy, happy event than as a sort of hazardous emergency sapping the strength of the mother just before the demands of motherhood are placed on her. But further changes in viewpoint cannot be ruled out as long as disharmony remains.

As Thou Sowest

The very act of observing disturbs the system.
—Werner Heisenberg

For whatsoever a man soweth, that shall he also reap.
—Galatians 6:7

Nothing comes into experience uninvited.
—Thomas Hora, *Dialogues in Metapsychiatry*

Some say the greatest variable in scientific observation is the scientists' own preconceptions, and that these preconceptions are actually reflected in the phenomena being observed. Technique might then be of little importance. If we believe the sun revolves around the earth, then a bigger, more powerful telescope may only augment our experience of that belief. If the belief is erroneous, truer understanding can occur only after the belief is relinquished. And if the external phenomena themselves are influenced by the viewpoint of the beholder . . . !

It makes little difference what technique is employed in the pursuit of truth if the basic premise or belief is erroneous. Any technique employed by the mother during childbirth may only augment her experience of what she unconsciously or secretly believes and values. To the extent that belief is in error, the experience is likely to be disharmonious.

It is at least clear that there is a mental factor to all experience that is worth taking into account. To leave your house, you first head for the door. But suppose as you near the door you become more concerned with the door itself than with passing through it. (Oh, what a beautifully carved door!) Perhaps you fear that the door will not open or that you personally will not be able to open it. (Oh, what a huge, heavy door!) Depending on the degree and nature of your conviction you may soon find yourself pausing to admire the carvings, frame, latch, knob, wood grain of the door, or struggling with the lock, trying to bash down the door, or calling for help. Either way, as long as you remain fascinated with the door it is not possible to pass through the doorway. Thought precedes progress; if thought does not pass through the doorway, neither will you—not unless someone forcibly gets you through.

This is analogous to the experience of many parents and children at the time of birth. After a healthy pregnancy and happy anticipation of the birth, many mothers (prepared and unprepared) experience long, painful labors in which both they and their children seem stuck in the doorway.

For both scientist and parent, then, perhaps the primary challenge is to relinquish false beliefs or concerns. Only in letting go of one idea does it become possible for another one to occur; if there is such a thing as truth, the only possibility of conflict or disharmony is through belief in or devotion to something else. The object is to realign one's thought with what really is. What then is the essential event of childbirth?

One common assumption is that childbirth is the bodily separation of the mother and child from each other. But perhaps on an idea(l) plane, the moment of childbirth could be something else entirely. It is at least something more. The true event that from the side of the child is called childbirth is from the side of the parent, parentbirth. Perhaps, then, delivery is not a matter of expulsion but of revelation, since what is essentially happening for both ourselves and our babies is the further coming to light of what we already truly are. Perhaps it is when we reach for the idea of motherhood that the child is finally released.

The moments of birth are as significant in the lives of parent and child as passing through a doorway is in any journey outside. It is only a matter of moments, a mere transition, and yet during pregnancy the whole focus of many of us is on labor and delivery. We spend the days of pregnancy preparing for childbirth, when it is parenthood with which we will be largely concerned from the moment of delivery on.

Perhaps it is impossible for a child to be born to a woman who still thinks of herself as a pregnant woman, just as it is impossible to pass through a doorway while giving one's full attention to the door. And isn't it also a mistake to think of childbirth as something between mother and child, since it is also the father's parenthood that is brought to light in the moment of delivery?

Since the true event of childbirth takes place in consciousness, we now concern ourselves during pregnancy not merely with childbirth or embryology, but with heightening our consciousness of motherliness and fatherliness, seeking to become parently in thought and mode of being. Reliance on a method does not preclude understanding, but the basic issue during pregnancy remains preparation for parenthood.

During labor, too, we need to center on these qualities of parentliness and on the real nature of the event. Such focussing keeps the event in perspective and prevents us from becoming disproportionately involved with the door, instead of the vista before us. This also helps to free us from pain—both physiological and psychological, both during and after birth—and fosters an atmosphere of peace and gratitude in which to greet the child.

A child is being born! We are here to welcome him. He is bringing new love, light, wisdom, and purpose into our lives. We are witnessing vitality and intelligence and power for good at work. We are becoming parents! We are about to begin to learn to love and give as we have never been motivated to love and give before.

Besides expediting the birth process, such an orientation is obviously best for the arriving child. Whether or not the labor goes smoothly or with a little distress is of small consequence. For most the result will be fine regardless. But for the child it is clearly more important to be welcomed into the arms of a consciously parently individual than someone skillful at pushing or pulling babies out into the world. And the relative value of these two orientations is no greater for the newborn child than for the newborn parent. To be happy we must become what we are.

> *Before she was in labor she gave birth; before her pain came upon her she was delivered of a son. Who has heard of such a thing? Who has seen such things? . . . Shall I bring to birth and not cause to bring forth? says the Lord; Shall I, who cause to bring forth, shut the womb? says your God.*
> —Isaiah 66:7–9

> *i am so glad and very*
> *merely my fourth will cure*
> *the laziest self of weary*
> *the hugest sea of shore*
>
> *so far your nearness reaches*
> *a lucky fifth of you*
> *turns people into eachs*
> *and cowards into grow*
>
> *our can'ts were born to happen*
> *our mosts have died in more*
> *our twentieth will open*
> *wide a wide open door*
>
> *we are so both and oneful*
> *night cannot be so sky*
> *sky cannot be so sunful*
> *i am through you so i*
> —e. e. cummings, *Poems: 1923–1954*

Getting Used to and Sustaining the Idea

Eating and sleeping are likely to become suddenly heightened concerns in any home with a new baby. *Struggle* describes what goes on in most families. Eating and sleeping are both forms of nourishment, and the following pages are loosely concerned with these issues and their significance. Some good questions to ask are: Just who is being nourished and with what and by whom? What is the sustenance that truly sustains and nourishes this idea that has become our child, and this idea that we are? What nourishment helps us and our children to become more fully what we really are?

A Mountain Is a Mountain, and a Baby Is Not Quite What We Expected

Ch'ing-yuan said: "Before I had studied Zen for thirty years, I saw mountains as mountains, and waters as waters. When I arrived at a more intimate knowledge, I came to the point where I saw that mountains are not mountains, and waters are not waters. But now that I have got its very substance I am at rest. For it's just that I see mountains once again as mountains, and waters once again as waters."
—A. Watts, *The Way of Zen*

Almost everything we encounter has two meanings: its apparent meaning, which is what we first experience (through the senses), and its deeper meaning, which we can come to understand (in consciousness). The experiences that go along with the apparent meaning tend to be discordant, and slowly force us to consider the deeper meaning.

Materially we may experience rock as an obstacle—dangerous, harsh, slippery when wet—whereas, looking deeper, we find qualities of steadfastness, strength, reliability, security, protection, immutability. The difference is in the viewpoint. With the material perspective also comes the dualistic: To Me, Inc. self and rock conflict. (Will the mountain conquer the climber? or the climber conquer the mountain?) Mastery, control, power, dominancy become the issues.

But to the seeing being the same rock calls strength to mind and reminds us that we are safe, supported, upheld, secure, and can count on one infinite underlying reality. Which viewpoint is true? What produces conflict, injury, discouragement, or frustration, must be false; what brings us peace, harmony, strength, assurance, must be true. We are not quick to learn, *first* hitting our heads against the wall, *then* wondering what hit us.

Now substitute the baby for the rock. At last, we hold her in our arms. So tiny, so cute, so weak and helpless! We can hardly wait to cuddle and feed and teach and care for her. All aglow, we take her home, and the crying starts and the sleepless nights begin. And she isn't cuddly, she's struggly! Instead of expressing beautiful parental love we seem to be engaged in some sort of marathon power struggle in which she is winning the no-sleep event hands down. Within a week we are so worried about the mess we are making of her life or so furious over the mess she is making of ours that we can only remember how cute she is when she is asleep.

But suppose we looked at her that other way? Suppose instead of tininess we saw life's vastness; instead of weakness, vitality; instead of helplessness, wholeness; instead of ignorance, intelligence and alertness? Suppose we could also recognize that these same qualities which are the baby's true nature are the fundamental truth about us and life as well?

When I was pregnant I thought, "A baby is a baby and a mother is a mother." But when we came home I found a baby is not a baby and a mother is not a mother. And ever since I have been learning.

> *Twinkle, twinkle, little star,*
> *How I wonder what you are,*
> *Up above the world so high*
> *Like a diamond in the sky.*
> *Twinkle, twinkle, little star,*
> *How I wonder what you are.*
> —Traditional nursery rhyme

> *If you know what, you know how.*
> —Thomas Hora, *Dialogues in Metapsychiatry*

That is the question, isn't it? The supreme question for parents? *How I wonder what you are?* If we would be good parents—then parents of what? What are our children? What are we? When we see what we are we shall be what we are. Lord, Lord, what on earth, what in heaven's name, do you have in mind?

O Lord, our Lord,
how majestic is thy name in all the earth!
Thou whose glory above the heavens is chanted
by the mouth of babes and infants. . . .
What is man that thou art mindful of him,
and the son of man that thou dost care for him?
—Psalm 8:1-2, 4

It is not yet clear what we shall be; we only know that when He shall
appear we shall be like Him for we shall see Him as He is.
—1 John 3:2-3

Like the rock, every child has two meanings. On the one hand he is an image and likeness of his parents. As such he not only bears physical resemblance to them, but will also evolve a mode of being that is the spitting image (though at times a mirror image) of their mode of being. This is true for our children; it is also true for us. What is apparent (what seems real) to the parent and is thus the central issue around which the parent's life is conducted will also be the parent of the child's experience and way of being. Thought is the parent. Every child is thus a model child. To the parent then, the child becomes a teacher. Through his being as an image and likeness of the parent, the child explains (makes plain by bringing out into the open) the parental thought of which the parentchild is also an image and likeness.

Parenthood has two meanings. On the one hand the weakness and helplessness of the child as an immature organism dependent for life, safety, sustenance, training, and education on a greater, stronger, more mature organism reflects an idea of parenthood that is an ego trip and a powerplay. To Me, Inc., haver and doer, the baby is only a smaller Me, Inc.—a possession and a project. This belief is constantly proving itself false in the parent/child experience through exhaustion, frustration, and discouragement. We lug, prod, stumble, and fumble over our children, which only and at last (if we have the least inclination to learn) proves to us that this is not what the child is and not what he is for; and that this is not what we are and not what we are for; and that this is not what parenthood and childhood and family life are, and not what they are for.

At the same time that what isn't so is being made plain, we are also being shown and shoved toward what we really are and what we really are for.

The other, truer meaning of the child is brought home two ways. Beautifully, quietly, amazingly (if we have eyes to see) right where there seems to be a little body produced by two big ones, we see *awareness* and *vitality* taking place. We know right off the bat that that vitality (being) and that awareness (seeing) are not something that we *did.* And we can only recognize and marvel.

Insofar as we do not recognize the child as this seeing being, the true spiritual nature of the child is bringing itself home to us in other, less pleasant ways: as problems and mandates. When we have done everything *necessary*—provided food, toys, diapers, exercise—and she is still hungry and restless, we are brought face to face with the fact that her *essential* needs and being are spiritual. We can do all the right, all the loving things, as diligently and perfectly as we like, but if our consciousness is filled with resentment or worry or frustration she remains unsatisfied, uncomfortable, restless. Because she *is aware* of when love is present and when it is not. So what the child sees (is aware of) determines her being (how she is).

Often at the time of birth we are so preoccupied with bodies —the mother's big one, the baby's tiny, breathing one—that we do not stop to consider what is the most outstanding characteristic of the newborn baby. Look at his eyes. Evidently they are seeing next to nothing, and yet seeingness or alertness is what they express most of all. Clearly he knows next to nothing and yet there he is, *conscious, aware, alert,* above all interested in seeing— not judging, not liking or disliking—just seeing what is so.

This consciousness is his definition. Any mother thinking back to the first moments when she and her baby looked at each other can remember it—the wide-awake looking. This quality of awareness is most memorable because it more than anything else is the truth of the child. As the wave is to water, the baby is to consciousness. He comes of it (conception), is made of it, and to it he returns. Only insofar as he becomes fully conscious does he become fully himself.

This recognition on the part of the parent is basic to true

parental love. Indeed, there is no more practical definition of love than that it is the realization of the truth of being of the beloved. The idea of love as a way of treating each other, as a feeling between each other, puts it on a have and have-not basis. Such love is always experienced as loss (in fact, theft) on the part of both the lover and the beloved. Between parent and child it is tinged with anxiety, worry, frustration, weariness, and resentment on the part of the parent, and with insecurity, dependence, rebelliousness, and depression on the part of the child. For the implication is always that the child is *un* whole, *in* adequate, *un* safe, *in* capable, even bad. The beloved is belittled. And life as a context is also seen as *in* complete, *un* fulfilling, *im* perfect, and *un* reliable.

But now we are going about love differently. We recognize, affirm that, and proceed as if our child really is perfect consciousness; and we treat everything else as a passing illusion. We still deal with the immaturities—ministering, caring, correcting, comforting, teaching, serving as needed—but we do not affix them to our child. Instead, we consciously separate him—his true, perfect, conscious, whole self—from everything else that seems to be. In this way an environment of letting be occurs in which the child most effortlessly becomes what he truly is.

So also are the true meaning of ourselves as parents and the circumstance of parenthood and family life brought to light. The child we thought we bore bears us toward the discovery of ourselves as spiritual consciousnesses, seeing beings. Our children both demonstrate and force us to see that life in general, parenthood in particular, is less a matter of doing and having than of seeing.

The child is not the only one who is maturing. We, too, are on the path of becoming what we truly are, that is, consciously conscious. Since consciousness is our true substance, it is interesting to note that the word *substance* comes from the Latin meaning *under* and *to stand,* that is, to stand under or *understand.* Love as the perception of that which is substantial is itself substantiating. To be loving is to be understanding. To be understanding is to be conscious. If the truth of the child's being is perfect consciousness and we perceive this, then we have become conscious ourselves. In perceiving the true substance—the consciousness of the child

—we become ourselves conscious, and thus realize, or substantiate, our own lives more fully. In the instant of perfect consciousness there is oneness—the realization that there is only one mind, one self, and that it is all good.

So the child is the parent and the parent is the child and our time together becomes a joyful participation in the process of our evermore coming, childparent and parentchild together, to see and express our true nature.

What Have I Done to My Life?

Parenthood always comes as a shock. Postpartum blues? Postpartum panic is more like it. We set out to have a baby; what we get is a total take-over of our lives. But even in the surprising early days there are many blessings to even a little spiritual awareness. We are eased of resentment, for we realize that we have not given up our lives for our children but that rather our life with our children is part and parcel of our own path toward self-realization. We are eased of our sense of personal responsibility (blame, guilt), for we realize that each child is what he is: awareness seeking awareness. We did not make him; we cannot break him. Our children are freed of our overbearing, overzealous trespassing, for now we view them less as projects than as revelations. And we look at their problems as opportunities for learning rather than as something wrong.

Assurances

For the many of us for whom the early days with the new baby are fraught with one trial or another, here are some assurances:

• For some people what you find difficult is incredibly easy. This does not mean you are terrible or ungifted parents or that you got a dirty deal. It means that the difficulties *can* fall away.

• For some people what you find easy is terribly difficult. This does not mean that you are superior parents; it means that God is God.

• The really dependent days are so few that you could almost miss the whole course. Suppose you live ninety years and your child who is born when you are about thirty heavily depends on you for three and a half years. If you wish away those three and a half years, you may spend fifty-six and a half years being nostalgic over what you missed. *That's* unhappiness.

• The baby needs peace more than sleep. Believe it or not, so do you. So don't struggle over sleep; just learn to be peaceful together.

• The baby needs love more than food. So don't struggle over eating; just learn to be loving together.

• Give yourself over for the time being. Learn what is to be learned. Enjoy what is to be enjoyed. See what is signified. What could be more important to long-range happiness than learning true peace, love, beauty, harmony? Money? Career? Tennis? Certainly there is a place for all these, but there's no rush about them.

• So look for peace, love, beauty, order, harmony unconditionally. Find them in the baby and in yourself. Enjoy being together. Together enjoy being.

• Good news! The baby doesn't want to die, and he does not depend on you to do all his living for him. Parents are servants, suppliers, helpers, and colleagues—not prime movers. Having loving parents can make all the difference in the smooth unfolding of the baby's life. But let's not exaggerate our own importance with illusions of guilt and pride. Our children certainly need mothering and fathering, but they do not specifically need *us* as their mothers and fathers. The best reason for being with our children is not simply that they need us, but that we need to become what we are, motherly and fatherly. Hardly any experience could change our lives more beneficially or faster than a correct appreciation of the significance of this one called parenthood.

• If you have to go to work, you have to go to work. No big deal. If it's a good idea, you can find someone loving to care for the baby; and when you leave, you need not think you are abandoning her. You are not her *source* of love. You are just one place that love is taking shape. You are not the only shape that love can take. She lives in your consciousness. You can guard her in your thoughts, knowing her to be in perfect health and in perfect love and care. What you can know, she can experience. The biggest task of parenthood is in thought. Parental consciousness can be maintained anywhere. This does not mean worrying and fretting and

49

calling home every five minutes. As a parent, seek simply to be aware of parentliness.

● New experiences such as this overwhelming one of parenthood do not exist so that we can put what we already know to the test or on display, but rather so that we can learn what we need to know. So don't worry about what you don't know—what you don't *yet* know. The new situation that demands new understanding of us is also the channel through which that understanding may come. What we need to know is always a given in the situation that requires this knowledge. Prior experience is not necessary. Urgencies are provided, and all we need is to be seeing beings, sincerely receptive to what *is* revealing itself to us.

> *My people will abide in a peaceful habitation, in secure dwellings, and in quiet resting places.*
> —Isaiah 32:18

Diet for a Seeing Being: Essential Ingredients

Almost invariably the arrival of the new baby brings about a tremendous involvement with food and feeding. Whether we are breast- or bottle-feeding, our entire lives are suddenly wrapped up in bodily processes. *Is it time for a feeding? Is the baby getting enough? Has she eaten too much? Hungry again? or just tired? I've been feeding her the whole afternoon, so I haven't even started to fix supper.*

What happened to parenthood? Is there nothing to it but maintenance? Somebody told us that babies are nothing but little eating and pooping machines. At the time we didn't think that was a nice joke—now we don't think it is a joke at all.

So after a few months the digestive difficulties are sure to abate. The breast/bottle struggle has worked itself out. The baby doesn't die; neither do we. Enter solid food—tidbits everywhere and little jars of this and that. Now on top of the concern with eating enough, we have the worry of whether or not he's eating the right things. Next he begins to feed himself—and his hair and his eyes and the highchair and the floor. Oddly enough he's a little shy of messing up his clean hands with the fingerpaints we paid good money for. He likes squash and beans and creamed chicken better. (I used to toy with the idea of feeding my child in a different room at every meal. That way, I could be sure the house would be thoroughly washed every twenty-four hours.)

All this time the regular grocery shopping, cooking, and cleaning up go on, getting more and more complicated as the baby becomes mobile and wants to play an active role in the kitchen. Somewhere along the way we've translated our lunch into an all-day snack, and though we feel we're eating nothing we are putting on weight. Our hungry baby woke us at 5:00 A.M.; here it is 10:30 P.M. and we're just starting to wash the dinner dishes.

But all the time we sort of know—we even say from time to time—that *there just must be an easier way.* We can't quite believe it has to be so hard. Yet many of us never find the way—we simply endure. As with everything else, the answer lies in a right understanding of who we really are and what it is that we are really about.

We tend to think of our offspring in material terms. We "made" a baby, "gave" it birth, and now we have to feed him so that he can become big and strong. But *did* we make the baby? *How* did we do that? Did the baby make the baby? When we hold the seed of the sweet pea in our hands or when we plant it in the soil, where is the colorful blossom? Is it in the seed? Do we put it into the seed? Can we say that it doesn't exist? No, only that it is not material. With the seed we participate in the materializing of an idea. What is the substance of an idea? Spirit. And what or where is the beginning or end of an idea? No beginning. No end.

> Oats, peas, beans, and barley grows,
> Oats, peas, beans, and barley grows.
> Nor you, nor I, nor anyone knows
> How oats, peas, beans, and barley grows.
> —Traditional nursery rhyme

Yet here we are with this baby on our hands, stuffing her full of food as if that will make her into something more or other. It's as if we tried to make a sweet pea blossom out of a seed by stuffing the seed with soil. But oats, peas, beans—*and babies* grow! It is written into the very nature of the oat, pea, bean, and barley to grow into fruitful plants. Nobody questions whether they want to do this, or can. So why do we doubt our children? When the farmer sows a nice, round, healthy oat and it doesn't grow well, he doesn't say, "What's the matter with this oat? It must be lazy or sick or emotionally disturbed in some way." He assumes that something is wrong with the environment in which he knows that oat is trying to grow. Then he sets about trying to perceive what is needed.

Parenthood is similar, although in two ways it's harder than farming. First of all, we have a less clear picture of what a healthy man or woman is than we do of a mature crop of oats. Secondly, the growing environment of the young child is not made up of soil and weather conditions; it's us—what we know, our consciousness. On this our perspective is not quite so panoramic and detached as the farmer's. But in one way our task is easier than farming, for, unlike the oat, the child is constantly telling us what he needs.

What is needed for this growth to take place? As we have begun to see, the answer is not simply material food; it is nourishment. As mothers and fathers, our job is not to create but to nourish. In nutrition the concern is with maintaining life— strengthening, building up, and promoting health. And what is health? *Health* and *holy* have the same Old English root, the word *hale,* which means *whole.* The difference between the words *healthy* and *holy* is only the distinction historically made between the physical and the spiritual. But a strictly physical concept of health is not whole; at best it is partial.

If we feed our children only food, no matter how much they consume, they will be at least half-starved. The body can never be whole—it is at best a partial representation of a spiritual idea. Doctors correctly refer to the baby's breathing and the beating of his heart as vital signs. They are not vitality, they have not vitality, but they express and signify the presence of vitality. It is the unfolding of the whole ideal self of the child with which we are concerned. Since the substance of an idea is not material but spiritual, it is obvious that spiritual nourishment is what the child needs. So we need a whole concept of the child and a whole concept of nutrition.

The ideal food for the ideal child must be love, since, after all, the ideal individual is above all a loving individual. There is a sense in which we can say that food makes the man. If we want our children to become peaceful, assured, joyful, and loving adults they must be nourished with peace, assurance, joy, and love.

We don't have to look to the end result to see that love is the prime food for sustaining the life of the child. Our children are primarily spiritual and their nourishment is primarily spiritual. Whenever love is present, all is well. Whenever love is absent, nothing is going well.

Our own children take us a step further. Even when we fondle and frolic with as well as feed and change them, if love is not a present state of consciousness or if it is—the condition of our consciousness registers directly in the child's consciousness and is accordingly translated into well-being or distress.

Nursing Child

Like everything else, breast-feeding has two meanings: material and spiritual. On a material level, in theory at least, it is the most fussless way of feeding the infant. If it goes well it can spare us messy feeding days. Many mothers feed their children nothing but breast milk until around five months. Then food is gradually introduced (by this time most babies can eat without slobbering everything all over the place). By eight or nine months, babies are proficient with training cups and largely able to feed themselves. No bottles ever! Further, breast-feeding may be a mutually sensuous experience which gives the mother pleasurable excitement and a sense of power and importance while the baby has an experience of closeness, security, and oral pleasure.

That this may not be an entirely true or complete picture is suggested by certain frequent difficulties. Breast-feeding may not "go well." It takes much more time than you anticipated, and you (mother or father) may come to resent this, feeling either used or neglected or both. In proportion as you find it pleasurable, you may be reluctant to give it up. In proportion as you do not, your child's need to suck becomes a tyrannizing demand.

LaLeche League deals extensively with all these contingencies, and *Whole Child/Whole Parent* has nothing to add in the way of technique or advice about what to do, whether to nurse, how or how not. But there is one essential thought to be considered: whether or not we breast-feed our babies, whether or not they are actually at the breast, even whether our children are tiny milk-sucking infants, or ten-year-old hamburger wolfers, whether they are feeding or sleeping, or playing or studying, or at home or away from home, *our children are ceaselessly nursing on our consciousness and being nourished or malnourished accordingly.*

This point cannot be made strongly enough. When the question is asked, "Do you plan to nurse the baby?" or "Are you still nursing your baby or have you given it up?" we should all be laughing. *Whether we plan to nurse the baby or not, the child will nurse; and she will never stop nursing as long as she is a child; and she will nurse not only from the mother's but also from the father's consciousness.*

For the sake of new parents we happen to be considering the early days of parenthood—breast-feeding, feeding, etc. But the fact is that through all the years childhood, and, indeed, through all their lives, our children will continue to nurse from our consciousness. If this doesn't make us quake in our shoes, then we haven't really understood it. But if we have understood it, after we finish quaking in our shoes, we can begin to seek and to find relief, harmony, beauty, and inspiration.

So what is the new parent feeding the new baby? Often mostly milk and worry—also discouragement, guilt, resentment, and general uptightness. No wonder if things have been going badly. Fortunately the baby is not yet conscious enough to learn these things from us or even to experience them emotionally. He is so largely a material translation of his ideal self that most of the mental nutrition (or malnutrition) we pass on to him is translated into temporary physical terms. He is not conscious of our worry or nervousness as worry or nervousness, but in some way he is aware of whether peace is there or not; of whether love is there or not. And in some way he experiences or encounters our secret mental anguish and displays it to us as physical discomfort, struggling, spitting up, etc. However, when we feed him on love—the true stuff of his true self—we see this translated into a physical state of peaceful well-being.

Nursing Parent

But we can only feed him what we have, and spiritually we can only "have" what we are aware of while we are aware of it. Once we reach physical maturity, our nourishment is more and more a matter of pure idea. As ideal selves, our fulfillment ultimately depends upon our consciousness of the truth about ourselves. This means knowing and expressing love, peace, gratitude, assurance, generosity, joy.

Having discerned that *all children are always nursing,* we arrive at yet another principle of nutrition, which is that *the nursing child needs a nursing parent.* Nursing mothers have to drink plenty of liquids; nursing spiritual parents, both father and mother, need a nourished spiritual consciousness.

> *Like newborn babes, long for the pure spiritual milk, that by it you may grow up to salvation; for you have tasted the kindness of the Lord.*
> —1 Peter 2:2–3

> *But I have calmed and quieted my soul,*
> *like a child quieted at its mother's breast,*
> *like a child that is quieted is my soul.*
> —Psalm 131:2

We can see that the baby is as much an instrument of nourishment for us as we are for him. We can foster his growth as a peaceful and loving individual only if we nourish him with love and peace. We can express love and peace only if we know love and peace. And we can know love and peace only if this is what we hunger for and feed upon in consciousness. Most of us would do more for our babies than we have ever been willing to do for anyone, even ourselves. In this way the child (seemingly so helpless) performs the mighty work of awakening in us a tremendous appetite for understanding and so brings us to the table of love.

We stand there in awful hunger, asking two huge questions. Our whole lives have been the asking of these questions, but only as we consciously frame them does the pre-existent truth become receivable as answers. *To be loving we need to be aware of being loved.*

But how can we do this? How, apart from doing or saying or thinking, how can we fill to overflowing our consciousness with love? How, apart from getting and having and feeling, can we know that we are loved?

After long years of searching and studying, and not a little struggling, the following has brought itself home to me. It may be the most important idea expressed in this book; and yet it may seem meaningless, academic, even irritating to some. If that is so for you, then skip it for now. Don't struggle with it, don't even reread it unless or until something makes you want to come back to it. For me, at least, it answers these questions: *How can we fill our consciousness with love? How can we know that we are loved?*

Song of the Seeing Being

The more we realize that seeing is the issue in life,
the more interested we are in seeing.
The more interested we are in seeing,
the more we look at everything for what it has to teach us.
The more we look at everything for what it has to teach us,
the more we see that we are being taught.
The more we see that we are being taught,
the more we know that we are loved.
The more we know that we are loved,
the more we see love.
The more we see love,
the more lovingly we are seeing.
The more lovingly we are seeing,
the more loving we are being.
The more loving we are being,
the more we realize that seeing is the issue in life . . .
The more . . . [start over]

Seeing is being. Intelligence expresses itself as love. Awareness expresses itself as being. Knowing is loving. Loving is knowing. And what we are feeding on in consciousness is what we are nursing on. And what we are nursing on is what our children are nursing on.

Just as it is not possible to bring love into the life of the child simply by doing loving things, neither can we achieve a loving state of mind simply by believing that we should, or trying to think loving thoughts. In fact, we could just about drive ourselves crazy trying to do that. But once the need for spiritual realization is recognized and the interest sincere, it is possible to nourish spiritual consciousness. Just being alert to the deeper significance of everything helps, and further study, prayer, and meditation can be helpful as they are understood and appreciated aright. But nothing can or needs to be forced.

I have meat to eat that ye know not of.
—John 4:32

My meat is to do the will of him that sent me.
—John 4:34

Truly, truly, I say to you, the Son can do nothing of his own accord, but only what he sees the Father doing.
—John 5:19

Besides the Bible, I have found the books listed here helpful in nourishing spiritual consciousness. Different things are helpful at different times, and a book that seems offensive at one point may be helpful at another. And one book may be inspired by truth while another by the same author may not. So don't feel frustrated if you find some, even all, of these books inaccessible or uninviting. When a book seems too obscure or too "religious"—just lay it aside and wait. There are other books; there are other ways altogether. The same is true of prayer and meditation; there are ways and there are ways. The main thing is simply to be receptive to some spiritual nourishment, to give some attention to it, some quiet time, some consideration.

Chute, Marchette, *The Search,* E. P. Dutton, New York 1941.
———, *The End of the Search,* E. P. Dutton, New York, 1947.
The Cloud of Unknowing, Underhill, Evelyn (edited from the British Museum MS: with an introduction by Underhill), Stuart & Watkins, London, 1946, 1970.
The Dhammapada, Lal, P. (translator), Farrar, Straus & Giroux, New York, 1967.
Fausset, Hugh L'Anson, *The Flame and the Light,* Theosophical Publishing Society, Wheaton, Ill., 1958, 1976.

Fox, Emmet, *The Sermon on the Mount,* Harper & Row, New York, 1934.

Goldsmith, Joel, *The Infinite Way,* DeVorss, Marina Del Rey, Calif., 1954.

————, *Realization of Oneness,* Citadel Press, Secaucus, N.J., 1974.

Graham, Dom Aelred, *Zen Catholicism,* Harcourt Brace Jovanovich, New York, 1963.

Holm, Nora, *The Runner's Bible,* Houghton Mifflin, Boston, 1913, 1915, 1941, 1943.

Hora, Thomas, *Dialogues in Metapsychiatry,* Seabury Press, New York, 1977.

————, *Existential Metapsychiatry,* Seabury Press, New York, 1977.

Linthorst, Ann, *The Gift of Love,* Paulist Press, New York, 1979.

Meister Eckhart, Blakney, Raymond (translator), Harper & Row, New York, 1946.

Prabhavananda, Swami, *The Sermon on the Mount According to Vedanta,* Vedanta Press, Hollywood, Calif., 1964.

The Way of Life, According to Laotzu, Bynner, Witter (translator), John Day, New York, 1944, 1962.

Nursing Creature

Whether we happen to be parents or not, honest reflection reveals that we continue to nurse on our parents' consciousness long after childhood, if only in the sense that our parents' values, their perspective on life and on us, continues (positively or negatively) to be the central, governing concern in our lives. Struggle to reform our character, behavior, or experience is fruitless until the human parental thought of what we seem to be, whatever that may be, is replaced with an essential, spiritual understanding that we are children of *Our Father Which Art.*

We are, after all, fundamentally nursing creatures. Our consciousness hungers for but cannot produce its own content. So it suckles constantly on some conscious content which in turn is transformed into our way of being alive and experiencing life. But consciousness is primary to all our being and experiencing. As Me, Inc., we cannot in any way personally reshape ourselves or our experiences, but as seeing beings we can learn to exercise choice over what we nurse on and discern whether it is true or false. As Me, Inc., most of the time we conduct our lives in terms of doing and having and feeling, but eventually we need to begin to *be aware of what we* seem *to be aware of.* Because *whatever it is that we put in charge of our consciousness we are putting in charge of our life.*

Our children are not our children. We are neither parents of our children nor children of our parents. We are all God's children, and to the extent that we are nourished in this truth will our lives be reformed and transformed.

> *And be ye not conformed to this world; but be ye transformed by the renewing of your mind, that ye may prove what is that good and acceptable and perfect will of God.*
> —Romans 12:2

Just who do we think we are anyway? Just who in the hell do I *think* I am? Just what—just who—am I trying to prove? The proof is in the pudding, or in the sticky situation.

> *By their fruits ye shall know them.*
> —Matthew 7:16, 20

Looking at ourselves and our children and at nursing in a spiritual light brings benefits to parent and child. Before, breast-feeding was an interruption in our life; it now becomes a welcome lull and a time for our spiritual nourishment. While the child nurses, we may read or consider spiritual ideas, or simply take time to commune (become one with) certain spiritual qualities. Nursing becomes a refreshing rather than a draining time, a time of self-fulfillment rather than self-sacrifice.

In breast-feeding, once we are no longer anxious, the milk flows freely and does not "sour the stomach." The baby, no longer surrounded by worry, becomes his peaceful, comfortable self. Now, though we enjoy them more, we may have fewer feedings, also fewer diapers and spit-ups, less laundry, and (though we need it less!) more sleep. We are suddenly struck by the fact that the milk (which we did nothing to make) *is there!* The love we wish to express and wish to receive is also simply there whenever, like a child turning to his mother's breast, we sincerely turn our attention to it.

The work of nursing, preparing food, spoon-feeding, and cleaning up is also decreased to a large extent. Having greater faith in the wholeness of the child, we don't manufacture seven-course trial menus anymore, or spend hours trying "to get him to eat." (One couple reported that they used so many pots and pans fixing supper for their baby that they had to wash dishes before cooking dinner for themselves.) All mealtime proceedings become more enjoyable—because it is pleasanter to be concerned with fellowship and generosity and love at mealtimes and because we understand that we need to express love.

Feeding the Whole Seeing Being and Allowing Him to Feed Himself

What is the wholesome food for the wholesome child? The child is not a body but a seeing being. So now the question becomes: *How do you feed the whole spiritual seeing being?* Food is necessary, but what is essential? In what way do the essential and the necessary become one in the feeding of the child?

In the discovery that there is a seeing being rather than just a body to be fed many things already become clear that were problematic before.

Almost as soon as she starts receiving solid food (assuming it isn't introduced for a few months) she begins to want to feed herself. While she is not likely to eat unless hungry, she is not simply feeding herself *because* her stomach is hungry either. Her feeding, reaching, feeling the food, pulling it into her mouth, is learning. And almost more than the food it is learning for which she hungers.

When she is popping peas with her fingers rather than eating them, she *is* eating! Her seeing self is nourished through finding out what it hungers to know. This recognition already leads to many blessings. Before we feared (*is she eating enough?*); now we are amazed (*how insatiable is her appetite for learning!*). Before we felt resentment and frustration (*so much mess, why won't she quit fooling around?*); now there is an atmosphere of love and a flooding in of intelligent ideas. Did we take squished peas personally before? We don't anymore. Were we frustrating her by trying to prevent her from doing what she starved to do? Now—seeing it in a fresh light —we find it somewhat easier to put up with, and are provided with more ideas for nourishing her consciousness at less inconvenience to us.

Before we conceived of the child as a seeing being we were preoccupied with what she should eat and how to make her do that. After we recognize her as a seeing being we become aware that she is already constantly feeding and that there is something in her that knows what she needs. When she is older the same thing will apply to her interests, her preferences, her hobbies and passions. We can trust her. We can trust life. We can entrust her to life. Life itself is working in her—one thing leading to another. "Sheep may safely graze."

Seeing what our children are trying to learn inspires us with many thoughtful ideas on how to prepare food—not only to nourish their bodies but also to help them learn what they are trying to learn. Realizing that they are not simply "playing with food" when they should be eating it, but rather learning, it occurs to us that there are many "foods for thought." Whether or not they get eaten, the peas in a pod are amazing; the star in the apple is a wonder.

Later, after we finish with the feeding fuss, we enter the under-foot phase: Someone's in the kitchen with Dinah. And she isn't strumming on the old banjo, she's clawing at our stockings, fussing to be picked up, grabbing at and tipping over bowls and pans. Left alone it would take you five minutes to fix supper, but she wants to be held. Ever try to operate an eggbeater with one hand?

Before you perceive the child as a seeing being, cooking is either a chore or an emergency. You are Dinah, slave to your child's physical needs and limitations. You would like her to stay out of your way while you get your chore out of the way so she can eat what you believe she so desperately needs but won't let you fix. After you begin to look at both your child and yourself as seeing beings, your kitchen time together takes on a different meaning.

There are two reasons for including our children in our kitchen activities. One is that we can't keep them out and get anything done at the same time. The other is that this may be the best place in the house for both parent and child to learn what we most need to know. We all have certain material and certain spiritual work that can best be done in the kitchen. The child's biggest task is to explore the material properties of her world and learn how to deal with them. And where could you find a finer, better-equipped learning laboratory than the average kitchen? Here such spiritual nutrients as love, humility, abundance, order, beauty, gratitude are concretely expressible. Here especially we can discover and demonstrate what these qualities mean.

The spiritually alert parent reviews every activity in an essential light. In the kitchen, without this perspective, as Me, Inc., we are giving up "our thing" to cook for others. Or we may try to become a gourmet and win praise from others. Either way the presence of a toddler underfoot or the absence of more help and appreciation becomes a problem. But when task and circumstance are viewed spiritually, essentially, the necessary work is accomplished more easily—and joyfully.

For the child the kitchen is a learning museum. Supplied with endless tools and activities just right for his learning needs, the toddler is happily busy with his work while we are freer to accomplish ours. No manufacturer's toy exceeds the drip coffee pot for the baby who wants to grab and lift and bang and take apart and in and out and put together. No sandbox offers the two- or three-year-old more than the kitchen sink or a basin of rice with spoons and measuring cups. No museum, science program, or junior chemistry set offers the grade school child so much as the freedom to bake and cook and experiment in the kitchen. No classroom, play group, or other family situation provides such regular opportunities for learning to work and love together as the kitchen. As the years go by and you see your children growing up, and away, over and over you will seek meaningful communication—"before it's too late." Though my children are still young, I can already say that we have told more stories, sung more songs, shared more profound thoughts, exchanged more deep secrets, confessed more doubts and received more assurance, hugged and laughed harder, and been kinder and freer and jollier together drying dishes in the kitchen than we ever have sitting at dinner or before the fire.

A monk told Joshu: "I have just entered the monastery. Please teach me."
Joshu asked: "Have you eaten your rice porridge?"
The monk replied: "I have eaten."
Joshu said: "Then you had better wash your bowl!"

At that moment the monk was enlightened.
—*Zen Flesh, Zen Bones,* compiled by Paul Reps

Jesus said, "Therefore I say unto you. Take no thought for your life, what ye shall eat, or what ye shall drink; nor yet for the body, what ye shall put on. Is not the life more than meat, and the body more than raiment? Behold the fowls of the air; for they sow not, neither do they reap, nor gather into barns; yet your heavenly Father feedeth them. Are ye not much better than they? Which of you by taking thought can add one cubit unto his stature? And why take ye thought for raiment? Consider the lilies of the field, how they grow; they toil not, neither do they spin: And yet I say unto you, that even Solomon in all his glory was not arrayed like one of these. Wherefore, if God so clothes the grass of the field, which today is, and tomorrow is cast into the oven, shall he not much more clothe you, O ye of little faith? Therefore take no thought, saying, What shall we eat? or, what shall we drink? or wherewithal shall we be clothed? For after all these things do the Gentiles seek: for your heavenly Father knoweth that ye have need of all these things. But seek ye first the kingdom of God, and his righteousness; and all these things shall be added unto you."
—Matthew 6:25–33

Man shall not live by bread alone, but by every word that proceedeth out of the mouth of God.
—Matthew 4:4

When a hungry monk at work heard the dinner gong he immediately dropped his work and showed himself in the dining room. The master, seeing him, laughed heartily, for the monk had been acting Zen to its fullest extent. Nothing could be more natural; the one thing needful is to open one's eye to the significance of it all.
—D. T. Suzuki, *Introduction to Zen Buddhism*

Of Purer Eyes

The baby cries. But we just fed him! He can't still be hungry. Maybe he's tired? Maybe he just needs a change. Oh, yes, see? Diaper rash. That was it, wasn't it? Or is it something else—something more . . . ? He cries, or maybe he *doesn't* cry! What's the matter with him? What's *wrong?*

No matter how well we cleaned our mental closet, worries come and worries go—and worries come . . . wishes and fears, acceptable—and dread. Some worries precede problems; sometimes problems provoke the worries; but they keep bobbing up and have to be dealt with somehow—responsively, lovingly, *continuously.* What a huge responsibility! What if we make a mistake? What if there's something really terrible the matter and we don't do anything? We can feel our imagination running away with us. What if it *isn't* our imagination?

> Nobody teaches little ducklings to swim, and nobody tells the water to hold them up. And as for the mother duck, what does she say, or do—or know? Not much. But when it is time she gets the idea to lead her ducklings down to the water. What does she do then? She just wades in and the ducklings follow. One minute they are waddling awkwardly on the land, and the next they are swimming. It all comes so naturally. There doesn't seem to be any doubt. And unless it is polluted, the river does not let them down. So whatever it is about the river that can hold things up is fulfilled in the little floating ducks. And whatever it is about ducks that can float and glide is fulfilled in the river. And the unseen quality of buoyancy expresses and fulfills itself in its oneness with them both.

We have said that the child lives in the parents' consciousness. So let's say that in parenthood the water is love (which implies well-being) and the river is the individual consciousness of the parent. The duck is the child—fully equipped for floating (and thereby expressing love as well-being)—paddling through our consciousness. Love is there, abundant, sustaining. The child is whole. Love then will flow through us to uphold the child as long as there are no interfering pollutants in our stream of consciousness.

With the rest of the world we share many worries concerning our children's potential for ill-being and our own shortcomings as parents. There are two major mental pollutants: one is all the thoughts about what can go wrong; the other is Me, Inc.'s belief in itself—that we are or should be in charge. Two things the mother duck has that we seem to lack are confidence in the water and no illusions about herself. Conveniently for her, she is just too dumb to get confused.

Actually the same self-starring Metrogoldwyn Me character that we saw featured in wishes is often featured in our worries as well. We depend on some troubles as excuses. *So that's what's the matter with him!* she sighed thankfully. Who is relieved by the bad news? The self-blaming parent. Who is the self-blaming parent? The disillusioned, frustrated superparent.

Watch. See how we sometimes count on little problems to break up the humdrum of everyday life. Everything is going fine, but nobody's noticing. We feel lonely with our children. The phone rings:

"I just thought you'd want to know. Johnny has been throwing up all evening—ever since he played with your Suzy in the park."

"Oh, poor you! I'm so sorry. But thanks eversomuch for letting me know. What are his symptoms? Fever? Headache? No? That's good. It was so thoughtful of you to call."

Like Snow White biting into the poisoned apple, we bite and are immediately asleep and dreaming. In the dream we are searching for something. For what? The signs of sickness. We know exactly what to look for. We hope she won't get it, but we are watching and waiting for it to start.

"Hi, it's me. Suzy has it, too. Only she also has a headache. Oh, now Johnny does, too? Well, then they do have the same thing."

Now we are less lonely and bored:

"Who was it they were playing with? You're right. I'll call them right away."

Now we are also more important:

"Got to go now. Suzy needs me."

It isn't enough to say to ourselves that just because one child has the flu our child doesn't have to have it. We need to go further, beholding the essential, spiritual child in her truest, purest light— not as my baby with stuffy or not nose and hot or not cheeks, but that other lasting child, the seeing being floating in and expressing God. And we need to recognize and relinquish any tendency to seek credit or blame in relation to others or through our children, realizing, instead, the fact and fullness of our lives as expressions of divine love.

It is important constantly to seek awareness of our children's essential perfection. *Despite all appearances, rumors, diagnoses, and experiences to the contrary, we constantly hold in the forefront of our thoughts the perfect, whole, unmarrable, essential nature of the child and the power of love to bear us both up.* This is not simply wishful, positive, or magical thinking. We do not cause good any more than we make rivers pure by not dumping garbage into them. If we don't dump garbage into the river its purity remains evident. Wholeness, goodness, and perfection are the truth of essential being. By not entertaining contrary thoughts we allow this wholeness freer expression.

Rivers get polluted only when their essential purity and value as a support of life is not appreciated. So even with rivers the real pollution is mental. This is only more true for us as parents. Even before the phone rings and our well-meaning neighbor gives us a lesson in precisely how to be sick, we are full of thoughts about various disasters, some of which we are sure will befall us sooner or later. The only question is which, when, how. We are waiting in suspense.

Like the waterways, the rivers of our minds are already polluted and need purification. We need to recognize and rid our thoughts of old unquestioned beliefs (whether cherished, feared, or hated), and to exercise discrimination over the new ideas we admit into our consciousness.

But there is no purification without appreciation of purity. If we don't know what the river is, how do we know what doesn't belong there?

The baby is dirty all the time. We are constantly changing his diapers and wiping his bottom. Yet it's easy to see that he is pure. His mess has nothing to do with him; he doesn't even know about it. And his ignorance of the mess he makes has nothing to do with him either; he will learn. We are not deceived by the mess into thinking that he is either impure or stupid. We have never seen such purity! No matter what he does to sheets, diapers, clothes, or our laps, purity remains to us an obvious characteristic of the child's true self.

This purity we see—that's truth! And the distinguishing we do between the purity and the mess—that's love! We deal with the mess twenty-four hours a day, but we do not allow it to become confused in our thoughts with the perfect picture we have of the child; hence, it does not interfere with love. And let's not confuse the love with the diaper-changing, just as we do not confuse the baby with the mess. Love is not the diaper-changing or the fixing of meals or disciplining or whatever it is that we must do along the way. *Love is the sorting out in thought of the perfect child from all suggestions to the contrary.*

No matter how orderly and clean the parents may be, if they continuously include their child's waste products in their picture of the child, the child may become involved with his excrement too, perhaps smearing it or relieving himself in inappropriate places. Likewise the child who is held in thought to his errors will manifest them steadfastly. He cannot do otherwise. But a clear picture of the perfect child in the parent's consciousness, which sees (unsees) all imperfection as irrelevant to the child's true being, allows the child to develop truthfully with the speediest and most effortless falling away of all irrelevant behavior.

The best way to help separate someone from his mistakes is to put a credibility gap between them. We begin by making a distinction between who they really are and who they really aren't, conducting ourselves as much as possible in relation to the real instead of in opposition to the false. This goes for everyone—including ourselves. We can practice and prove it with our children.

It is fairly easy with diapers because we more or less know what we have to do. But crying? Staying awake late? Hitting? Demanding? Whining? Being sick? It seems so much harder as we become more and more concerned with what to do instead of what we need to know. But just as we can see purity right in the middle of the diapers mess, so also must we learn to see gentleness in the middle of the violence, innocence in the face of guile, health where there seems to be sickness, perfection where imperfection seems to be, intelligence where there appears to be stupidity, goodness and the desire to be good right where there seems to be willful badness.

These spiritual qualities of purity, innocence, intelligence, gentleness, and goodness are true. Whenever we see them, we see

God (good). When we find them in our children, we discover them in ourselves. When we start finding them everywhere, we begin to see that they are true—not as personal virtues but as the truth of being. When we see that they are true, we are conscious. Now we are what we are, which is one with all that truly is. Discord, conflict, effort, ill-being, drop away; instead there is only love. This love, this perfect consciousness, is now all that we meet and all that we express, just as the water at one with all water expresses fluidity, the essential quality of water.

Here we are with a fingerful of ointment in one hand and somebody's bottom hanging by two feet from the other. What kind of oil are we applying? And what is going on in consciousness? We think of oil as both an environmental pollutant and, since time immemorial, the substance used for anointing the beloved and chosen of God.

> *Thou anointest my head with oil; my cup runneth over. Surely goodness and mercy shall follow me all the days of my life, and I will dwell in the house of the Lord forever.*
> —Psalm 23:5–6

Anointing is a way of honoring essential wholeness, perfection, and worth. It is an act of hallowing that really occurs in the mind of the one doing the anointing.

We can grease away as necessary; but at the same time let's discard the notion that the baby has to have diaper rash because that's what babies do, along with the notion that the baby is the diaper rash. ("He's a rashy baby.") We can bathe our children, washing away impurities, and then oil them with fine ointment that no friction may occur. At the same time we purify our thoughts, washing away the fears that our children are not quite perfect, that love is not enough protection for them or sufficient fulfillment for us. The choice is not between the necessary and the essential; it is just here with the necessity that we are brought to conscious awareness of the essential.

> *And when the dragon saw that he was cast unto the earth, he persecuted the woman which brought forth the manchild. And to the woman were*

given two wings of a great eagle, that she might fly into the wilderness, into her place where she is to be nourished for a time, and times, and half a time, from the face of the serpent.
—Revelation 12:13–14

Our two wings are spiritual consciousness, the ability to distinguish *what is* from *what isn't* and having done so to place *what is* in charge of our consciousness rather than fear of *what isn't*.

Once we had a sick pet which I was bringing to a vet for emergency treatment. All the while I was hating doing so, certain that there was a better, higher route and no real need for the animal to be sick. Yet it didn't seem right to be ungrateful either. I did not know much about prayer, but I thought about God and waited for some understanding. Immediately an idea came to mind very strongly: *Do what you have to do until you know what you need to know.* It was very obvious to me that I had not thought of this myself. This was the first time it was perfectly clear to me that a prayer had been answered.

Better is to *do what we have to do while seeking to know what we need to know.* With problems we can often wait to do what we have to do until it is absolutely *necessary.* And before and during and after that point we can keep our attention focused on the *essential.*

As we do whatever seems necessary to cope with and cure our difficulties, the important thing is to remain concerned with the possibility of transcending them and to focus on the lasting, the essential, the spiritual in life—by keeping sight of it, addressing ourselves to it, and expressing it.

I have seen the retarded child of a devoted parent who focused on the child's potential for consciousness float across barrier after supposed barrier, expanding and transcending not only his own diagnosed limits but the limits of medical consciousness as well. I have read of autistic children whose parents tirelessly and successfully drew them out of themselves because "what else could we do?" after all doors of help and promise had been closed to them. In my own family I have seen both major and minor symptoms disappear as mysteriously and suddenly as they came when some one of us got desperate enough to turn to God with sincere receptivity.

Take no thought for what should be or what shouldn't be; only seek to know the good of God that already is.
—Thomas Hora, *Dialogues in Metapsychiatry*

Some difficulties can be seen through and annihilated. Sometimes even in the middle of fears come "true" they can be transcended. But the real wonder and joy and purpose of our being here is not to gain power over what isn't, but to wake up to what is.

Zen Cow

Most times a cow is content to mill around in the middle of the pasture with the other cows. But when the idea of going beyond the pasture occurs to her she begins to have trouble with the barbed wire fence around the pasture. Or perhaps it is when she bumps into the barbed wire fence that she begins to be aware of the freedom beyond and to know that she is confined. The fence goes all the way around all the cows. But this cow is having a problem with the fence at a particular point. It is this particular section of the barbed wire fence that is hurting this particular cow. Now this piece of fence isn't her fault! It is just that here she becomes acutely aware of her confinement and begins to appreciate what freedom means. The cow does not get through the fence by chewing through the barbed wire or by complaining to the other cows or being angry at the farmer. But at some moment when her vision of what lies beyond gets very clear and dear to her, she just begins to go there. She becomes unaware of the fence. Following her vision, mindless of limitation, heedless of pain, she simply leans down the fence and goes. If we have a serious difficulty, or if our children do—then for now at least this is our place to break through the universal fence of ignorance. Sometimes where the fence is down, others get free, too.

Hui-neng said: "From the first not a thing is."
—D. T. Suzuki, *Zen Buddhism*

Lao Tsu said: "The nameless is the origin of heaven and earth; Naming is the mother of the ten thousand things."
—A. Watts, *The Way of Zen*

Job said: "The thing I greatly feared is come upon me!"
—Job 3:25

Paul said: "Whatsoever things are true, whatsoever things are honest, whatsoever things are just, whatsoever things are pure, whatsoever things are lovely, whatsoever things are of good report; if there be any virtue, and if there be any praise, think on these things."
—Philippians 4:8

Jesus said: "In the world ye shall have tribulation; but be of good cheer, I have overcome the world.
—John 16:33

John said: "Beloved, we are God's children now; it is not yet clear what we shall be; we only know that when he shall appear we shall be like him, for we shall see him as he is. And every man that hath this hope in him purifieth himself even as he is pure.
—1 John 3:2–3

Habakkuk said, "O thou who art of purer eyes than to behold evil, and canst not look on iniquity.
—Habakkuk 1:13

Lullabye and Good Night

A distinguished teacher was once asked, "Do you ever make any effort to get disciplined in the truth?"
"Yes, I do."
"How do you exercise yourself?"
"When I am hungry I eat; when tired I sleep."
"This is what everybody does; can they be said to be exercising themselves in the same way as you do?"
"No."
"Why not?"
"Because when they eat they do not eat, but are thinking of various other things, thereby allowing themselves to be disturbed; when they sleep they do not sleep, but dream of a thousand things. This is why they are not like myself."
—D. T. Suzuki, Introduction to *Zen Buddhism*

A lot of people have trouble going to sleep at night or waking up in the morning. According to Thomas Hora both difficulties reflect the belief that we author our own existence. But sleep is not something we can do. It is allowed. If we think we are the authors of our own existence we may be reluctant to wake up—it is so risky and strenuous to be alive. By the same token we may be reluctant to sleep; even while yearning to rest we may harbor the secret fear that if we stop thinking and doing we shall cease existing. I know a woman who can never sleep unless she falls asleep before her husband does. She equates being alive with being paid attention to. When *he* sleeps *she* feels ignored, even afraid. If no one is paying attention to her, maybe she doesn't exist. So while she is dying to get some rest she has to stay awake. Well, at least then somebody knows she exists!

If we have an exaggerated sense of responsibility for our children, we may keep them awake in the busyness of our minds. If we believe we author their lives, we may also be unconsciously involved in the process of trying to author their sleep. This is impossible, since sleeping is a process of letting go, something that is allowed. If a baby is busy, restless, struggling at bedtime, and yet you know he yearns to rest, see if you are not busy, too—with ten thousand thoughts. The thoughts can be anything—he's got to sleep, he needs it; he's got to sleep, *I* need it; I have to get some time to myself; maybe if I do this; maybe he wants that; why won't he sleep? Is it so? Then try to acknowledge that, at least for the moment, neither you nor the child has any needs beyond the awareness of love. Corny? Well, just try it.

> The Lord is my shepherd, I shall [need] not want.
> He maketh me to lie down in green pastures.
> He restoreth my soul.
> —Psalm 23:1–2

Turn the child over to love. Turn yourself over to the idea that love and peace simply are. For just a few minutes do not *think* of what you have to do or what you want to do or what the baby needs. Whether or not you remain in the room with the child, for a brief time before and after bedtime, simply give some quiet thought to the possibility that love is. Behold the child not as a burden or a body in need or a responsibility too great or a cherished possession, but as an expression of love. Behold yourself the same way, acknowledging that love is bearing you up and flowing through you unendingly. No matter what has to be done, allow yourself to be peaceful. Hold or don't hold the child, but be very honest. It is not easy to be peaceful. You are not being peaceful if your mind is racing. Cultivate peaceful consciousness; rely on the idea that love is sufficient. And in that silence it may happen that love, the only discovery of ultimate importance, breaks in upon you as a reality. If this happens, the baby will surely be peaceful and you will surely find yourself refreshed for any task.

Learning to be even momentarily truly peaceful, still of mind as well as body, takes much practice. It tends to be especially difficult in the early days of parenthood, when our lives are so suddenly so different and we are worried about how ignorant we are. We are constantly fretting mentally, so the child may continue to be restless and his sleeping habits unpredictable and brief. It will be suggested to you that the baby is manipulating you and that you are spoiling him. Don't believe it. He doesn't know anything about power struggle. If you start a power struggle with him, even when you win, you lose. Because in the process you teach him that power struggle is what life is all about. So just hang in there and seek a still and loving consciousness, that stillness of mind into which love pours itself. Let the problems fall away, let sleep, let be.

> *Unless the Lord builds the house,*
> *those who build it labor in vain.*
> *Unless the Lord watches over the city,*
> *the watchman stays awake in vain.*
> *It is in vain that you rise up early*
> *and go late to rest,*
> *eating the bread of anxious toil;*
> *for he gives to his beloved sleep.*
> *Lo, children are a heritage from the Lord.*
> —Psalm 127:1–3

High and Lifted Up

A bed, a highchair, the kitchen counter—these can become either focal points of power struggle, battlegrounds of wanting and won'ting; or they can be places where we are high and lifted up. In the morning we often do better. We say we are refreshed. I think we are more childlike: not certain of what the day will bring, we are more open to its will and less willful ourselves. But by the end of the day we are doers and don'ters, succeeders and failers, willers and won'ters, martyrs and victims. So what is bedtime, then? A time to lay down our controllingness, our feeling that we are or ought to be in charge. It is an exercise in entrusting ourselves to a greater power; as we lay down our own ideas of what our lives are, we allow ourselves to be lifted up out of power struggle.

So much of the toddler's work is physical. The physical navigating on the floor and around the furniture, the lifting of this and that, becomes tiring and deteriorates from joyful discovery to a struggle. Then mercifully it's mealtime. But mealtime, bedtime, anytime can become part of the struggle—or an opportunity for rising out of the struggle. They are places and occasions to realize that seeing more than doing is being.

> Now is the judgment of this world, now shall the ruler of this world be cast out; and I, when I am lifted up from the earth, will draw all men to myself.
> —John 12:31–32

> To thee, O Lord, I lift up my soul. O my God, in thee I trust. . . . Make me to know thy ways, O Lord; teach me thy paths. Lead me in thy truth, and teach me, for thou art the God of my salvation; for thee I wait all day long.
> —Psalm 25:1–2, 4–5

> Seek the Lord while he may be found, call upon him while he is near; let the wicked forsake his way, and the unrighteous man his thoughts; let him return to the Lord, that he may have mercy on him, and to our God, for he will abundantly pardon. For my thoughts are not your thoughts, neither are your ways my ways, says the Lord. For as the heavens are higher than the earth, so are my ways higher than your ways and my thoughts than your thoughts.
> —Isaiah 55:6–9

SEAL LULLABY

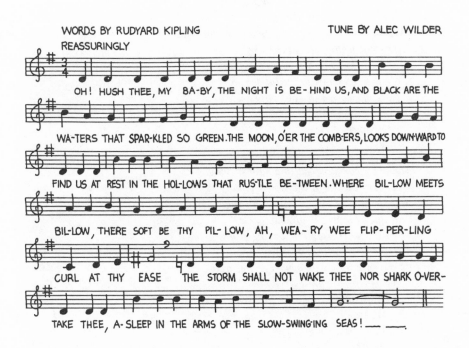

WORDS BY RUDYARD KIPLING   TUNE BY ALEC WILDER

REASSURINGLY

OH! HUSH THEE, MY BA-BY, THE NIGHT IS BE-HIND US, AND BLACK ARE THE

WA-TERS THAT SPAR-KLED SO GREEN. THE MOON, O'ER THE COMB-ERS, LOOKS DOWN-WARD TO

FIND US AT REST IN THE HOL-LOWS THAT RUS-TLE BE-TWEEN. WHERE BIL-LOW MEETS

BIL-LOW, THERE SOFT BE THY PIL- LOW, AH, WEA-RY WEE FLIP-PER-LING

CURL AT THY EASE THE STORM SHALL NOT WAKE THEE NOR SHARK O-VER-

TAKE THEE, A-SLEEP IN THE ARMS OF THE SLOW-SWING-ING SEAS! __ __

STAR WISH

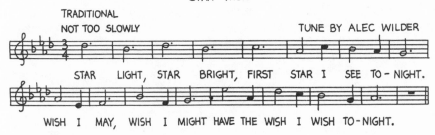

TRADITIONAL

NOT TOO SLOWLY   TUNE BY ALEC WILDER

STAR LIGHT, STAR BRIGHT, FIRST STAR I SEE TO-NIGHT.

WISH I MAY, WISH I MIGHT HAVE THE WISH I WISH TO-NIGHT.

Wynken, Blynken, and Nod one night
  Sailed off in a wooden shoe—
Sailed on a river of crystal light,
  Into a sea of dew.
"Where are you going, and what do you wish?"
  The old moon asked the three.
"We have come to fish for the herring fish
  That live in this beautiful sea;
  Nets of silver and gold have we!"
    Said Wynken,
    Blynken,
    And Nod.

The old moon laughed and sang a song,
  As they rocked in the wooden shoe,
And the wind that sped them all night long
  Ruffled the waves of dew.
The little stars were the herring fish
  That lived in that beautiful sea—
"Now cast your nets wherever you wish—
  Never afeared are we";
  So cried the stars to the fishermen three:
    Wynken,
    Blynken,
    And Nod.

All night long their nets they threw
  To the stars in the twinkling foam—
Then down from the skies came the wooden shoe,
  Bringing the fishermen home;
'Twas all so pretty a sail it seemed
  As if it could not be,
And some folks thought 'twas a dream they'd
    dreamed
  Of sailing that beautiful sea—
  But I shall name you the fishermen three:
    Wynken,
    Blynken,
    And Nod.

Wynken and Blynken are two little eyes,
  And Nod is a little head,
And the wooden shoe that sailed the skies
  Is a wee one's trundle-bed.
So shut your eyes while mother sings

Of wonderful sights that be,
And you shall see the beautiful things
As you rock in the misty sea,
Where the old shoe rocked the fishermen three:
Wynken,
Blynken,
And Nod.
—Eugene Field, "Wynken, Blynken, and Nod"

I see the moon, the moon sees me—
over the mountain, over the sea.
Please let the light that shines on me,
shine on the one I love.
—Traditional camp song

As far as I know, all children are moonstruck. Even in the city where the lights blink and blaze insistently, where the sky is often only a straight-up chimney patch, even in the daytime, if the moon is out—just a pale, pale sliver moon—the child will find it at once. "Oh, look, there's the moon!" Is the friendship between this round, clear wonder whose hand holds mine and the one in the sky (both with their whispers of faces) founded on a deep, inborn awareness of true calling? Does he already know, can he still remember, that the beauty and happiness of his whole life are to reflect a greater light? Does he already suspect that the darkness lies only in the shadow of turning away from the light in whom there is no shadow of turning? Does he already guess that in standing under (understanding) the light there is no shadow to be cast? See how he already casts about in the darkness for the light! This moonchild of mine keeps on reminding me that I must be moon for him as he is one to me.

Every good endowment and every perfect gift is from above, and cometh down from the Father of lights, with whom there is no variableness, neither shadow of turning.
—James 1:17

The child's wonder
At the old moon
Comes back nightly.
She points her finger

LORD, BLOW THE MOON OUT, PLEASE

UNKNOWN

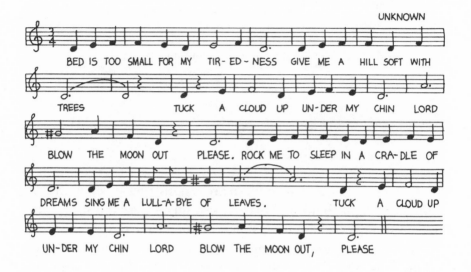

BED IS TOO SMALL FOR MY TIR-ED~NESS GIVE ME A HILL SOFT WITH TREES TUCK A CLOUD UP UN-DER MY CHIN LORD BLOW THE MOON OUT PLEASE. ROCK ME TO SLEEP IN A CRA-DLE OF DREAMS SING ME A LULL-A-BYE OF LEAVES. TUCK A CLOUD UP UN-DER MY CHIN LORD BLOW THE MOON OUT, PLEASE

WEE BABY MOON

UNKNOWN

THERE'S A WEE BABY MOON JUST A LY-IN ON HIS BACK* WITH HIS LITTLE TI-NY TOES IN THE AIR; AND HE'S ALL BY HIM-SELF IN THE DEEP BLUE SKY, BUT THE FUNNY LITTLE MOON DOES'NT CARE

*For a long time someone we know thought this meant that the moon had a lion on his back

To the far yellow thing
Shining through the branches
Filtering on the leaves a golden sand,
Crying with her little tongue, "See the moon!"
And in her bed fading to sleep
With babblings of the moon on her little mouth.
—Carl Sandburg, "Child Moon"

There is a blue star, Janet,
Fifteen years' ride from us,
If we ride a hundred miles an hour.
There is a white star, Janet,
Forty years' ride from us,
If we ride a hundred miles an hour.
  Shall we ride
  To the blue star
  Or the white star?
—Carl Sandburg, "Baby Toes"

Practical Information for New Parents

If you are a new parent, you are probably overwhelmed by the many different things you have to deal with and the variety of products designed to help you. If you aren't confused, you're exceptional. This "Practical Information" section provides guidelines to make things easier for new parents. Topics include: baby clothes, equipment, feeding, and books on child-rearing. None of these things is truly important and there is no "right way" to do anything. There are easier and harder ways, and determining what's best and simplest is easier once the issues are understood. So if you are a new parent, even as you concern yourself with selecting a highchair or setting up a crib, the more important task is to learn to be discerning, to tell what is from what isn't. With the exception of "What? No Books on Child-Rearing?" (page 94) I should think parents of older children will want to skip directly to the next chapter (page 99).

Get Ready, Get Set

Equipment purchased ahead of time is better kept at a minimum, but in making ready for your newcomer, you'll want to consider the following:

Birth Announcements. If you wish to send some these can be planned and addressed ahead of time. In all hospitals babies are automatically footprinted on arrival. If you remember to ask in advance or at the time (but not later) it is usually possible to have an extra print made for a keepsake or to use as a birth announcement.

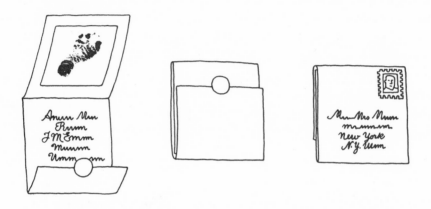

Baby seat. A sort of bookstand for babies to eat, sleep, be awake, and travel in—a place where the baby can see what's going on and be a part of things without straining to hold her head up or being held. These are a fairly recent development and so nice that it's hard to imagine what parents ever did (with us!) without them. Dinner is ready and your baby won't sleep. Put her on the table in her baby seat. You'll have a more peaceful hot dinner, and she'll soon be lulled to sleep by the conversation. For the wide-eyed two- to five-month-old who wants to use his hands, the baby seat has one drawback: dropped toys fall out of sight and reach. But put the whole seat into a highchair with some interesting things on the tray to look at and learn to pick up. Or turn a cardboard carton the right size on its side to make a desk. There are various combination seats available: baby seat/car seat, baby seat/carrier, baby seat/highchair/stroller. See what exists; choose what you like.

Comfortable chair. A rocking chair with armrests *is* all it's cracked up to be for nursing and lulling a baby in. But whether it rocks or not, be sure to have some very comfortable place to sit down on in the baby's room.

Baby bath. If you have enough counter space beside your sink a babytub is handy. First baby? Then you may appreciate the kind with a slanted back support. If you don't have enough room for the tub near its water supply, forget it. It's easier to bathe the baby in a tub at waist level, but it is not easier to carry the whole thing to and from the sink. Heavy and sloshy. Anyway, as soon as she can sit up she will have more fun in the big tub. Meanwhile the kitchen sink makes a fine babytub. And the regular bathtub is perfectly good if you don't object to getting down on your knees. Just put an inch or two on the bottom and let her lie on her back, kicking and splashing as much as she likes. Once in a while take her into the bath with you. Then the water can be deep and with your help she can float again.

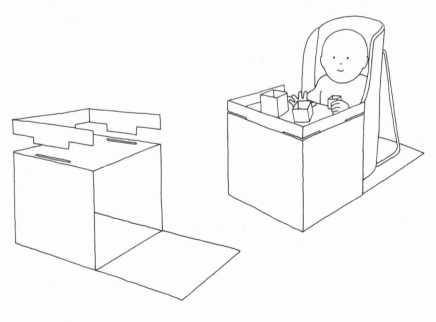

Changing table. Buy or improvise. As long as the mattress is in the high, infant position you can use one end of the crib. Or, if you have an auxiliary portable crib for trips, use it for a changing table.

Changing mat. Especially at first an extra changing station near the kitchen or in the living room is handy. Just a good-size rubber sheet will do, or a vinyl-covered foam changing pad with raised edges to prevent the baby from rolling off. Whatever arrangement you use, a *safety strap* of some sort is a good idea. If your changing setup doesn't come with one, improvise. A webbed luggage strap is fine.

Indispensable dispenser. Mount a toilet paper dispenser on the wall beside the place where you will be changing diapers, and forget about tissues, tidy wipes, cotton balls, cozy cleans for clean-ups.

Get Dressed

Considerations in buying clothing include:

● Ease in putting on and taking off.

● Ease of changing diapers in (should have snap or zipper crotch or be open at the bottom).

● Ease of care (should be no-iron, machine washable, machine dryable, or drip-dry).

● Season of birth (warm or cold, and take the usual temperature of your house into account, too).

● Size of infant (a big newborn of 8 or more pounds at birth will wear "newborn"—or small-size things—for only a short while, if at all. Even smaller babies grow fast. So don't overdo on the initial wardrobe).

● Effectiveness as clothing—comfort and freedom for the baby—warm enough? cool enough? doesn't ride up, fall off, come undone, bunch or lump up, stop circulation, fall over face or cheek?

● Looks? As you like. But a word about *boy and girl clothes for babies.* There's no need to hurry. The growing up happens very quickly. Little boy suits with separate tops and bottoms always result in bare midriffs with pants below and tops above the belly. So select one-piecers or those two-piecers that snap or button together. Little girl dresses are almost irresistible and now come in drip-dry fabrics. Never fall for one that needs ironing or she will very likely outgrow it between the first washing and the time you get around to ironing it.

Layette clothing sets include a variety of knitted cotton kimonos, nighties, pants, and tops and are generally not useful. Within a few days of the baby's birth you have found which of these is easiest to put on and does the best job. Everything else is either a drag to put on or doesn't fit comfortably. More extra decisions than you need at the outset.

Stretch suits are probably best at first, provided it isn't too hot. If you have enough stretch suits, you don't really need anything else. They meet all the criteria for baby clothing superbly and can adequately replace nighties, booties, sweaters, and undershirts. Long-sleeved, footed, snap-crotch stretch suits are the most useful throughout the year. Short-sleeved, legless romper and sunsuit versions are available for hot summer days.

Nylon-tricot infant suits cost more and are outgrown sooner than stretch suits, but they dry in no time at all—2 minutes in a dryer or about 30 minutes in the bathroom (squeeze out in a towel first). One or two are a boon for those clumsy early days when everything may be wet before breakfast.

Cotton knit nighties (be sure to get the kind with a drawstring at the bottom to keep the gown from riding up) are reasonably inexpensive, a breeze to change diapers in, and can be washed and dried at the hottest temperatures. Too warm for the hottest weather in un-air-conditioned or unbreezy homes. Some people get extra mileage out of these gowns by resurrecting them as nightwear when the children learn to walk. Crawling children cannot wear them because they crawl into the chest of the gown, but they are perfect for beginning walking, when nonskid bare feet are an asset.

Wee Willie Winkie runs through the town
Upstairs and downstairs in his nightgown,
Rapping at the windows, crying through the lock,
"Are the children all in bed?
Now it's eight o'clock."
—Traditional nursery rhyme

Undershirts are an unnecessary encumbrance. Since you are constantly picking up the baby under the arms, any undershirt that is not pinned to the diaper rides up and becomes a constricting wad across the chest and under the arms. Undershirts mean double laundry and extra dressing. For extra warmth, a sweater, jacket, or blanket that can easily be donned or doffed as you go in and out of heated and air-conditioned buildings is better. The most prevalent tendency is overdressing, not underdressing, babies.

In winter a *bunting* is most useful. Best are those with hoods, mittened sleeves, and no legs. The sack-type bottom makes it easier for changing diapers and allows plenty of freedom for kicking without kicking off the carriage blanket. Also a good place for an extra tissue or diaper. The sleeved kind is better than the straight sack kind because it allows the baby to move her arms without becoming uncovered. Get a machine-washable one, and if possible one with a hood that ties snugly under the chin and does not brush constantly against the baby's cheek. Such brushing makes some infants want to nurse at inconvenient moments.

When the time comes for standing and walking, bare feet are the best non-skid base. But if it happens to be cold, you may want some kind of footgear for toddling on bare floors. Footed stretch suits are slippery. Booties fall off as fast as you put them on and are slippery. Leather moccasins are a good idea, but most fall off because they are designed to tie too high (above, rather than below, the anklebone). Shoes seem premature and are awkward. Make a pair of *knitted mukluks* with non-skid soles by cutting pieces out of leather elbow patches and sewing them to the bottoms of socks or booties.

Coated electric wire (bellwire) is handy for keeping booties and mittens on. Weave pieces through booties at the narrowest point of the child's ankle (just below the ankle bone) and mittens (just below the wrist bone). Bend and tape the ends of the wires so that there's no danger of scratching. Once the booties and mittens are well on, simply twist the ends of the wire once. There's a period between 1 and 2 years when children *will* shake their mittens off to touch the snow, then cry for you to put them on, only to immediately shake them off again. At such times this idea is very helpful.

Night! Night!

The main factors to be considered in selecting a child's bed are budget, space, safety, appearance, quality, and durability. Your life style will come into play here, too—whether you travel much, whether or not you plan to have more children. No one can say what's best for you but here are some issues to consider.

Cradles, baskets, and car beds. Even though babies look cozy in them, for the most part they are not necessary, and they are outgrown very quickly, often in a few months. Nevertheless, if you have the space and the money or a lending or giving friend, you may be very happy to have one as a temporary or auxiliary sleeping place. In the very early days of night feedings, it may be handy to have the baby next to your bed at night instead of in a separate room. Small beds are also useful for the traveling baby, although the baby young enough to be in a basket can also be safely bedded down on a normal adult bed with a bolster on either side, or in a big deep bureau drawer. Some carriages have separable baskets with carrying handles that are good for small-bed purposes. Just don't make the mistake of thinking that any small bed or basket will do for very long.

Cribs. There are three basic types: portable inexpensive, standard moderately priced to expensive, and unusual and expensive. There is something to be said for each. Regarding the quality of standard models, you can check *Consumer Reports.* But before buying a standard crib, here are a few other things to consider.

If you can avoid or transcend the bedtime power struggle most people have with their children, it will not be necessary to keep your child in a crib much longer than a year and a half. After that, crib sides are really not needed for safety. Using them as restraints to keep the child in bed doesn't have to be harmful, but it is desirable for both the parents and the child to find a better reason for staying in bed than not being able to get out.

By this time the child can choose to lie down at will or to get up in the morning and play quietly alone without disturbing anyone. (Of course, what is implied here is a harmony for both parent and child with the ideas of sleeping and waking that many people never attain in their entire lives.)

In any case, unless you plan to keep the child in a crib for longer than two years, the standard cribs are really larger than necessary. Smaller cribs are perfectly adequate and leave more room for play space.

Whatever crib you buy, look for simplicity and openness as well as sturdiness, safety, and convenience. Remember that you are buying a bed, not a safe deposit box or a learning center. If there is anything to be learned in bed, it is the fine art of grateful retirement, peaceful sleeping, and cheerful waking.

Small collapsible cribs are perfectly adequate, quite inexpensive, and attractive beds for babies up to at least two years. Of course their main claim to fame is collapsibility for traveling or storage, but they are also nice on a permanent basis. The foam-filled, vinyl-covered mattress can be placed in two positions, and the top of one side is hinged for opening outward. Mattresses are available in two thicknesses. The thicker one is firmer, stays made up better, and is preferable if the crib is to be used on a permanent basis. The fitted knitted sheets of most manufacturers come in portable as well as standard crib size.

Most *standard cribs* have solid headboards and footboards that make them seem unnecessarily dark and confining. So, if you decide to buy a standard crib, you may want to look for one with simple spindles on the ends. Don't buy a double drop-sided crib —they are more expensive, less sturdy, and, even if you have the crib in the middle of the room, you will probably fall into a routine of picking up the baby from only one side.

Unusual, expensive cribs include a variety of the worst and the best. Among the worst are some highly elaborate, extraordinarily ugly contraptions that are supposed to expedite early learning. They are all cluttered with built-in toys for stimulating the baby in bed! Entirely overlooked is the idea that bed is a place to sleep.

Some perfectly lovely expensive cribs convert to junior beds. A junior bed is not a necessary purchase (see below); therefore, a combination crib/junior bed is not much of a bargain. One crib combination that does seem worthwhile is the smaller than standard crib that converts to a settee or small sofa for a child's room.

Finally, it seems necessary to mention that, of course, no bedstead is really necessary. Around the world undoubtedly more

people are sleeping on the floor on simple mats than in beds as we know them. This same procedure can be followed with mattresses if you prefer. Then, of course, there is never any danger of falling. I happen to appreciate the idea of getting off the ground (see "High and Lifted Up," p.73) that a regular bed seems to suggest. But you don't really have to have a bed for that to take place.

How to move from crib to bed. Do not make the mistake of believing that you need a "junior" bed, that is, something with guard rails and between a crib and a twin bed in size. Guard rails are not necessary, and if you do use them it will be only for a week or so. Sooner or later you will have to buy a normal-size bed for your child. If you have the space buy a twin bed whenever you think he is ready to leave his crib. Making the move is easy. Place a chair or small table of the same height as the mattress beside the bed at the child's head. If he rolls off the bed onto the chair, his feet will land on the floor. By the time this has happened, he will be awake enough to climb back into bed. Within a week or two this will probably stop occurring altogether, as he will now have a built-in awareness of the limits of the bed. Also by then you will have discovered how nice it is to sit beside the open bed at bedtime for a song or story, so you will probably leave the chair there anyway. At first, as an extra precaution, you may want to put some pillows or a quilt on the floor by the bed. If you're superprecautious, simply place the mattress on the floor until the child becomes used to sleeping without sides. But this seems a little melodramatic, and most children make the move without ever falling.

Bedding. Determining factors in deciding how much bedding is needed for these early days are laundry facilities and savoir-faire. If it's a first baby and you're a rank beginner at diapering, you may need a few extras for leakage, especially if you don't have easy access to a washer and dryer.

On our first day home from the hospital, we ran through all the bedding before noon—two crib sheets, four receiving blankets, three rubber pads, and about four layette nightgowns. We had no washing machine in our apartment, so we sent out for more receiving blankets and did hand laundry until the humidity verged on rain. But after the first day we never got to the bottom of the pile again. The four extra receiving blankets became dustcloths.

Even if you are a beginner with no skills, a few tricks can help to keep the laundry level low:

● Never wake up a sleeping baby for a change.

● Until the baby learns to move around in bed, it isn't necessary to change the whole bed just because there is a damp spot in one corner of it. Move the baby instead.

● Let the baby sleep on a baby-size pad of cottonized rubber on top of the sheet. If small spit-ups or wetnesses occur, just change the pad.

Knitted, fitted crib sheets will be useful as long as the baby stays in a crib, so if in doubt, buy more rather than fewer—you'll use them eventually. Still, three to six should be enough. These are soft to sleep on, and a breeze to launder. If you like to tie-dye, try a crib sheet Two crib-size *cottonized rubber sheets* should be sufficient. If the mattress is vinyl-covered you don't have to have any, but you will still probably want them to soften the mattress surface beneath the sheet and to avoid always having to wash off the mattress. Four to six so-called *puddle pads* will be handy for sleeping on (see tips above) and as lap pads and places for changing. They can be bought precut in almost any infant supply department or variety store. In some good-size fabric and department stores this material can be less expensively bought off the bolt and cut with pinking shears to the desired size. Don't put in a very hot dryer. *Mattress pads* are optional. Some people like to use them to soften the mattress surface or instead of a rubber sheet. But a rubber sheet is really more practical and all that's necessary between the cotton sheet and the mattress.

Bedmaking. Once the baby begins to move around (about a month), the bedmaking arrangements have to be revised a bit. There are two approaches. One is to make the baby, to dress him in warm enough clothing so that it doesn't matter whether he stays covered or not. The other is to make up the bed like a real bed, with tucked-in top sheet and blanket.

If you follow the babymaking approach, you will want thermal, blanket-weight sleep suits for cold nights. The disadvantages of this approach are that the suits are expensive, a bit cumbersome for diaper changing, somehow a bigger project to launder, and often too warm for running around in before bed.

If you follow the bedmaking approach, you can use season-weight pajamas and just toss on or take off extra blankets as the temperature changes. The bed-making approach seems easier all the way around except for one thing. Most ready-made top sheets and blankets for cribs are too narrow. It is crucial that the top sheet and blanket be wide enough to tuck in well under the mattress on both sides without being stretched tightly across the child. Otherwise the child becomes uncovered and tangled up. About the only solution is to cut down larger sheets and blankets. Ideal dimensions for a 5-inch-thick standard crib mattress are $5\frac{1}{2}$ feet long by $4\frac{1}{2}$ feet wide for top sheets and 5 feet long by $4\frac{1}{2}$ feet wide for blankets. Extra blankets may be smaller, of course.

A good washable *quilt* is unbeatable. Beautiful patchwork ones can be made or bought at sizeable expense of time or money, but we received one that had been made by covering a ready-made, synthetic baby blanket with drip-dry cotton. The top layer of cotton was a quiltlike print. The bottom was covered with a plain, bright yellow. The whole thing was stitched together on a sewing machine, and the top was decorated approximately 3 inches from the edge of the quilt with a strip of grosgrain ribbon to match the bottom. There was something almost magically right about the thickness, stiffness, and weight of this quilt. As a cover, it was stiff enough so that the child could turn over without becoming tangled up, and it was light enough to stay across his shoulders when he inched his way toward the head of the crib. As a floor pad, it was the closest this family ever came to using a play pen. It provided a soft cushion under the baby and yet was stiff enough not to crumple up under him.

Or you can make a special *blanket* using fake fur, fake lamb's wool, or scraps of cotton appliquéd to a cut-down blanket or blanket-size piece of washable suit fabric (buy 5 feet from a 58-inch-wide bolt). Make a happy-faced clown from old scraps of cotton, a fake fur teddy bear with print-bottomed paws and button eyes and a soft velvet or kid-glove nose, a fake fur kangaroo with a print-lined pouch that holds a removable baby kangaroo stuffed with a thin layer of alpaca or polyurethane foam. It is best to machine-stitch around the edge of each piece to be appliquéd, to prevent raveling. Then fold and iron along the stitching, baste or pin, and sew to blanket. Fancy appliqué stitches may be learned from sewing books, or you can make the stitches invisible.

Glow-in-the-dark stars and moon. It is possible to purchase luminous paper stars, comets, and moons that self-adhere to the ceiling. Really nice when the lights go out.

Bedtime Books

Here is a list of some of our favorite bedtime books.

> *Catch Me and Kiss Me and Say It Again, Goodnight Moon, Goodnight Richard Rabbit, Jamie's Story, Ladybug and Dog and the Night Walk, The Little Fur Family, Lullabies and Night Songs, Midnight Moon, The Sailor Dog,* and *The Runaway Bunny*

Yum! Yum!

Highchair. The biggest concern is the clean-up. Be sure to buy a highchair with a detachable tray (for washing in the kitchen sink) and with a space between the back and seat (for easily sponging off squashed food). The bigger the tray the better, since there are so many other nice things to do in highchairs besides eating. Some trays extend back a little under the arms, which prevents a few of the inevitable spills. It should be possible to set the tray in several positions (nearer or farther from the child). Try taking the tray off and putting it on once or twice to see if it goes easily. Make sure that, when mounted, the surface of the tray is level. This seems so obvious, but we once used one with slanted arms. Everything slid toward the child and ultimately wound up in his lap! Chrome and vinyl are easier to clean than wood.

Pyrex pie plates make good plates for preschoolers who have outgrown the "cereal" dishes designed for babies, but who still need sides to help them load their forks and spoons. And *clothes pins* can be used to convert anything—dish towels, cloth diapers, table napkins—into bibs. Use a small, plastic clothes pin (the kind with a spring). Use two clothes pins and you can fashion yourself an apron out of any hand towel.

The child who wants to feed himself will eat the soft foods you prepare more happily if you also give him something to be busy with. He has important problems to solve. At first the whole loaded fist arrives inside the mouth. But it cannot be opened there. How to remove the hand without dropping the food into the lap? It's not easy, and it's not neat. But it's very funny and quite beautiful if beheld aright. He will like to pick up and feed himself pieces of canned, peeled fruit, of bananas, cheese, macaroni (it dissolves even if swallowed whole), small meatballs of puréed cooked meat, a slice of toast, five or six peas, soft sandwich cubes, and all kinds of omelets. A full set of teeth is not necessary for chewing—all of the above can be managed without any teeth at all. Also don't forget that the baby does not have to be made to eat or worry that he will like only what's bad for him. The most important thing about the meal is the friendly, appreciative, peaceful coming together. Try the following "Foods for Thought":

● *Fresh green peas in the pod*—a bowlful is a miracle of abundance and beauty and mystery any two-year-old can appreciate. A whole afternoon of package-opening and healthy (unsticky) nibbling, and perhaps talking a bit about growth and how the peas got there.

● *Corn on the cob.* Give her one ear as a present. Let her husk it leaf by leaf (help only when she finds it too difficult), discovering the silk and, at last, the amazing hundreds of row-by-row kernels. She will like it raw as well as cooked. *Popcorn on the cob* is even more amazing, if you can find it. For best protection of your house, don't butter.

● *A pumpkin.* On Halloween a one-and-a-half- year-old and his mother made a jack-o'-lantern. The process filled nearly a whole day of waking time. The child mostly sat and watched in his high-chair, delighting first in the revelation of the seeds ("What do you suppose we will find?") inside the huge, round, orange ball. While the mother carved the face, the child helped with the sorting of seeds from meat. They roasted the seeds for a snack and cooked the pumpkin meat (with brown sugar and butter) for a vegetable to be eaten that evening by the glow of the smiling, candlelit jack-o'-lantern. The second year he was too busy to sit so long, but enjoyed choosing a face, did a little scooping, and still appreciated it a lot.

● *Apple.* If you slice an apple in half horizontally, you can see that the seeds are positioned in the form of a five-pointed star. If you've ever tried to draw such a star, you will marvel at the perfection of this one which got there without your help. Try the same thing with a *pear.* "Hey! How did those seeds that look like a star come there?" Then later, "And on the tree there came a bud. And the bud became a blossom, and the blossom became an apple, and I am eating that apple! If I eat its seeds will a tree grow?"

The *highchair* is not only an eating place, but can also be used as a place of quiet refuge, heightened concentration, and change of pace and perspective. At the end of the day when she may be a little restless and tired and you are fixing her supper, let her sit beside you in her highchair. She will like to watch what you are doing, to help, or to play with some kitchen tools. And at the end of a family meal when she would like to get down but you would like to finish eating first, give her a simple puzzle to work in the highchair. The highchair is a wonderful place for creative projects that might otherwise be hazardous to your decor. A small pad of paper and some watercolors, crayons, or felt-tip markers (water-based ones), play dough—the very young child will enjoy all these activities with greater concentration and less mess in the gentle confinement of the highchair.

Kids in the Kitchen

For children under a year, the *potato and onion bin* is delightful and, relatively speaking, creates an easy mess to clean up. The onions are fascinating to peel, and washed potatoes are great rumblers and rollers.

The *coffee pot* (nonelectric, metal percolator, or drip pot) is the world's best first puzzle and stack toy.

Have some low *cupboards* and *drawers* that are all clear for the baby. Putting in and taking out *pots and pans, colanders, strainers, plastic containers,* or just opening and closing the doors themselves —all are absorbing and edifying activities for tiny hands.

Until label-peeling is discovered, *canned goods* can be used for blocks and are especially fun if you happen to store them on a *turntable.*

From the kitchen drawer come endless delights of *smaller utensils:* spoons, spatulas, pinchers, an old egg beater, measuring cups, whisks (we never really needed to buy a rattle). Egg and apple slicers, cookie cutters, potato ricer, and butter knife make a fine modeling set when play-dough age is reached.

A set of *cookie cutters* is especially nice to have when there are children around; though it isn't always easy to find good ones that have nice shapes and aren't too sharp. Besides cookie-making, these are good for cutting sandwiches (an effortless way to teach shapes—eat a semicircle!), play dough, and even watermelon and apples.

The *kitchen sink* with a little water and some ladles, cups, sieves, and the wonderful coffee pot or some boats will last for hours. Almost all educators agree that this water play is important for children, and the children's own deep interest in it seems proof.

A *cannister of rice* is *the* indoor substitute for sand and water play. It is good for pouring, piling, stirring, scooping, and shoveling. It is clean, not sticky, and okay to eat. If you insist, it can even be washed and cooked later.

Helping means being like Mommy and Daddy. And even before they know the words, they will aspire to that. Before the age of two they can and will already appreciate the challenge of:

● "washing" unbreakable dishes and vegetables and *drying* silverware

● sponging off cabinets (let her have her own sponge) and *dusting*

● unwrapping a stick of margarine (while you season the meat, put it in the oven, peel the potatoes, and wash his hands)

● peeling off the outer layers of an onion (while you peel and finely chop six)

● breaking the yolk of an egg before you beat it and *dumping* the pudding mix into the pan

● telling you when it starts to bubble

● throwing anything away

● carrying things from here to there (the littlest ones have a tireless love of missions and cooperative efforts)

● putting the bread on top and wrapping sandwiches

● sorting and putting away knives, forks, spoons

And so on. The more *we* cooperate, the more we will be inspired with the appropriate ideas at the appropriate times. And we will be blessed a hundred times over for our generosity in priceless companionship and incredible beauty—for there is nothing quite so grateful or so perfectly lovely as a child who is merely being allowed to learn.

Worse than not allowing our children to help is expecting too much or insisting. This happens, too. You hear people hissing things like "Can't you do anything right? You're no help at all!" That is devastatingly not the point. Watch a child try to put a cloth table mat on the table for the first time. He will try to lift it from the bottom edge, not realizing yet that the material will flop down. All these things have to be learned. Then if he hasn't come to hate the failure connected with his efforts to be helpful he will indeed be a help.

What? No Books on Child-Rearing?

The best thing to read when trying to raise a child is the child. Maybe it is even more important that we learn to read ourselves. Most of the time when we try to read books that tell us how to deal with problems we get problems. Problems are very contagious.

Look how easily our children catch them from us.

The trouble with most problem-solving books for parents is that they start with the idea that the child has a problem. Then they try to tell us how to fix the child, or else, after blaming the parent, they suggest how we can fix ourselves. It is better to think that there are no problems, only ignorant beliefs and their symptoms. We experience problems because we have certain beliefs that don't work. We try to make them work, but they don't because they are false. We are only ignorant. But we are not ignorant because we haven't read the right books; we are ignorant because we haven't discovered the right questions.

In the beginning our children don't have any problems. They simply reflect our ignorance, just as a thermometer registers a fever. There is nothing you can do to the thermometer that will change the illness. You can shake down the thermometer so that the fever doesn't show, but the fever itself is not affected. Likewise even if we can shake the symptoms of error out of our children (and sometimes some of us in frustration do literally shake our children into obedience), nothing will have happened—at least nothing constructive. The problem is not in the child any more than the sickness is in the thermometer.

When a man who has had a fever becomes healthy again, he can put a thermometer in his mouth and it will not register a fever any more, only health. That's how it is with our littlest children. If we become healthy, they will stop registering ill health as symptoms.

Now the interesting thing is that *we* don't *have* problems either. We are only ignorant of truth. Actually ignorance is a positive step for most of us. We have to move from the wrong ideas we are certain of (ignorance of ignorance) to knowing that we don't know (conscious ignorance—receptivity). Once that occurs, understanding comes rapidly, for there is nothing to interfere with it.

But we must not *blame* ourselves for not knowing or for having wrong beliefs which are reflected disharmoniously in our children. If we already knew all that we needed to know to raise our children harmoniously, we probably wouldn't be having children. Perhaps it would even be invalid for us to have children then. Children are children so they can become adults; parents are parents so they can become understanding (which is the same as loving). Learning seems to be the point of it all.

Likewise we must not fear that we can wreck our children with what we don't know. The thermometer isn't sick just because somebody's fever is registered on it. Neither is the baby. As a matter of fact, until the child is about two years old, there seems to be a sort of grace period in which the symptoms of error disappear in the child the very instant the errors are corrected in the parents' thought. All this time the child is becoming more and more self-aware, and sooner or later he begins to take on the parents' errors in the form of his own mistaken beliefs. But even then, perhaps even more then, the crucial progress has to be made in the consciousness of the parent, and it is really a kind of condemnation and trespassing to think that the child must be fixed.

Recognition that parenthood is even more for the parents' growth than for the child's also helps us to ease up on our children. From this standpoint we can look at the child as a sort of hand mirror in which we can perceive and improve our mental image of ourselves and life. It is necessary to know how to look into the hand mirror and to understand clearly its significance. Our children are not images of our selves but of our thoughts about ourselves. The image itself cannot be faulted or corrected, nor can we even fault or correct ourselves as causes of the image. In this mirror we do not see either our true selves nor the true self of the child, but only the reflections of our beliefs about ourselves and about reality. So we must not view what we see with fear or guilt or blame or any thought that gives reality to the image. The image has value only in that it signifies to us what we do not know about reality. Otherwise it is of no consequence. To try to correct the child is like putting a lipstick smile on the reflection of an unhappy face in a mirror. To correct or try to change ourselves is like putting a lipstick smile on the unhappy face itself. Both actions are absurd; only the knowledge of something truly happy can transform the face and the face's reflection with a genuine smile.

Our children need to be comforted, cared for, encouraged, trained, protected, instructed, reprimanded, forbidden, and prevented. But we must also have regard for them, for their right to be wrong or, more correctly, for their ability to learn to be right. Where their mistakes are not dangerous to themselves and do not impinge radically on the rights of others, we must allow them their freedom. We must respect their privacy as much as we must respect the privacy of a complete stranger, an adult with whom we have no family ties whatever. This isn't just being nice; anything else is a denial of truth and of the child as a truthful, competent being.

Sooner or later he must consciously seek truth as we are doing. When this time comes (rarely before adolescence), he must have confidence that truth is and that he can perceive it. If we are constantly fixing our children (in effect affixing error and lack *to* them), they will not have this confidence. Instead they will think of themselves only as needing to be fixed—or needing "a fix"? (See also pages 122 and 319)

> *The kingdom of heaven may be compared to a man who sowed good seed in his field; but while men were sleeping, his enemy came and sowed weeds among the wheat and went away. So when the plants came up and bore grain, then the weeds appeared also. And the servants of the householder came and said to him, "Sir, did you not sow good seed in your field? How then has it weeds?" He said to them, "An enemy has done this." The servants said to him, "Then do you want us to go and gather them?" But he said, "No, lest in gathering the weeds you root up the wheat along with them. Let both grow together until the harvest; and at harvest time I will tell the reapers, Gather the weeds first and bind them in bundles to be burned, but gather the wheat into my barn."*
> —Matthew 13:24–30

The field is each man's consciousness. The seeds are truthful, fruit-bearing ideas; the weeds false, hindering ones. We are all the sowers striving, servants sleeping, and reapers discerning. The enemy is ignorance passing for knowledge. The farmer is the One Mind. The harvest is the reunion of the individual mind with the One Mind in consciousness. For us "the time for the harvest is now." The time for our children is also always now, but that is their business, theirs and the farmer's. With regard to our children, as parents we must simply tend to the wheat.

3
Happiness

Verily I say unto you, Whosoever shall not receive the kingdom of God as a little child shall in no wise enter therein.
—Mark 10:15; Luke 18:17

And a little child shall lead them.
—Isaiah 11:6

Let both grow together until the harvest; and at harvest time I will tell the reapers, Gather the weeds first and bind them in bundles to be burned, but gather the wheat into my barn.
—Matthew 13:30

Wheat and tare, the seeing being and Me, Inc., cohabit in each of us. By the time we are parents, Me, Inc. is full grown and proving itself false, ever more untenable, coming to the end of its rope. Like a bud breaking apart to make way for the flower, the self is having more and more trouble keeping itself together. Now along comes this child to make the increasingly difficult utterly impossible. Unaware of our true nature as seeing beings, Me, Inc. struggles in us—angrily, fearfully, futilely —to be self-sufficient, now even self-sufficient for two! As a parent caring for a child the self is being forced to confront its insufficiency and to let go of itself. Yet what a tender mercy this child is! In the child, Me, Inc. is just beginning; so for a time the seeing being, which is the true one, shows through more clearly. And we can see it if we know what to look for. And what we are able to see is what we are free to be. And in this way the wheat outstrips the tare and the weed dies back, never to be missed.

Work and Play

Does the newborn baby already experience himself to be one thing and life or other people another? When his blanket is unwrapped or he is lowered too quickly into bed, he flails his arms, and perhaps cries. Does he feel his *self* unwrapped and exposed? Does he feel his *self* falling from some goodness? Maybe his startle reflex shows that this sensation of being a separate self comes as a sort of unhappy shock, that it feels wrong. With the experience of being a self comes the experience of limitation and the desire to overcome it—to sit, to walk, to crawl, to run, to fly; to find security, connection, freedom, love. To be happy.

Having entered upon the experience of being a separate self, he also embarks on the struggle to get his self taken care of or to become an adequate separate self, one that can take care of itself. But on a deeper level he remains a seeing being. Though he does not know what he is searching for or even that he is searching, we can see that everything he does is part of a search to understand what he is and what life is and how the experienced separation is to be overcome. He wants to make a connection, to see how he fits in and into what.

Play: The Serious Side

Well-timed and at their best, toys are a means through which a child experiences certain spiritual qualities. Through playing with puzzles and blocks he experiences unity; through learning to walk or riding a tricycle he experiences freedom; through music and art, beauty; through books, meaning and truth; through pets and friends and family, love.

Experience is not really an adequate word. It may be *through* experience—that is, through the senses—that the child meets up with spiritual qualities. But we only need to watch a child's face light up with surprise to realize that these events (literally *e-venire*, forth coming) are really taking place in consciousness. However rudimentary it may be, awareness is happening. Through various sensory experiences the child is made aware of and on some conscious level participates in and appreciates certain spiritual realities. The happiness does not come from the experience but from the awareness.

Perhaps *encounter* describes it best. He is not conceptually aware of anything. Yet there is clearly some conscious recognition taking place. If you take his hand, put a piece of a puzzle in it, and use his hand to fit the puzzle piece into the puzzle, he has experienced unity with his senses. But if he does not *see* something; if nothing clicks in his consciousness with some semiconscious question of his, then there has been no encounter and no real event.

> *The toddler at the beach at sunset, surrounded by a vast panorama of sky and sea, cannot see it; he is totally preoccupied with the pebble, the wavelet at his feet. His eyes can see it all, but his consciousness cannot recognize beauty, grandeur, vastness, order, harmony, all the formless realities which make such a scene so breathtaking. However, he is capable of growing into an appreciation of these things; indeed, he must do so if he is to fulfill his potential. That expansion of consciousness to the realization of aesthetic*

and, finally, transcendental values is the essence of our human growth process.
—Ann Linthorst, *A Gift of Love*

So, while much of the child's learning occurs *through* his senses, the learning itself is taking place in consciousness. It is not purely sensory; it cannot be called instinct. Encounters are spiritual events that take place when sensory experience is accompanied by a meeting with spiritual reality in consciousness. Whether brought by a pebble, or a wavelet, or the sky, it is a moment of oneness—the oneness of seeing with being—when the seeing being supercedes the strugglesome Me, Inc. When this happens there is always an explosion. It may be an explosion of light, de-light on the child's face, or an eruption of laughter. Children do not laugh only at what is funny, but even more often at what they find *wonderful.* One-derful. And by the fact that they find it so wonderful we recognize the depth and truth of their yearning.

Children search constantly for encounters. It is the absence of encounters that renders any toy or activity a bore or frustration. Encounters are what motivate and please a child at play. Whenever they break upon him we see that he is happy. For a moment the sense of gap between self and what it belongs to is overcome and the seeing being rejoices. Without quite realizing it, but without doubting it either, he has a momentary sense that the unity, beauty, truth, freedom, love he innately desires (because they are the truth about him, too) are *so. That's* the joy of play. Because the child's work with his toys brings him happiness, we call it *play* and buy more toys. But *having* toys is not the fun; the toy is just a means. This is evident from the fact that children lose interest in a toy (or in the treasured pebbles brought home from the beach) as soon as they have learned all they can from it. Whatever toy does not offer him a conscious encounter does not interest *or animate* him either.

So again we observe that the child is primarily a spiritual being, a seeing being. Even as he is being mis-educated to be Me, Inc. and take care of himself, he is really vitalized and rendered happy only by what he *sees.*

Work: The Lighter Side

My meat is to do the will of Him that sent me.
—John 4:34

As Me, Inc. has grown up in us we have tended to divide our lives into categories of "work" and "play." Work is more or less unpleasant; play is pleasant. As full-grown selves looking out for our selves we have forgotten that happiness has something to do with seeing. Having divided our lives into work and play we find joy elusive. Where has it gone? No matter—for our children bring it back to us by showing us what it is. And just when we had begun to notice it was missing!

Watching our children we are reminded that happiness depends on learning. Unity, freedom, beauty, love, are not things Me, Inc. can *have*, but ideas that can only be real for us as we consciously realize that they are so. A good toy is one through which a child encounters these spiritual principles through experiencing their effects. It is the encounter that is happy. And as mature beings we need to move beyond even encounter to conscious realization. Yet somewhere during Me, Inc.'s growing up, the joy of conscious encounters has gotten confused with the things or conditions that facilitate the encounters. ("Why don't you take better care of your things? I laid out good money for that toy, and now you've broken it!") Somehow we get distracted. Instead of moving smoothly from experiencing to encountering to seeking to understand or realize principle, we get all involved with trying to acquire things or set up situations in which we can *have* the experiences. Detached from principle, these efforts fail, and from the failures we infer that the spiritual principles themselves are not so.

But the true self, the soul in us, goes on yearning and will not give up seeking its truly happy, idea(1) fulfillment, the conscious overcoming of our sense of separation.

Beyond Work and Play

In thy presence is fullness of joy, and at
thy right hand are pleasures forevermore.
—Psalm 16:11

A child is not a toy, but as we have seen, a toy is not merely a toy either. Like good toys our children express concretely certain qualities of spiritual reality. We know that they do not possess or understand these qualities; we know that we have not put them there. Yet there they are. Marvel at it! The incredible fact of these qualities—peace in the sweet sleeping and still watching, love in the fearless expectancy of perfection, intelligence in the alert searching, vitality in the perpetual activity, unity in the working together of all parts and functions for good. Where did all this come from? What is it if it isn't so?

Just as a good toy invites a response from the child, children invite us to be involved with these qualities and elicit them from us. So here we are confronted with the fact of goodness and the necessity and possibility of being good. In proportion as we give ourselves over to this goodness we begin to experience the overcoming of the self/other gap, much as the child experiences unity when he consciously participates in fitting a puzzle piece into a puzzle. On the child's level it is a matter of spiritual encounters; on our level it is a matter of consciously realizing the truth that is the one nature of self, other, and life itself. In this way the struggle of Me, Inc. can finally come to an end as the seeing being replaces Me, Inc. altogether and finds itself at home and at one with the reality of love-intelligence.

In the last chapter we considered how the necessary becomes a point of conscious contact with the essential. The toy, the game, the child, and the task are all concrete points of expression for infinite spiritual reality. In working with our children we have an unmatched opportunity that can lead us toward the spiritual realization we have in fact been seeking since birth.

As parents we may begin to perceive the true nature of play as work and discover that the purpose and pleasure of both is the learning of principle. And having made the discovery, we will surely be as happy in our so-called work (whatever it may be) as the child is in his play.

> *Our attitude toward the newborn child should be one of reverence that a spiritual being has been confined to within limits perceptible to us.*
> —Maria Montessori, *The Secret of Childhood*

Toys, Playtime, and Learning

Our ongoing task is to do the necessary while keeping sight of the essential. Having discerned the essence of play as seeing work, we find that the principle of discernment has as wide an application to the playing and learning child as to the new baby's early care and feeding.

Until recently toys were usually associated with childish pleasure, feeling good, and love, as compared with books and lessons which were associated with childish displeasure, intellectual success, and discipline. Recognition that child's play is learning has led to a tremendous proliferation of educational toys. Side effects are parental confusion, budgetary distress, domestic clutter, and rampant materialism. With older children the possibility of lessons and special adventures adds to the confusion. Now we are supposed to provide both fun ones and educational ones. When we aren't tempted to buy something just because he wants it, we are subject to the strong suggestion that we should buy it because he *needs* it. Fresh understanding is needed to help us provide appropriate toys and opportunities at appropriate times.

So much seems necessary. Even when we succeed in the struggle to meet all these "needs" we find our very success backfiring in our faces. It is never enough; our children may have "everything" and still seem unhappy, ungrateful, discontented, never satisfied. No matter what we do, we may sense that they feel unloved. They may have every educational opportunity and still be apathetic or anxious, easily frustrated and discouraged. Maybe they don't seem to try. Or they try and fail. Or they succeed and are unhappy (the success is a failure).

If such is our experience, we need to apply the principle of discernment anew. We can ask: What is the essential idea behind this scramble to provide our children with the best of everything? The idea behind an action is called motive. If the motive is *esse*ntial, that is, if it is consistent with the truth of being, then the best can be expected. But if the best is not what is happening, there may be something false or impure, something essentially mistaken, underlying our action. And we can be sure it is some plan Me, Inc. has hatched out for itself.

So what is our motive? It seems simple enough: we would like our children to succeed, and to feel good and happy. We associate success with personal intelligence, and pleasure or feeling good with being loved. But is pleasure a true measure or motivation for love? Is success a true measure or motivation for intelligence? And are we really so selflessly concerned about our children as we think we are? There are two ways in which almost all of us parents attempt to exploit our children as the supporting cast in our own Metrogoldwyn Me productions: one is based on a false idea of love as personal pleasure; the other is based on a false idea of intelligence as personal power.

False Love and Toy-Buying:
The Hedonistic Motive

Give her what she wants so she'll feel loved (and so she'll love me in return). Though we all know that this is an invalid motive, in floundering moments we are sometimes seduced by it. It may be a toy or some other treat, but whatever it is, watch for the thought that precedes the thought of going out to buy or do something special. Often it is Me, Inc.'s secret desire for acceptance. So then we are not really giving love to the child, but attempting to use the child to feel loved ourselves. Also, to the extent that we look upon our children's lives as remakes of our own childhood, buying things for them is like buying them for ourselves. We get vicarious pleasure out of it. Or we may look at the child as existing for our pleasure. Either way the tendency is to define love in terms of pleasurable sensory experience. We equate not feeling good with not being loved. If our children feel (or look or act) good we feel (that we are) good. We equate feeling good with being loved. So we try to love ourselves through our children by making them feel (or look or act) good.

False Intelligence and Toy-Buying: The Ambitious Motive

Buy it for him to help him get into Harvard—to increase his I.Q. If you don't buy enough educational toys, he'll have a low I.Q. The flip side of the materialistic pleasure-seeking inclination to buy toys to show love is a kind of intellectual materialism which says we must provide toys (also experiences and lessons) to make him smart. Implied (even statistically verified) is the idea that if he doesn't learn enough before he is four he will never get into (the) college (of our choice). It's very intimidating.

Whereas formerly parents saw themselves as providers and caretakers of the child's physical and emotional well-being, with the discovery of the preschooler's intellect we now see ourselves as having to be early-learning specialists too. The belief is that the child is a sort of empty thing to be trained, educated, and stuffed with knowledge; otherwise he will fail. Fail? Our exaggerated sense of personal responsibility turns the discovery of the preschooler's potential into a frustrating, discouraging, anxious, exhausting, competitive frenzy.

Just as the so-called loving motive for buying toys may conceal a selfish motive, behind the so-called educational or intelligent motive we can also discover an essentially selfish one: ambition. Through the success of the bright child we expect to demonstrate how knowing and smart and successful and powerful *we* are both as the source of and the force behind the child.

The Love-Intelligent Approach to Toys and Learning

With both false motives, love and intelligence are confined to the very narrow context of self and other (Me, Inc. among Me, Incs.); love as a feeling to be gotten from each other, and intelligence as a personal power to be had against each other (success, competition, comparison). Everyone is either a tool or an adversary.

As long as we adhere to these definitions neither love nor intelligence is possible. Love becomes exploitation; intelligence becomes conquest. So then love is not love after all; and clearly any intelligence that defines love as something that love isn't must be unintelligent. So these ideas of love and intelligence are clearly unloving and stupid.

If we provide our children, via toys and tools, playing and learning, with such perverted ideas of love and intelligence, is it any wonder that there is a certain perversity to the result?

When does the light-obsessed clown become happy? (See page 19.) Only when he sees. At that moment he is no longer a clown; he is both intelligent (seeing) and endowed with and able to express (be) every goodness (freedom, creativity, harmony, etc.) —he is at one with love (loved). Now love and intelligence are not something he gets from or has at the expense of another. The encountering of both love and intelligence is one event. *Love-intelligence takes place where the tendency of life to reveal itself is fulfilled in the essential nature of the individual to see what is being revealed.* And it makes harmonious participation with others (love) both possible and good. A clear appreciation of this liberates us to discern both the loving and the intelligent response to our children's quests for love and intelligence. We are no longer distracting them through materialistic or dualistic misapprehensions of what wisdom and learning or love and happiness are all about. For example, a discerning parent reports:

> I think it is better to show love by meeting needs than to keep telling my son that I love him. Right now he is learning to tie his shoes. He is old enough, so even though it's hard for him, sometimes I insist. But once in a while when I see he's tired I still do it for him, and I have noticed that while I am tying his shoe, he says, "I love you, Mommy." When he says, "I love you," I know he knows that he is loved.

The Idea(l) Gift, the Idea(l) Toy

If we recognize child's play as the seeing work of the seeing being, certain intelligent questions arise when we consider providing a particular toy or experience. What idea does this toy express?

What will our *giving* of it show the little seeing being to whom it is being given? What does it mean to me? What does it mean to the child? Is the idea being expressed a good one? Is there a better way to express this idea?

For the most part, toys are an unnecessary encumbrance for parent, home, and budget, and they can even become obstacles to the child's learning and happiness. Whenever a child is given the notion that he needs to be entertained, learning comes almost to a halt. If we keep in mind that the purpose of play is learning and that toys are tools of learning rather than possessions, we will be more successful in choosing appropriate toys. Children learn so quickly. If we treat them as objects of our affection by tossing them a lot of objects (toys) when we are at a loss for love, they may get the idea that they are themselves no more than objects and become quite miserable and difficult to live with. Painful object lessons.

Sometimes particularly with young children an idea is more clearly expressible through things than by word. But when it comes to love there is often a better mode of expression than through things. Sure, children need to know that they are loved. Sure, a gift of a toy can express love. But a smile when you see her, a minute of helping her do something she's trying to do, a minute of letting her do badly by herself something you could do better in ten seconds, the loving refusal to meet an illegitimate demand, a moment of abandoning everything just to listen to what she has to say —no toy can equal the power of these gifts to show her the joy of being loved, lovable, and loving.

> I was inspired by a mother I saw. Her son came running up to her, fretting and frowning, all frustrated over something. Undisturbed by his disturbance she smiled the loveliest smile at him. I saw his face change, relax. Before anything had been said, his problem had shrunk. Now they could talk about it—if he could remember what it was.

Sometimes people give our children things without our approval. It may be the gift itself or the excessiveness of the giving that troubles us, but what others give our children is no big problem. Gifts from others—or from Santa Claus—can be appreciated by both parents and child as demonstrations that the parent is not the child's only source of good.

The Idea(l) Teacher

As the nursing child needs a nursing parent, so the learning (seeing) child needs a learning (seeing) parent more than a teaching one. We do not have to get our children to learn; only to allow and encourage them in their learning. We do not have to dictate what they should learn; only to discern and respond to what it is that they are learning. Such responsiveness is at once the most educational and the most loving.

If we approach parenthood as a seeing rather than knowing or feeling parent, if we approach life as essentially a process of realization rather than an arena for success or failure, pleasure or pain, then our children will not be distracted from the seeing/learning work that is their natural inclination. And they will learn constantly, and whenever they understand something they will sense that they are loved. No child who is learning is ever doubting that he is loved. And every child who does not doubt that he is loved is learning. And such children cannot help but realize their potential to be both intelligent and loving.

> *All things work together for good to them that love God.*
> —Romans 8:28

Life itself is loving and guiding (teaching) us along. The more we regard our children as seeing beings rather than as projects or possessions, the more we see that this is so. All things work together in favor of realization to them that love truth. Observe how all things are working together to show our children what they so eagerly want and need to see.

At first the baby is mainly reaching with her ears and eyes. She almost seems to focus her eyes with her ears, using hearing to aim her face at you when you talk, then peering out for you through those incredibly sincere, intelligent, unfocused eyes.

When she begins to "speak" to you, you will see this same reaching for focus—a sort of generalized groping for the specific.

She sees you, smiles, and then her whole body reaches for the means of communication. Her shoulders, and maybe even arms and legs, come forward, she exhales through rounded lips, and a soft "Ho" comes forth. Answer softly, "Ho," and her face lights up. Your first conversation!

Slowly the hands come into play—first as unrecognized servants of the mouth, then more and more as a means of reaching out to explore what she now sees and hears.

Reaching is the crux. Everything follows from the reaching, meticulously and minutely ordered in favor of progress. For example, at a certain period a baby will open and close his hand several times when reaching for a desired object. He does not know to raise the hand and bring it down upon the toy. We watch compassionately as his opening fist actually pushes the toy farther from his grasp. Soon he becomes frustrated. But in the meantime we notice something wonderful. In striving to reach the toy, he now draws up one leg. The beginning of crawling! The very inadequacy of his grasp initiates his discovery of the possibility of mobility!

Ain't Misbehavin'

Intelligent seeing leads to loving responding. The seeing parent recognizes what is happening and is able to work with rather than reacting against seemingly inconvenient or contrary behavior— sometimes lovingly helping; sometimes lovingly not helping; sometimes lovingly allowing; sometimes lovingly forbidding.

> At a certain point diaper-changing became almost impossible. Our baby was suddenly overcome with the desire to see what was behind his head. He would look up, crane his neck, and arch his back, so that you really had to fight to get a diaper on him. But he wasn't just being ornery. He was trying to do something. One day he looked up, craned his neck, arched his back. He reached with his arm, then with his leg—reaching, reaching. I didn't know what he was reaching for. I don't think he knew it either. But it turned out to be the beginning of turning over. No one was as surprised as he was when—plop—he suddenly found himself on his tummy!

We don't have to know every stage of child development to be responsive rather than hindering. The key is to recognize our children's reaching as an impulse of life itself seeking expression. We can then trust and respond in the most helpful, least interfering, most meaningful manner. We can gauge our response by the baby's reaction. A "ho" back to the "ho-ing" baby may evoke a smile or laugh of pleasure that seems to mean *mission accomplished. We have reached each other.* From "ho" we may go on to repeated, one-syllable, explosive sounds—"Buh! Buh! Buh!"—which bring almost startled laughter. But "Hey diddle diddle" we see is still too complex—just part of the background din that doesn't penetrate consciousness. From the lack of reaction we see that nothing has registered, that no *encounter* has taken place.

Sometimes we bring an out-of-reach toy within reach to relieve the striving baby before he becomes discouraged. But sometimes instead, perceiving the link between reaching and crawling, we place our hands beneath the soles of his feet, helping him to discover the possibility of pushing off toward the desired toy. Truth itself guides us both through our seeing—if we are seeing.

The Responsive Parent

The seeing parent is freed from reacting for or against things simply on the basis of pleasure/pain or success/failure and self/other. When we perceive what in essence is taking place, the necessary response that is both loving and intelligent becomes clear—even when what takes place appears as pain or failure. As seeing beings we recognize that what we do or have or feel is less important than what we understand. We are less inclined to take things personally or to distract our children from learning by suggesting to them that life is an interpersonal experience. We know that in any situation it is what is signified and whether or not we see it that is important. This insight transforms our experience and provides a sound, love-intelligent basis for responding to our children.

Child [on telephone, crying]: Hello, Mom? I forgot to bring my homework, so I have to stay after school and miss basketball again.

Ambitious or Pleasure-minded Parent [inward experience: fear, hurt, anger, worry, embarrassment, guilt; inward thought: *Oh, no! He's going to fail! He's got the same problems I had. What shall I do? Who is to blame?*]: What? Again? Won't you ever learn? It's your own fault! Where's your homework and what if I bring it right away? I'm going to dock your allowance. Why don't you do better? How do they dare? This is going to show up on your report card, you know. Your father isn't going to like this one bit. The coach is going to be mad. Other children don't do this. What's the matter with you? What's the matter with that woman? I'm going to have a talk with that woman.

Seeing Parent: Too bad. I'm sorry. But it is a lesson. I know you have been trying not to be forgetful, but it has been hard for you to be organized. Maybe this will help. Maybe from now on it will be easier to remember. Won't that be good?

From looking at the concrete, everyday moment in the light of the spiritual, from looking at the necessary in the light of what is essential, from viewing our children and ourselves at work or play as seeing beings in the process of realization—at every juncture what is at once immediately practical and in the long run most helpful is revealed to us. When it comes to responding to our playing/learning children, certain practical guidelines and priorities emerge. Each follows from and is subsidiary to the other.

1. The Parent as Model. Insofar as we approach everything for what it has to teach us (rather than what should or shouldn't be or what is pleasing or displeasing), we reinforce our children's innate conviction that life is a learning place and that learning is our purpose in life. Thought is parent. The thought that parents the parent is parent to the child. If *seeing what is* governs the parent, it will govern the child as well. Then harmony and wholeness take place because seeing beings is what we really are. To be really seeing is the same as to be really alive. The children of learning parents are resilient, creative, interested, and efficient in their learning; and they are comparatively free from experiences of hurt and failure in relation to others because they are not learning to compete or please but to understand.

2. The Parent as Beholder. Insofar as we behold our children as seeing beings rather than as pleasing/displeasing or succeeding/failing ones it becomes evident to us that they are both good (lovable) and learning (intelligent). They are neither obedient nor disobedient, neither smart nor dumb, only relatively aware or unaware, ignorant or understanding. A benefit of this for the parent is freedom from reactions of fear and anger, pride and guilt, credit or blame, and, in their stead, a growing firsthand appreciation of infinite goodness, beauty, order, infinitely taking place. A benefit to the child is the preservation of his sense of worthiness. The beholding parent recognizes that a sense of worthiness is the child's greatest possession and so protects it by never calling it into question. Beholding means "holding to being." We constantly uphold the child in consciousness in the light of what is. The beholding parent is able to be both patient and firm in a nonpersonal way. (See also "Worthiness," page 117 and "Discipline," page 208.)

3. The Parent as Preparer of the Way. By perceiving the child as a seeing being we understand that while we do not have to make our children learn or be happy, we do have a role in making way for the learning child. This relieves us of the enormous burden of thinking we can make or break our children. It relieves the child of being pushed or prodded ambitiously or "spoiled" and distracted by materialistic overindulgence. Now we realize that the way to be loving and educate our children is through recognizing, making allowances for, and facilitating the learning child in his learning. With such an understanding both greater freedom and discipline are possible.

4. The Parent as Preparer and Maintainer of the Learning Environment. We can take a cue from the teaching of Maria Montessori about this. She saw that the way to facilitate learning is to set things up in such a way that the child can find and reach and select whatever he needs to help him in his learning—as much as possible on his own. Looking at the home as a learning environment, it is helpful to keep two objectives in mind: access and invitation are one; freedom and order constitute the other.

Access and invitation. With the youngest children, this may depend on such simple means as providing a low table for the child's work, a stool from which to reach the sink, setting up a bottom drawer of kitchen things they can and may easily get at, providing a bookshelf which displays the inviting covers of the books rather than just the narrow spines. Especially with older ones, access often means simply helping them find time for everything worthwhile. Partly it means not distracting them—for example by constantly switching on the television to bring them under control. Setting aside space and time for quiet learning and creative enjoyment is part of access and invitation. Older children are relieved and happy to make and keep to schedules, rather than being constantly reminded and scolded. Keeping the dictionary and encyclopedia near the dining table is another concrete example of access and invitation.

Freedom and order. Freedom and order are two sides of the same coin. In Montessori classrooms the "prepared environment" is one in which everything has an intelligent place and in which there is an intelligent (and intelligible) procedure for maintaining this intelligent order. Children are taught simply that they may play with anything whatsoever in the room (as long as someone else is not using it) and for as long as they like, but when they are finished, before taking out anything else, they must return it to its proper place. The beauty and simplicity of this is stunning. It can be applied beautifully to the orderly home. As children grow, different accommodations have to be made, but new parents may wish to see also pages 33, 136, and 159.

5. *The Parent as Teacher, Guide, and Companion.* Notice how low on the list comes the place of parent as teacher. While willingness and availability to help our children learn should never be denied if genuinely needed and sought, it is best for both parent and child if the child is allowed to learn on his own whenever possible. This means not neglecting but being present in a somewhat removed way. Rather than either leaving the child alone or overdirecting her, the seeing parent recognizes various ways of participating in her learning. If you think of learning as a path, you can picture yourself walking beside her rather than either pushing or dragging or carrying her along. Over*seers* only in a spiritual sense, we participate in our children's learning mostly thorough seeing beyond, appreciating, respecting, encouraging, and celebrating whatever it

is that they are trying to learn. Only sometimes and less and less do we actually instruct or help or demonstrate—and then as non-personally as possible.

> Once my son came to me with a math problem that he could not solve. He had filled two sheets already, but he could not solve it. He explained the problem to me, but my background was such that I couldn't even understand the problem. When I did understand it, I still had no clue as to how to approach it. Whom could we call that would know how? One call was made, but no one was home. "Anyway," my son admitted, "we're supposed to do it ourselves." Well, he could go to school and say that he had not been able to do it. But then realizing that there was no other mind to rely on I remembered the One Mind. I thought, he does not know how to solve this problem. I do not know how to solve this problem. But he does not have to rely on himself or on me or on anybody else. The only mind there is can reveal to my son what only it knows. "I have confidence that an idea for solving this problem will come to you," I said. "Let's sit down here and see." We sat at the kitchen table and waited. I read. In a minute he picked up his pencil. In another minute he shouted, *"Oh!"* and began to write furiously. When he came home from school the next day, I asked about the problem. Was his solution correct? Did any other students solve it? He answered yes to both questions. "But you know what?" he said. "I was the only one in the whole class who got it the short way."

There is one mind which is fulfilling itself as individual consciousness. Intelligence and love take place strictly between individual consciousness and reality, not between personal minds. While neglect is tragic, by far the more prevalent parental error is well-meant trespassing.

6. *The Parent as Supplier of Tools, Toys, Equipment, Lessons, and Experiences.* Most of our assistance should not be given in the form of toys at all; but where toys are appropriate the main guideline for what and when is *reach.* Month and age criteria are uselessly arbitrary and part of a detrimental tendency to question the unique perfection of our children and compare them (and ourselves) with each other. The time to introduce a toy is when our children are in fact or in principle reaching for it. It is most useful if we can see beyond their reach to the ultimate principle being sought. Their desire to walk is the quest for freedom; their love of bright pictures

and music is a quest for beauty; their urge to speak is the quest for truth and meaning; their wish to be held is the quest for love. If we appreciate that principle is the central issue, we need only watch our children to perceive what is most helpful, and when. The child whose essential spiritual perfection is constantly beheld in his parents' consciousness will concentrate raptly, and develop speedily, securely, and happily. At the same time, such parents are readily inspired with the right idea for the right activity or toy at the right time. Toys must be introduced as fruits of rather than substitutes for understanding. Partly it is a matter of improvising, partly of literally offering our children tools instead of toys. Mostly it is a matter of providing a good work/play environment both spiritual and material.

Worthiness

A sense of worthiness is a child's most important need. The American self-made-man ethic says that we are what we make of ourselves. This is an improvement over the Old World class systems which said you could never rise any higher than your father. But the implied converse—that you are nobody until you prove yourself to be somebody—is troublesome. The suggestion is that our self-worth depends on external measurements—such as money, power, and popularity. On a child's level, worthiness is often measured by good behavior or achievement.

Comparisons are always being made between ourselves and others, between our children and others' children. Whenever these comparisons favor others we tend to feel unworthy or ashamed. This also has a serious effect on our human relationships. As long as we measure our worthiness in relation to others, we are constantly at odds with each other. It may be subtle, but often we are either putting others down or feeling put down by them.

I know two teenage children who always seem to stand out in a crowd. People often comment on how natural they are—how attractive, assured, and graceful. Their particular family is a highly cultured European one with a long tradition of high social standing —tempered nicely by the more democratic American viewpoint.

While teenagers frequently seem self-centered, awkward, and ill at ease, these two are poised and good-humored. They excel academically, yet they appear to be free from both fear of failure and excessive ambition.

How is this possible? They have never had reason to seriously question their abilities or essential value. Evidently they experience almost no need to prove themselves. They try to do everything with excellence, not to prove anything, but because excellence befits them.

A sense of superiority is not the same as a sense of worthiness, and both of these children have had to develop a higher regard for others. But watching them it is easy to appreciate the value of growing up without questioning one's essential worth.

How can we raise our children to have such a sense of worthiness? Just recognizing its importance is helpful. But there are several concrete areas in which we can cultivate an attitude of confidence in our children's worthiness and convey it to them.

Freedom and Independence

Basic to an awareness of self-worth is a sense of competency. This is less a matter of achievement than of not doubting our capability to begin with. If we perceive our children as capable, so will they. An old Anacin ad showed a young woman protesting, "Mother, *please!* I'd rather do it myself!" The mother was hanging onto the headache of trying to run her grown daughter's life. Having a parent like that was a headache to the young woman.

> A four-year-old I know will tackle anything with assurance and stay with it. She is also unusually comfortable with adults, starting up conversations with the refreshing poise of those children you see on "Candid Camera." One evening I was invited to her home for dinner, and the mystery of her assurance was solved.
>
> After eating, the child was excused to prepare a surprise dessert. She had a tall step stool which she lugged around the kitchen, climbing up to open first this cupboard and then that one, choosing the ingredients for her "surprise."
>
> There was no fanfare, no anxious glances from the watchers at the table. Once she consulted her mother in loud stage whispers.

Agreement was reached that honey would probably taste better on yogurt than chocolate syrup. Before long, delicious individual desserts of yogurt, grapes, and honey began arriving at the table. Each had a cookie sticking up like a candle in the middle.

"Doesn't she ever try to go too far?" I asked.

"Sometimes," her mother answered. "And of course we do more complicated desserts together when there's time. But mostly she's happy with ice cream or yogurt. She fixes yogurt and bananas, yogurt and applesauce, yogurt and seven raisins. She likes experimenting with different combinations, and she likes to make them look pretty."

Most revealing was the mother's surprise at my enthusiasm for the idea of child-styled desserts. "I never thought much about it," the mother said. "She likes doing it, so she's just always done it."

Never miss an opportunity to allow a child to do something she can and wants to on her own. Sometimes we're in too much of a rush—and she might spill something, or do it wrong. But whenever possible she needs to learn, error by error, lesson by lesson, to do it better. And the more she is able to learn by herself the more she gets the message that she's a kid who can.

I.Q.: The Inhibiting Quotient

Retarded? Average? Gifted and talented? It's hard to say which is the more harmful label. All children are gifted and talented. There is only one mind, so all manifestations of intelligence are *given.* True intelligence is neither had nor not had. Intelligence is awareness of what really is. All judgments made in the light of what really is are intelligent. In counseling a blind individual, it became clear to me that real seeing is seeing the real. In that light it was evident that by comparison to everyone else this individual was not so radically handicapped after all. If real seeing is seeing the real and if the real is spiritual, then as long as we are judging by appearances we are equally blind. The potential for seeing beyond appearances is no less in blind than in sighted individuals. Handicapped people may be less handicapped than we think they are; likewise, "advantaged" people laden with ideas of self-sufficiency and superiority are more handicapped and weighted down than we recognize.

To quantify intelligence and locate it in somebody's physical head and call it himself (whether superior or inferior) is handicapping him. When you credit a child with having much intelligence, when you objectify intelligence *as* the child, you have interrupted that intelligence. You have changed the subject of his life from learning to self. It is like thrusting a mirror between a reader and his book. His own appearance interferes with his vision. When a child is identified as gifted and talented, he begins to think of himself as special. Being gifted and talented becomes an excuse for all kinds of license and suffering.

True intelligence cannot be gotten or done. It can only be obstructed or unobstructed. When intelligence takes place in an individual it is an event or coming to light of what really is. It is an awakening, a dawning or seeing. An intelligent event occurs when the tendency of reality to reveal itself is fulfilled in a moment of conscious realization. As the nature of light to illumine is fulfilled in individual seeing, so the intelligence is fulfilled in understanding. Intelligence is a universal force seeking expression through universal consciousness. When it takes place it is not a matter of credit or pride or success or personal virtue; it is a matter of freedom, joy, beauty to be rejoiced in and appreciated.

A preschool director commented that she used to have mostly children of families in which the wife was in her twenties and at home, but that lately, there is a new breed of mothers who are thirty-five years old or older and taking time off from their careers to have a couple of children. Asked whether there were noticeable differences between the children she said, "Oh, indeed, yes. The children of young stay-at-home mothers tend to be quiet, 'nice,' at first fearful of leaving their mothers' sides to take advantage of classroom opportunities. The children of older professional couples tend to be extremely verbal, extraordinarily bright, and outwardly poised, but nervous and subject to tempestuous times." Is this the choice?

The hidden selfish motives: that the child be good (be pretty, behave, be close) for the parents' sake; or that the child excel, achieve, be superior for the parents' sake—these backfire in a variety of perverse and paradoxical ways.

I.Q. tests do measure something. Perhaps they record the flow and relative unobstructedness of a certain function of intelligence; maybe they measure interest, focus, and pace of learning; primarily they seem to record the relative earliness of language development, something largely determined by environment. But they do not measure intelligence itself. They cannot, because intelligence is infinite. Focused interest can have either a healthy or a pathological base. The so-called idiot savants, intensely focused to the point of obsession, are able to perform extraordinary, almost superhuman intellectual feats with seeming ease. Some, for example, can instantaneously calculate the day of the week on which any date (past or future) falls. Yet these same people barely function on any other human level. Is that intelligence? In a way, yes; in a way, no. On the one hand they demonstrate through utter single-mindedness an intelligent facility far beyond our usual level of realization; on the other hand it seems that here narrow concentration is used unconsciously precisely to remain unaware or unintelligent of reality in general. And that cannot be considered true intelligence. So-called gifted and talented children are frequently taught to use intelligence for personal power and superiority, for conquest and competition. But if true intelligence is awareness of what is and if what is is infinite love, then is the conquering genius truly intelligent? And if the so-called retarded individual, however unskilled and seemingly limited, nevertheless has a keen, simple awareness of goodness and finds joy and fulfillment in being good and useful, is he truly unintelligent?

If I were king of the schools, next to the nurse's office where children are sent for health emergencies, I would set up an office for learning emergencies. I would advise teachers to be on the lookout for passion fits or enthusiastic seizures. Whenever interest rose like a fever in a child—whatever the interest and whoever "afflicted" (retarded, gifted, or average)— I would have her sent to this office. If during math she doodles dinosaurs, if during writing she makes up a story about dinosaurs, if going to the library she selects a book about dinosaurs, I would consider her a bit flushed and in need of immediate attention. Unlike the nurse, whose concern would be to see the temperature go down, the resource person in the Office of Learning Emergency would be concerned to gently huff on the glowing coal of her passion and hope to see it break into a self-sustaining flame. He would have a variety of measures to take. Like the nurse, he might send a note home to the parent: "Your child is feverishly interested in dinosaurs. Perhaps you might like to keep her home tomorrow morning for the television special on paleontology." Further, he would call on other resources—perhaps a session with a retired senior citizen volunteer, a special trip to the librarian, a recommendation to the teacher, who (if he hadn't thought of this himself) might assign the child a related project. Whatever the budget for special remedial or enrichment services and whether or not classes are individualized or structured, such a service would be a relatively affordable way of helping many children with a minimum of upheaval. Small passions would be recognized as precious and critical opportunities for enhancing the child's sense of worthiness and possibility.

There is no such thing as a middle-of-the-road child; there is only a child who is standing in the middle of the road. An interest as yet unkindled? Some doubt about himself? Often just a little valuing of his momentary interest and some opportunity to follow it through is enough to set him off down the road at a gallop.

> In reviewing student applications, I often spot a sudden change in a student's record. After years and years of substandard performance, suddenly one semester he seems to pull himself together and "get his act in gear." Over and over I have asked these students, "What happened?" Over and over the answer has come, "I don't really know. All I remember is that that was the year I . . ."—built a canoe, bicycled through Nova Scotia, learned to juggle. Some success. Some interest allowed to come to fruition.
> —Dean of Students, Hampshire College

Shame and Blame

A child will behave according to what he thinks he is. Therefore, if he is addressed in terms like "You always . . ." and "You never . . ." and "You are such a . . . ," he will surely develop an image of himself as a "so and so" and continue engaging in "such and such." When correcting a child it is much better to make a clear distinction in your own mind between who he really is and what he is doing, between his essential being and his ignorant

behavior. It is absolutely necessary to behold our children as innocent. We can always assume that if they really knew better, really
understood the value of another way, they would do it.

As parents we are called upon for various responses to error.
Sometimes a firm and vigorous stand is called for, such as when
there is immediate danger of physical injury. Sometimes admonition is called for, the pointing out of a possible consequence.
Sometimes we simply have to stand by and let our children discover consequences for themselves. Sometimes reproof and explanation are appropriate. But the child's goodness is never the issue;
even behavior is not the issue; learning is.

In every instance something will be learned. If we view our
children as stupid, naughty, disturbed, or guilty of their misdeeds,
they will learn to behold themselves as foolish, faulty, or shameful
specimens of humanity. They will regard us as judges from whom
they wish to hide, and they will interpret everything we say as
further proof of their unworthiness. If we view them as innocent,
or at least merely ignorant, they will gain understanding from their
experiences, and they will continue to regard us as wise partners.

Write a no-fault clause into your family policy and apply it to
yourself and your children. With no-fault assurance, even if you
have to yank your toddler off his feet, you will be able to do so with
compassion and a sense of humor rather than fear or anger. You
will be able to issue warnings without insult, and to reprove without humiliation.

It is best not to reprove a child in public. Rather take him aside
and offer respectfully the information you think helpful. Remember, the issue is not what should or shouldn't have been done but
what needs to be understood. Always assume the essential goodness of the child. As much as possible be positive, nonpersonal,
and concrete. Instead of, "No. Bad boy! I told you not to touch the
scissors!" try, "Scissors are not a toy. They are for cutting. Here
is something better to play with." Whenever you can, instead of
giving directions ask questions that lead him to discover better,
more valid, truer alternatives for himself.

One afternoon I overheard our oldest child pestering the youngest.
Several times I told him to stop, but he couldn't give it up. Finally

it hit me that his pestering mood was as troublesome for him as for his brother. A feeling of compassion welled up in me. As I came out of the bathroom he went sailing by. I grabbed him, pulled him into the bathroom with me, and shut the door so no one could hear us. "What *is* this?" I asked in genuine bewilderment and some amusement. Startled to find himself confronted with a question rather than condemnation, he jerked his head up and smiled. "That's the only way I can be happy," he said, sheepishly. "I can't find anything fun to do."

"Oh," I said. "Well, it isn't working very well, is it? I'm sure you can get a better idea. Let's see, what *would* be nice?" He was soon happily absorbed in a constructive project that he had thought of and I had helped him to set up. The pesterer disappeared and did not return that day.

Praise and Celebration

Surprisingly, praise may be just as harmful as shame and blame. Personal praise suggests to the child that his personal worthiness rises and falls according to others' estimation of his accomplishments. In praising children we give them the idea that they are good because of what they do that pleases us. But when we don't praise them or when we praise others, they feel diminished and unworthy.

Praise also distracts the child from whatever he is doing by implying that the value of his activity is getting attention. It's a vicious circle. If a child has his eyes on his parents watching him learn to ski, he is more likely to fall or crash into a tree. This experience may at once injure, embarrass, and discourage him. His skiing progress is impeded and his enthusiasm and self-confidence undermined. Whether it's manners or artwork, the law is the same. A child cannot have his mind on seeking approval and on what he's doing at the same time. If his mind is not on what he's doing, he is unlikely to enjoy it or do it well. Paradoxically, the more a child's ego is bolstered, the more insecure, discouraged, and even incompetent he's likely to become.

It is good to express joy and to encourage our children in their growth. But there is a much better way than to make a big fuss over them. When a child says, "I did it myself!" usually this is not Me, Inc. speaking. He doesn't mean, "Aren't I great?" but rather,

"Isn't it a great thing that I am able? Isn't it wonderful that this happiness is possible for me!" In other words, he is grateful. The right kind of celebration heightens this enjoyment of discoveries and increases the child's sense of possibility. It is characterized by appreciation and gratitude rather than praise and pride. If you wish him to grow with joy and confidence, do not let the child become the issue in his own work and play. Let him be good-conscious rather than self-conscious. Instead of "What a great reader you are!" try "Reading is really getting much easier for you, isn't it? Soon you'll be able to find out almost anything you want to know." Instead of "Aren't you proud of yourself?" or "I am very proud of you," try "Wonderful! It sounds so lively now, and I can see that you really enjoy playing that piece!" (See also pages 205–206 and 254.)

Truthful Regard

Most of all it's good to consider what's right with our children, to focus on the true rather than the false. This truthful regard is the purest form of love and the most important aspect of parenthood.

> Robert is the older of two children. He appears to take everything personally and is thus constantly flying off the handle and getting upset. Whenever he is reproved he tends to become angry or discouraged. But nobody has to walk on eggs with his younger sister. Julie is spontaneously happy, cooperative, and her characteristic response to reproof is, "Oops! I forgot!" How can this be? They have the same parents. Or do they?

In a sense Robert and Julie do not have the same parents. Julie's are a little more experienced than Robert's, less anxious, and still preoccupied with Robert. The real difference between Robert's and Julie's behavior has to do with the way their parents regard them and the way, accordingly, that they view themselves.

Especially with our first child, we tend to take too much responsibility—both credit and blame—for everything. The more we want to be good parents, the more we tend to see ourselves as making or breaking our children. Experts everywhere alert us to problems until we are constantly searching for what's wrong with our children and then trying to fix them. As in Robert's case, our efforts to make our children prettier or smarter or nicer only suggest to them that they are not pretty, not bright, not nice—in short, unworthy.

Overzealous parenting—or what someone has called "smother love"—is undermining Robert's confidence. With his parents he views himself as a problem and life as a hazardous situation that he is incapable of coping with. Julie, on the other hand, is a revelation to her parents. Lo and behold, she cut her teeth—with no parental supervision! With a minimum of attention she is spontaneously cheerful, intelligent, and resilient. Her parents regard her as a constant source of pleasant surprise. She sees herself and life accordingly.

The child who lives in an atmosphere of truthful regard will know himself and others to be worthy. Then in the same way that a boat is seaworthy, he will float along—buoyed up, unsinkable— learning in due course to express his full potential as a loving, intelligent, assured individual. He is a see-worthy individual in an environment of self-revealing reliable truth.

All that is needed is continually to behold the perfect child right where the disobedient, failing, or disturbed one seems to be. The perfect child cannot be seen at a superficial glance any more than the flower can be viewed in the bulb. We must look deeper than complexion for beauty, deeper than behavior for goodness, and deeper than test scores for intelligence. Call it potential if you will, or basic goodness, or divine spark—every good and necessary quality of wholeness is given to the child and does not need to be imposed on him by us, only beheld. What we can see, he can be.

Anyone who has ever raised a child from diaperhood has a perfect example. We change hundreds of diapers without being deceived by sight or smell or repetition into thinking, "Why did I have to have a dirty one?" In fact, purity is usually regarded as the baby's most outstanding characteristic. And, indeed, in the end it is the child's own maturing purity that eventually does away with the need for diapers. It can happen quite effortlessly. Those of us who, doubting, fall for the idea that we have to "toilet train" our children, learn the hard way that children are not *made* to use the toilet. Rather they just do when, sooner or later, it becomes perfectly clear to them that it is good to do so and that they can. Once they perceive the worthiness of the idea (provided they do not question their own worthiness), the idea itself takes charge of them and thereby of the situation. So what we do or don't do, say or don't say, is not too important. But the way a child is viewed by his parents—and the way he views himself—is crucial.

View him as a promise rather than a problem or a project. Enjoy him. When he is around, smile often. When he speaks, listen. When he proposes, consider. "Well, let's see. Would that be a good idea or not?" If you tuck his shirt in do it because he deserves to be comfortable, not because he looks like a slob. See him not as a success or a failure, well- or ill-behaved, but as a fully equipped participant in the process of living and learning. When he fails offer comfort rather than condemnation. "It doesn't matter. Now you know that doesn't work, so it won't have to happen again." Show respect for his effort even when his work is imperfect. Sometimes let him all but hang himself to discover something he needs to learn and above all demonstrate to him your truthful regard for others as worthy individuals to be loved and respected. Then he will do likewise. And no one who has truthful regard for others ever has time for self-doubt.

This is my beloved son, in whom I am well pleased.
—Matthew 3:17

Receptivity

You road I enter upon and look around! I believe
you are not all that is here;
I believe that much unseen is also here.

Here the profound lesson of reception, neither
preference or denial. . . .
—Walt Whitman, "Song of the Open Road"

The baby's repeated craning of his neck suddenly results in his being able to turn over. But this is not at all what he had in mind, so his increased freedom comes as both a great shock and a tremendous blessing. Likewise to us our children come as something of a shock yet bring a great blessing. To receive it we only need to become like the children themselves—meek, teachable, receptive seeing beings. This is what is best for our children, and it is best and happiest for us as well.

In thy presence is fullness of joy; and at thy right hand
are pleasures forevermore.
—Psalm 16:11

We spend so very much time trying to get our work done—the laundry, dishes, bookkeeping, what have you—with the idea that once all that is out of the way we'll be able to "devote our full attention" to our children. Yet in those rare moments when our sense of self-importance is diminished or satiated enough so that we feel we can "take some time off," we suddenly find that we are uninspired. We sit down to "be with" our children and find the moments almost awkward. It must mean that our idea of "being with" is invalid in some way.

As Me, Inc. we are inclined to believe that the purpose of being with our children is twofold: we take care of them, and we entertain them. But this narrow subject/object outlook leads to several kinds of unhappiness, such as feeling taken advantage of by our children, neglecting them, never having enough time for ourselves, etc. The valid motive for our being together is to further understand what really is. What is love? What is truth? What is life?

Children, who, of course, do not consciously know that seeing is happiness and their very nature, also never doubt it. They are learning machines, ceaselessly seeking new understanding of anything and everything. That is one reason they will not play with their toys and leave us alone for long. They love their learning work and feel loved through it. Furthermore, their learning is existential; they especially want to be learning what relates to their living. For the toddler this usually means whatever we are doing.

We, however, have long since divided our work and learning time into categories. Work is supposed to be the most time-consuming of all, and learning (which means reading or taking a course) is something else. "I have so much work to do that I don't have time to improve my mind anymore!" Medical science sometimes even seems to suggest that learning is only for children. Their brains are young and growing; ours are already deteriorating. But if we are not learning much anymore it is only because we no longer think that learning pertains to us. And if we *are* interested in learning we certainly do not expect to learn anything from changing diapers or folding the laundry.

But what the child has to learn is more obvious to us only because so much of it is so physical. If we allow our one-and-a-half-year-old to "help" us fold the laundry he will learn something about buttons, zippers, snaps, where things go, the physical properties of cloth, what happens when you drop it, how easy or hard it is to carry compared with everything else he has ever carried, what clean clothes smell like, how a big towel can turn into a small bundle, how the small bundle you just folded can turn into a big towel again, plus any songs we care to sing or stories or related or unrelated facts we care to pass on. If we are cheerful and responsive, he may also go on assuming that orderliness is an agreeable aspect of reality and that it's a joy to be together. And he may *not* yet begin to think that he is only a nuisance.

So it's easy to see that it is good for our children to be included in our work whenever possible. And, practically speaking, no matter how unhelpful the help of a toddler is, we will almost certainly get the task done faster with him than by trying to keep him busy in some other room.

In the meantime, what can *we* possibly learn from folding the laundry? It *is* possible to learn while folding the laundry. But first we may have to relearn how to learn. And this is one thing our children can certainly teach us.

The learning child unconsciously assumes two things that are crucial to learning. The first assumption is that *there is nothing standing between him and happiness but what he hasn't learned yet.* At least for a while, he does not think that having or doing something else would be nicer. As long as he's learning he's happy. He lives to find out. The second assumption is that *whatever comes along next is the next thing he needs to learn.* He does not doubt the fulfilling nature of life. These two assumptions are crucial to receptivity. And receptivity is crucial to learning.

So what might we learn when we are trying to fold the laundry (which we may think is a bore) and the task is being made more difficult by the fact that our toddler is aggressively in the way?

The basic issue in folding the laundry is orderliness. If this is the task with which we are presented, then a right appreciation of orderliness may be what we need to learn. Perhaps the interruption by our child signifies the truth that the perception and expression of love are even higher aspects of our lives. Or perhaps we need to see that love and order are not in conflict with each other. The possibilities are infinite, and we can learn some new dimension of reality each time we are confronted with this situation. Perhaps while the child is exploring the physical properties of cloth or material, we will come to see that what we do is *im*material, or that life is *un*foldment and that expressing life (in this case love, order, humility) is fulfilling. When we understand whatever there is for us to understand while folding the laundry, we will either be happy folding laundry or else we will be lifted into some other task altogether.

Like us, our children will become fulfilled, happy adults only in proportion as they come to understand and express life aright. We cannot teach them what life is or what orderliness is, even if we come to understand it ourselves; one day they will have to find out for themselves, just as we are doing. But as manifestations of life, they enter this world with a natural expectation or unconscious appreciation of order. As parents we can foster this appreciation and help it to become conscious. Then when our children become young men and women searching, order will be one of the realities they seek to discover and understand.

But the simple lesson of orderliness is only a small part of what we teach our children. The unspoken lesson for us all in our right appreciation of even the smallest tasks is that life—every minute detail of it—is significant and meaningful and worthwhile, that receptive understanding is the secret of happiness and that ultimately happiness is.

Lay disciple Ho said:
"My daily activities are not different,
Only I am naturally in harmony with them.

Taking nothing, renouncing nothing,
In every circumstance no hindrance, no conflict . . .
Drawing water, carrying firewood,
This is supernatural power, this marvelous activity."
—Huston Smith, *The Religions of Man*

Paul said: "Set your affections on things above, not on things on the
earth."
—Colossians 3:2

Jesus said, "Suffer the little children to come unto me, and forbid them not:
for of such is the kingdom of God. Verily I say unto you, whosoever shall
not receive the kingdom of God as a little child shall in no wise enter
therein."
—Mark 10:14–15

Suzuki said: " 'Childlikeness' has to be restored with long years of training
in the art of self-forgetfulness."
—Eugen Herrigel, *Zen*

Practical Information for New Parents

Included here for new parents are some guidelines regarding toys (buying, improvising, organizing, storing) and play. Parents of older children may prefer to go directly to Chapter 4, page 149.

Toys and Things

The first and last thing to know about toys is that buying toys isn't important. Love, that is intelligent love, is enough. If you cannot afford to buy any toys, your children can still have every educational advantage. On the other hand, we can buy all the best toys in the world and they won't help a bit unless we are present, maintaining without reservation the understanding, loving atmosphere vital to all children.

131

Not Buying Toys

It doesn't make much sense to buy many toys for babies. Play is work, and the baby is supremely motivated to do this work, which includes a thorough sensory examination of all the properties of everything he can get his hands on. When this work is done, the object ceases to be interesting. This doesn't take long, because every baby is enthusiastic and works fast. So as much as possible use things you find around the house—plastic measuring spoons, potholders, coasters, etc. Baby food jars, plastic bottles, and boxes can be filled with colored water or split peas or beads or buttons *until* the baby learns to open or break them or *unless* he has an older toddler sibling who doesn't know better than to do so for him.

From sitting to crawling is perhaps the easiest time of all. At this stage children like almost anything you put in front of them, and they work diligently with everything—patting, pounding, picking up and putting down, putting in and taking out, over and over and over. From standing to walking to running, things start happening very quickly and busily. When she tries to walk, set up a walking tour. Arrange a few chairs and low tables so she can progress from one to the other while still holding on. Put a cookie on one chair, some interesting things on another, a book on another, a favorite toy on another.

Every time you buy a toy, you make a commitment to having it around, to finding a place for it, and picking it up frequently. Despite the fact that your child may have lost interest within a few days, she will keep dragging it out, and you will think you have to keep it in case she regains interest or "grows into it" or is followed by a younger sibling who will be just as interested in the toy as she was . . . for about twenty-four hours.

There's no question but that most toy purchases are a matter of parental weakness. If we pay attention, we can find many ways to amuse and educate our children (of any age) with things that are already in the house. Furthermore, our children like to use our "real" things because they are trying to grow up into real people and accomplish real ends. Two or three sessions with a pincushion and a dish will satisfy the toddler's curiosity and give him some useful information and increased dexterity. Aren't pins dangerous?

Of course, but in the highchair with you right there it's all right. Between sessions the pincushion goes back to the sewing box.

Certain concept materials such as wooden parquetry design tiles are worth purchasing because their beauty and precision are difficult to duplicate in the home. But when you consider buying a toy, first make sure it is not something you could match with what you already have at home. Try some of the following *nontoys* (see also some of the books listed on pages 142–145, 235–236):

Under one year old try a: Telephone—the real one (if you have two) with the button taped down. Now when the child is in a banging phase. Transistor radio—they love turning the knobs and watching the dial move and hearing the stations and volume change. Jewelry box—with only good-size, safe, and durable things that cannot be swallowed; he will lift the lid and close the lid, take things out and put them in, and examine and examine and examine. Kitchen drawer—"This is your drawer," full of safe things to explore.

Over one year old try an: old manual typewriter, tool box—minus sharp things, sewing box—also minus sharp things.

Any desperate rainy day try: a ball of string, a roll of toilet paper (just once or twice), a little masking tape and a lot of newspaper.

Montessori teachers are past masters at setting up worthwhile and inviting *nontoy activities* that leave the child free to work and learn without adult assistance or interference. In a good Montessori classroom you may find dozens of children working at the most mundane tasks with the most sublime expressions on their faces. On one tray are a small bowlful of walnuts, an empty bowl, and a pair of tongs. Another tray, also with two bowls, includes some tinier objects and a pair of tweezers. Each activity is entirely self-explanatory and offers the child a practical skill. And their arrangment on trays helps to bring about a sense of security, definition, and peaceful order that could never be expressed verbally. Once the child has transferred all the nuts to the empty bowl (and probably back again and more than likely several times over), he will almost certainly replace the entire tray on the shelf from which he got it. (If not, this can be gently and firmly taught in only a few sessions.) The whole procedure is carried out by the child in complete independence. Whatever they may lack of the garish appeal of commercial toys, such activities more than make up for it in their appeal to the child's intelligence and innate love of order, freedom, and peace.

One of the loveliest Christmas gifts I ever heard of was a scrap of cloth with four buttons sewn on. A two-and-a-half-year-old child had sewn them on, taught secretly by her eleven-year-old sister. There are so many little things our children would learn with joy if we did not view them as dull work, too hard for the child, or too time-consuming for us. He is often happiest (and least bothersome) by our sides doing some modified version of whatever we are doing. How few toys we would buy if we really appreciated this.

Toy-Buying

Choosing what toys to buy is a small matter compared with the overall task of discerning from moment to moment how to respond to our children in an intelligently loving way. When buying a toy seems called for, here are some things to consider:

- *Physical quality.* Is it sturdy and safe? Is it strong enough to last as long as the child's interest or as long as you think it should for the price you are paying? It is a mistake to stress the safety issue to the point of fear, but given what your child is likely to do with her new toy (throw it, bite it, fall on it, take it apart?), is it safe?

- *Physical appearance.* Is it beautiful? There's no disputing tastes when it comes to beauty, but in general is it nicely designed and harmonious in appearance? Is it inviting? Can you stand the sight of it yourself? Remember, it's going to be around and probably in sight for quite a while.

- *Span of usefulness.* How long at a time will the child enjoy it and how many times?

- *Educational value.* What does it teach and is that worth learning? Is a toy really needed to teach this or is there a better way?

- *Your child's stake in the toy.* Does it meet a need or interest your child is manifesting now? Even the right toy at the wrong moment is the wrong toy. You can answer all the other questions by examining the toy, but this one can be answered only by watching and knowing the child.

• *Cost.* Balancing the price against all the above and in relation to your budget and space, is this toy worth buying?

Toys to Avoid

Many toys that seem worthwhile at first turn out to be disappoint-
ing. It is well to be circumspect about the following:

• *Terrific but too late.* Try to avoid buying things you wish you
had known about six months ago. If he's already learned what your
latest discovery teaches, the toy will be uninteresting to him. So
wait for the next child.

• *Terrific but too temporary.* Some beautiful, well-made, and edu-
cationally sound toys that are valuable in a preschool may be almost worthless at home because the child learns what they offer in
a few minutes. At least in the beginning, children are not interested in the having of toys (possessiveness is acquired), but in what
they can learn from them. As soon as the child has learned all he
can from a toy, he will lose interest in it. If he can learn everything
in one sitting, he will be through in one sitting. Glenn Doman
estimates that the average toy designed for the average eighteen-
month-old holds interest for about 90 seconds.

• *Babysitter toys.* Sometimes parents want to find a set or something that will "really keep her occupied so I can get some work
done." This hardly ever works because the motive is tantamount
to an open invitation to the child to cling. But if you are looking
for one "big" (meaning costly) thing that will last, try to test it out
at a friend's house more than once. Consider where you will keep
it and whether or not you have a good place for the child to use
it. For example, a model garage or farm is easier to use and more
interesting to the child if set at eye level on a table rather than on
the floor. Some use-up activity items such as sewing cards and easy
follow-the-dots, a small set of watercolors, or colored pencils may
occupy the child better, take up less space, and contribute more
while costing less. Just think twice.

• *Redundant toys.* While a toy can teach much and be of lasting interest, it may be that the child can learn what it teaches with things
around the house—for free. If so, you may prefer to save your
pennies for something that can't so easily be duplicated at home.

• *Baby home learning programs.* As soon as your baby arrives you are likely to find yourself on a surprising number of new mailing lists, some of which invite you to subscribe to *their* home learning program for *your* baby. They may offer to send each month new toys pretested to suit the development of the child plus various books, publications, and charts. Some such publications are full of helpful ideas and can be a real tonic, but check first to make sure the suggestions are compatible with your own philosophy. Avoid programs that claim to speed up the child's learning and may tempt you to push your child. Avoid publications that might tempt you to make comparisons between your child and others. Avoid programs that arbitrarily send preselected toys on schedule as part of your subscription. Direct mail is a big help, but it's best if you have the freedom to select and then to buy or not. All babies and parents are different, so the time progressions followed by these programs may not apply to you and your child.

Organizing and Storing Toys

The physical environment in which the child works with his toys is important. No matter how selective we try to be , by the time our children are only a year old they have accumulated quite a supply. Unless we discover an orderly way of storing them, we will slowly go crazy from looking at or trying to deal with the mess.

It is important to find some way of organizing and storing things in a reasonably effortless and orderly way. A jumble of toys only expresses possessiveness and the purpose of play as learning gets lost. Some "mess" has to be tolerated for the child to be free to learn, but pure chaos works out to be tyrannizing rather than freeing.

Children really appreciate order and, provided the order is *reasonable and apparent,* they will usually help to maintain it. They like finding things in the same place; they like knowing where things go. Order makes life easier. The only difficulty is finding a rationale to go on—not merely a place for everything, but a sensible place for everything.

Most preschoolers will not play long by themselves. So you

may find it nice to have a play area near where you spend most of your time. When there is a separate place for most toys, then the bedroom is easier to maintain and retains a certain sanctity as a high and lifted-up place of quiet refuge, peace, contemplation, privacy. A few toys of current interest can still be kept there as well as a nice selection of books.

Wherever you keep them, generally speaking, toddlers' toys can be organized by category: small-parts toys and sets, small to medium single toys, medium to large toys, medium to large unorganizables.

Small-parts toys and sets can be nicely stored in plastic containers or bins. Clear plastic kitchen containers come in all sizes, and you can see what's inside at a glance. When giving a small-parts gift, it's nice to give such a container as well. Frequently used sets such as Legos can be stored in stackable plastic bins and are thus easy for the child to get at and pick up on his own.

Small to medium toys, such as yo-yos, balls, and flashlights, are almost as troublesome as small-parts sets. They defy organization and are easily knocked off open shelves. For these, shallow plastic bins make good "drawers" and can be set on shelves or mounted on glides beneath shelves.

Medium to large single toys, such as a cash register, pounding bench, or xylophone, can have specific places on a shelf.

Medium to large unorganizables, such as dolls and stuffed animals, can be sorted into categories and stored in large plastic laundry baskets or large cardboard cartons (cover with contact paper, add rope handles). If these containers are placed on the floor beneath a shelf, they look neater and can be pulled out as if they were drawers. You might want three boxes: one for cars and trucks, one for costumes, one for dolls, stuffed animals, and puppets.

Big *toy chests* are not very useful, except for long-term storage without use. Things get lost at the bottom and nobody wants to wrestle them forth.

Shelves, built up rather than around the walls, take up less play space. Besides, it's wise to have some things out of reach so that not everything can be spread out in aimless moments or at inappropriate times. Obviously things of greatest interest and needing least supervision get stored within the child's reach, whereas those that need you (e.g., perhaps paints, glue) can be placed higher.

Closet. If most toys are kept in the bedroom, the closet may be more useful for toys than for clothes, at least while most of the clothes are too small to need hangers. Though it's good for children to have free access to their toys, having them in sight all the time may be a distraction that results in their moving from one thing to another in a superficial, unsatisfying way. Line her closet with storage shelves. She can still get at her things but is less likely to drag everything out.

Hooks are handy for tanglers and danglers that don't fit in elsewhere. And for some of the clothes you took from the closet to make room for the toys, provide hooks that she can reach: one for pajamas, one for bathrobe, jacket, raincoat. You'll be surprised at the daily difference it makes to both of you.

Pickup time. If you're overwhelmed by the task of picking up, just imagine how it looks to your child. For a quick pickup and a chance for her to experience the clean-up as a happy, rewarding event, give her a shopping bag in which to put "everything you find on the floor" or "everything you find around the house that really belongs in your room." Then have a sorting session. It is as much fun for the child as a treasure hunt, and the sudden improvement makes the value of order apparent. When the idea that we are seeing beings is kept in mind, it is easier to know what to expect of her and how much help to give in restoring order. What will help her to see the value of order? A time to demonstrate, a time to enforce, a time to help, a time not to help.

A Place to Work

In fostering the best use of toys and playtime, a good place to work is as important as a place to put things away. The former is partly taken care of by the latter, since a little space is about all a child requires to do her work. The only equipment that might be considered crucial are a table and a chair sized down to the child, and a step-stool for upping her size.

A child-size table and chair are almost as valuable as a bed. While it's perfectly possible for children to work or read in highchairs or junior chairs at adult-size tables, they are much more comfortable at tables and chairs that fit them. Activities tend to last longer at child-size tables than at a big one or on the floor. The children can pick up what they drop, work standing up for a while, move around and work from the other side, and come and go and come again. A clean, visible, reachable work surface inspires constructive work. Much greater concentration, independence, and freedom are possible. Heavy-duty plastic-topped tables such as those available through educational catalogs are ideal, but almost any smooth surface of the right height will do. Cut down an old table. A large piece of plywood covered with matte-finish white Formica makes a superb counter/table/desk that can grow with the child to adulthood. All you have to do is change the base from short legs to longer legs. Or rest it across small chests of drawers. A good minimum size is 20 by 30 inches. Most important is the relative height of table and chairs. During the preschool years, 24 inches is a good average table height. Ten inches between chair seat and table is about right. Have extra chairs for playmates.

A step-stool that brings the child up to sink, counter, toilet, workbench, and higher bookshelf replaces water table, play kitchen, and in many instances the long arm of Mommy and Daddy. Any untippy stool will do. We had a wonderful one that combined a two-step stair with a small rocking chair.

Kinds of Play

Facilitating the happiest and most fruitful use of toys and playtime is a much greater issue than what toys to provide. When the days are long, often what's needed is not a new toy or a change in the weather, but a shift in subject, a change of perspective, another way of carrying on, of shifting gears. Only clear seeing can tell us what and when, but there will be times for . . .

Playing alone. While we try not to abandon our children or push them aside, we must nevertheless stand back as much as possible—available but not interfering, helping and encouraging, but becoming ever more irrelevant as the child grows. It is also important to treat our children and their work with courtesy and respect, never abruptly interrupting a child at play any more than we would interrupt a fellow adult at work.

Playing beside each other. This is the most common mode of play throughout the preschool years. He does his work; we do ours. We do not interfere with each other unnecessarily, but we share the joy of working, understanding, learning, accomplishing. We keep company with each other and are near each other in love.

Playing together. Doing the same thing together. Anything from roughhousing, to artwork, to games, to cooking or making something together. Often it is something requiring two that first awakens the child to the benefits of cooperating. Whatever is happening, let it be characterized by gentleness and joy.

Planned play. With toddlers it is good to have some planned activities every day and some regular activities each week. They are too mobile and too thirsty for learning for us to respond adequately on an entirely moment-to-moment basis. Parent and child are likely to feel tired of each other at the end of any day in which there is no planned time.

One time of day that is unfortunately often trying for small children is early morning. They wake so expectantly, glad to see us and eager to get on with life. But sometimes we almost wrestle the morning away.

It may be that a little sooner attention rather than all that later attention would be better—just a little help to get her started in her own "work." So set up something after she goes to bed—a project or a toy she hasn't seen for a while or all her cars lined up in a new place. Try reading one story right off the bat. (See also page 294.) Afterward you may find you can go your separate ways for a time. And give some thought to what she might do beside you while you work. Such thoughtfulness expresses love and can help free everyone for a happier day.

Going out. No matter how responsive we are, we almost have to have an outing each day to break the illusion of being trapped by each other. If you are at home alone with your toddler for long stretches of time, you almost can't help revolving around each other. The more we think we are running our children's lives, the more we feel that they are running ours. We wake up glad to see each other, but by bedtime we are standing over our sweetly sleeping children, vowing that tomorrow we will give more of ourselves to them. But maybe less is the answer. Outings are great for changing the subject from me and him for and against each other to both of us in the big wide world, making discoveries side-by-side. Outings give life a chance to take charge of us and diminish our conviction that we have to take charge of life. On any outing try to arrange for the child to do some walking or climbing on his own. While a ride in a grocery cart or a quick tour of a nearby pet store can be as good as a museum expedition, long shopping trips are a trial to be avoided when possible. Besides regular outdoor explorations, frequent library visits are tops. Make both as shouldless as possible. Most libraries are relaxed about children talking in the children's section. And try the firehouse, an airport, a pajama walk just before bed. And don't let the rain keep you in. Hardly anything is more fun than a pair of boots, an umbrella, a puddle, and permission to splash.

Active play. A time to allow for climbing. You are available now, so the safety gate can come off the stairs and he can practice. Dancing. Marching. Walking like a duck or an inchworm. He does things and you copy him. Indoors or out, just some running around and jumping and climbing.

Quiet play. Separate private times. Quiet times together. Is there conflict and frustration? Then let's both go to our rooms— not as a punishment, but to get free, become quiet, and put something besides each other in charge. A time to be still together, to listen to the wind or what she wants to say. To look out the window, up at the stars, down at the street, into the woods. To walk once around the house before bed and hear the insect music. If we want to help them learn to pray, let's not teach them what to say, but how to be still and listen when there doesn't seem to be anybody talking at all.

Books About Toymaking and Play

One last thing to consider before heading off to purchase a toy is a good practical book on homemade toys and play activities. The true craftsman's books on toymaking are best reserved for enthusiastic grandparents and friends unless you already have the necessary skills or a mother's helper to take care of your preschooler while you learn to carve or sew or carpent. But improvisational books on toymaking and play activities are extremely helpful in inspiring us with well-tried ideas that can be done on the spur of the moment. One such book coupled with a little enthusiasm is worth a dozen toys and will probably cost half as much as one toy. (See also pages 235–236)

Child Care Tips for Busy Mothers, by Nancy Carlyle. Practical tips to make life with children pleasanter and easier. From coping with slippery-soled new shoes, to finger paint recipes, to long car trips. Sometimes silly, but mostly very helpful. Simon & Schuster.

The Cooperative Sports and Games Book, by Terry Orlick. We all say winning isn't what counts, yet we find it difficult to say what does. In chapters of games for every age group Orlick shows how to face challenges and have fun together through playing games that nobody loses! To us this book was a revelation well worth the price. Pantheon.

Easy Woodstuff for Kids, by David Thompson. Woodworking is one of the most appealing and discouraging activities for preschoolers and their parents. Unless you are experienced with both wood-working and children you are likely to set your sights too high. The result is either an unsuccessful project or a frustrated child, sighing, "I didn't make it. You did." *Easy Woodstuff* is full of projects that really can be managed by almost any parent and preschooler. Especially nice are the numbers of things children can make and give as gifts. Fosters appreciation of trees and nature, satisfying creativity, learning of basic wood-working skills, and resourcefulness. Gryphon.

The Everything Book, by Eleanor Graham Vance. Divided into "Things to Make" and "Things to Do," this is a real treasure chest of good ideas for parents, sitters, and grandparents. Among our favorites: directions for newspaper hats, boats, and giant trees; mice and dolls from knotted handkerchiefs; and a fabulous "impromptu dollhouse" from junk—sure to provide days of fun that you'd never get from a costly "boughten" one. Great for trips, rainy days, chicken pox. Handy throughout childhood. Golden.

How to Make Children's Furniture and Play Equipment, by Mario Dal Fabbro. Cribs, chairs, gyms, tables, sandbox, easel, playhouse, workbench—60 clear plans for the parent handy with some power tools. McGraw-Hill.

The Incredible Year-Round Playbook, by Elin McCoy. A book of over 100 season-related crafts, games, tricks, and stunts that promote resourcefulness, awareness of nature, and good times in families. Random House.

I Saw a Purple Cow and 100 Other Recipes for Learning, by Ann Cole, Carolyn Haas, Faith Bushnell, and Betty Weinberger, illustrated by True Kelley. An endless variety of things to do and make with young children. Includes play dough recipe, finger plays, toys to make. Compiled by four mothers who seem to know what they're talking about. Little, Brown.

Just a Box? by Goldie Taub Chernoff, illustrated by Margaret Hartelius. Many things to make from the endless cardboard boxes everything comes in. A toothpaste-box alligator, oatmeal box cradle, etc. Scholastic Book Service.

The Ladybird Book of Toys and Games to Make, by James Webster, illustrated by Robert Ayton. 23 toys to make from any old thing. Designed for older children to do by themselves, a bargain for mothers of preschoolers. A Ladybird Book. Penguin Books.

Learning with Mother, by Ethel and Harry Wingfield. Books 1 (up to 2 years), 2 (2–3 years), 3 (3–4 years), and 4 (4–5 years). Imported from England, these unassuming little books are unusually helpful regarding what to do and how to get along with the preschooler from babyhood until five. Arranged according to chronological development, the sequence is good, though many children will be ready for things sooner than the books suggest. As small activity books they don't contain many things to do, but each idea offered suggests a dozen other ways of helping your child to learn. A Ladybird Book. Penguin Books.

Making Things, by Ann Wiseman. A good craft and toymaking book that is mostly for older children but good to know about. Includes a wide variety of activities from printing, to xylophone-making, to carving wooden whistles. Little, Brown.

A Parent's Guide to Children's Play and Recreation, by Alvin Schwartz. First published in 1963, this book is not quite up to date in the materials and prices it mentions. Nevertheless, it is an exceptionally useful introduction to the activities most children enjoy, with rough guidelines for when and suggestions for how to provide appropriate equipment inexpensively. Collier.

The Playgroup Book, by Marie Winn and Mary Ann Porcher. A superb book about all the things preschoolers like to learn from doing. A highly useful resource for parents of preschoolers, whether or not you're starting a play group. Penguin Books.

Play and Playthings for the Preschool Child, by E. M. Matterson. Just what the title implies: a useful book brimming with suggestions for providing young children with a good play/learning environment. Special emphasis for the handy parent-with-a-hammer on building shelves, benches, gym equipment (doesn't give specific plans, just ideas to improvise on). Very useful presentations of the particular worth of various kinds of play. Penguin Books.

Puppet Party, by Goldie Taub Chernoff, illustrated by Margaret Hartelius. All kinds of simple hand puppets made from paper bags, socks, paper plates, and cups. Scholastic Book Services.

Three, Four, Open the Door, by Susan M. Stein and Sarah T. Lottick. At once just about the most conscious and practical book of activities for young children: what they accomplish, how to do them, and when. Very well thought out in response to society's growing awareness of the very young child's eagerness, ability, and right to learn. Wonderful for parents or teachers. Follett.

Toy Book, by Steven Caney. Clear instructions on how to make and get the most out of more than 50 toys and experiments. Many of the toys are for children older than preschool age, for whom much of the fun will be in the making. But the preschooler is growing up fast and in the meantime such things as soap crayons, tube telephones, sand combs, and a creature cage are wonderful. Workman.

What to Do When "There's Nothing to Do," by members of the staff of the Boston Children's Medical Center and Elizabeth M. Gregg, illustrated by Marc Simont. 601 truly practical play ideas that really work with younger children. Expresses very well the possibilities of learning and playing without buying a lot. Dell.

Workjobs, by Mary Baratta Lorton. Jar tops, safety pins, rice, and such can help the preschooler to help himself to language, math, and happy hours. Described as "activity-centered learning," *Workjobs* is a terrific mind-opener for the home. So often we don't recognize learning when it is taking place. On the one hand we fall for workbooks that bore or frustrate. On the other hand we overlook the educational dimensions of everyday materials and situations. Recognizing the child's play as respectable learning work, *Workjobs* is a catalog of child-proven activities. Photos and straightforward text demonstrate an enormous variety of learning games easily assembled from ordinary grocery-bag fallout. Addison-Wesley.

Direct Mail Sources of Toys, Books, and Equipment

It is often better to shop for toys and equipment from educational suppliers than from local toy stores and chains. A wider range of better materials is available from these school suppliers and whatever extra you pay in postage may well be offset by the convenience of shopping by mail.

The following list is far from comprehensive. To find additional sources in your area check nearby urban telephone directories and inquire at local schools.

Dick Blick, P.O. Box 1267, Galesburg, IL 61401. A large resource of art supplies and other educational materials. Blick has a number of catalogs, beginning with its comprehensive offering of art supplies. Most relevent to parents of preschoolers are Blick's "Early Learning Catalog," "Enrichment Aids," and "Invicta Educational Aids."

Childcraft Education Corporation, 4 Kilmer Rd., Edison, NY 08817. A large collection of toys and equipment for children, including many fine imported things not generally available in the U.S. Childcraft offers a 48-page catalog for free and a more inclusive and worthwhile one for $1.50.

Child Life Play Specialties, Inc., 55 Whitney St., P.O. Box 527, Holliston, MA 01746. Excellent indoor and outdoor gymnastic equipment for children. Big wooden gym sets plus all sorts of parts and attachments such as swing seats, hitching rings for doorway gyms, devices for mounting swings on tree trunks, etc. Free 24-page catalog.

Community Playthings, Rifton, NY 12471. The wooden climbing equipment, furniture, and toys manufactured by this Christian community are all beautifully made, superior products, strong enough for nursery school use. Black and white catalog: $1.00.

Constructive Playthings, 1040 East 85th St., Kansas City, MO. A large early-childhood and special-education resource, handy for western and midwestern families. No orders under $10 accepted. 200-page black and white catalog, free to teachers, $2 for private individuals.

Developmental Learning Materials, P.O. Box 4000, One DLM Park, Allen, Texas 75002. A highly selective catalog of excellent educational materials for young children. Of special interest and value to preschoolers are DLM's "pre-academic" materials:

parquetry, wooden cubes, and puzzles. DLM also offers a unique collection of learning materials specifically designed for Spanish-speaking grade school students. Write for free "Comprehensive Catalog" in full color.

Edmund Scientific Co., 800 Edscorp Bldg., Barrington, NJ 08007. "Astronomy, optics, science, hobbies, parapsychology, alternate energy . . . more than 4500 unusual bargains for hobbyists, schools, and industry." A wonderful catalog for experimenters of all ages, this does include a number of things to delight and inform the preschooler. Three-foot toy parachutes, cardboard periscope, large assortments of prisms and magnets, gigantic balloons. Their magnetic tape could prove to be the world's easiest way to make any place a bulletin board. Satisfaction guaranteed or your money back. This good-size catalog is free.

Educational Teaching Aids, 159 W. Kinzie St., Chicago IL 60610. Items for early childhood and special education. Includes a wide variety of manipulative materials selected for "their educational merit in terms of providing concrete learning experience." The 100-page "Vital Years" catalog available on request for $1.00.

Growing Child, P.O. Box 620B, Lafayette, IN 47902. These publishers of monthly child development newsletters "Growing Child" and "Growing Parent" also offer an excellent and extensive selection of preschool toys and books for sale by direct mail. Nearly all books listed in *Whole Child/Whole Parent* are available here. Growing Child will send free sample newsletters and Christmas catalog upon request.

J. L. Hammett Co., Braintree, MA 02184. Toys, art supplies, furniture and storage equipment, gym equipment, music, math and reading readiness, science—some good things in every category. Another institutional supplier with many worthwhile materials for the preschooler at home. Ask for the "Hammett Early Childhood and Special Education Catalog" (136 pages, 1 color).

Kaplan Corporation, P.O. Box 15027, Winston-Salem, NC 27103. "Catalogue of Play, Learning and Growth." A superb 200-page, full-color catalog of early-childhood and special-education materials. Both the comprehensive bi-annual catalog and smaller annual supplement are free upon request.

Learning Materials Workshop, 58 Henry St., Burlington, VT 05401. This is not a supplier of many toys, but the manufacturer of a few very special ones. Beautifully sanded, oiled, or painted hardwood shapes form various and variable constructions and vehicles and puzzles. The quality and educational and entertainment value of these handcrafted toys justify their high price. Free brochure available on request.

Scholastic Audio-Visual Materials, 906 Sylvan Ave., Englewood Cliffs, NJ 07632. A 44-page catalog of Scholastic's records, cassettes, films, filmstrips, posters, and charts. Free.

Scholastic Book Services, Starline Editions, 50 West 44th St., New York, NY 10036. A catalog of more than 800 paperback children's books. Free.

4
Freedom

We never did have tears over broken balloons because, knowing that they would rise when the string was released, the children always wanted to let go immediately. As parents we had a little trouble adjusting to this. While we secretly lamented the "waste" of our money, the children marveled at the freedom of each bright, rising thing. After a while they learned to hold on to their balloons a little more tightly and a little longer. So the kids are learning to hold on, while we are learning to let go.
—A parent

And ye shall know the truth, and the truth shall make you free.
—John 8:32

Freedom is a universal urge. Lack of freedom is a universal experience. From infancy on, whenever limitation is experienced we desire to overcome it in order to be free. The newborn infant, unable even to hold up her head, is almost completely restricted by the limitations of her physical body. As an immature being she is further in bondage to her parents. As she learns to feed herself, to walk and to climb, she experiences emancipation both from her own physical limitations and from her physical dependence on her parents. Each attainment increases her freedom and her awareness of freedom. You can see that she desires freedom and rejoices at every increased measure of it.

False Freedom

Me, Inc. can conceive of participating in reality in only two ways: by having and by doing. So we tend to approach freedom in two ways: by wanting (and not wanting) and by willing (and won'ting). We want to be *free to* (and not to) do what we feel like. We want to be *free from* others' expectations of us (and *freed by* others' compliance with our expectations of them). When we see someone "doing his own thing," we think that's freedom. Free time is time to ourselves, time for pleasure, time out, time to relax, time to enjoy ourselves and to do as we please. Implied is a sort of lawlessness, a freedom from or outside of the law. On the other hand, when we see someone in a "position of power"—say, the conductor of an orchestra, someone who is telling everyone else what to do—we believe he is free. He's his own boss. No one can tell him what to do. He is free to make decisions. He is in charge. He can get people to do what they should. Again, freedom seems to mean being above the law or having the power to create or impose law and order.

Free to Be Me

We sense that freedom involves both pleasure and order, yet we experience a tension, even conflict, between these aspects of freedom that results in little pleasure (except at the expense of order), little order (except at the expense of pleasure), and no freedom. Individually when we seek freedom as pleasure we find only self-indulgence, which proves enervating, enslaving, confining, and chaos-producing. So then we try the orderly route, making resolutions, trying to get organized and do what we should. But we keep meeting up with internal rebellion. The harder we try, the more something in us jumps up and down and refuses. And if we succeed, we find ourselves getting very serious and joyless, "uptight." Anything but free.

Free to Be Me and You

In relation to others, our efforts to find freedom through pleasure outside of the law or to bring about freedom through willfully imposing or complying with some set of laws is even less fruitful than our solo attempts. Most families experience a constant struggle to maintain freedom without trespassing and chaos, order without tyranny and conflict. There is a constant battle within each individual between doing what he feels like doing and what others think he should. The freedom of the individual is experienced by others as his "getting his own way." One's pleasure wreaks havoc on the others' order; one's order destroys everyone's pleasure.

Parentally, it's even worse. We try to find a loving and intelligent way of maintaining maximum freedom (pleasure and order), but we get confused. If freedom is identified with pleasure outside of the law, then loving means "being nice," which means letting our children do what they feel like instead of what they should. If freedom is identified with order, then being intelligent means being "right," and we find ourselves continually telling our children what they should do (so that everyone will have equal freedom and responsibility). But this way we meet with conflict, resistance, and frustration instead of freedom. Either way we wind up feeling tyrannized—by the chaos or the conflict, or the conviction that all the ordering is left up to us.

> *Parent:* You are bossing me around by making me boss you around by not doing what you should. If you would just do what I tell you in the first place then I wouldn't have to keep telling you.

Child: I think there's something fishy about that.
Parent: I think you're right.

For the child it is just as bad. When we equate freedom with pleasure (freedom from pain and work) we may become either overprotective, restricting, fearful parents or overindulgent, doting, spoiling ones. In the first case the child may become overly fearful and afraid to go forth and try new things; or he may become reckless and wild and wind up getting hurt or into trouble. Either way he is not free. In the second case, the child becomes demanding and self-indulgent. He approaches everything with the question of whether or not he "feels like it." So he is confined by his feelings to a very narrow world in which ultimately he finds little happiness. His freedom to fulfill his potential and to enjoy and participate in an ever-widening (freer) world is curtailed.

If we identify freedom with order, we may think more in terms of responsibility, duty, commitment, discipline, and become strict, demanding parents. The short-range objective is to try to get our children to take responsibility and do what they should so that then (in the future) they will be free to do what they like, and so that others might be freer in the meantime. But this argument, no matter how sensible it seems to us, does not impress our children. (I overheard one despairing parent say to her son, "Asking you to hurry is like telling you to take a nap.") The long-range objective is for the child to be successful—free to make something of himself, to get ahead, free to get somewhere, free to take command, to compete, to be powerful, a freewheeler, a free agent. But right now he is feeling pushed around, and he is getting the idea that freedom is a matter of power over others. So somehow he is never doing what he should, or he is doing it and failing, or he is succeeding and feeling miserable, or he is succeeding and being obnoxious. He may feel mad as hops or guilty as hell; he may be either a bully or a sissy. But one thing he surely isn't is free.

I Will, Therefore I Am

Strangely, all these seemingly different approaches to freedom are based on a common idea. All of them (and all combinations of them) equate freedom with the exertion of personal will power in a fundamentally chaotic or conflicting universe. Whether as wanting or not wanting or as willing or won'ting or as should or shouldn't or as feel like or don't feel like—and whether selfish or altruistic, active or passive, strict or permissive, individual or collective—there is a hidden assumption that life is a chaotic situation and that freedom depends on our ordering, on human will power. Freedom through will. "Free will." As we fail to see but variously and unvaryingly experience, this is both a preeminently tyrannical idea and a preeminently chaotic one. So it is no wonder that as an idea of freedom it is constantly proving itself false in our experience. Wherever freedom is sought in vain, we can expect to find an underlying idea of personal will power in combat. Beneath that is a fundamental misperception of who and where we are: a body among bodies, a personal mind among personal minds—Me, Inc. The idea that each of us is a body among bodies tends toward pleasure-seeking (wanting and not wanting) and a self-indulgent life outside the law that leads to chaos and confinement. The idea that each of us is a person among persons (an embodied mind among embodied minds) leads to competition, ambition, and power struggle (willing and won'ting). Different people have different emphases at different times, but for all of us life is a bewildering mixture of both.

Let Freedom Ring

The girl did not fall asleep readily and when she was ten, she began to switch on her radio at night—which was against the rules. She hardly ever broke rules, and did so only fearfully, switching the radio only "on" and not turning it up at all. Sometimes she was still awake when the stations signed off playing the "Star Spangled Banner." As she had been taught at school, she would climb out of bed and stand —shivering sleepily—while "our national anthem" was played. But she couldn't hear it with the volume so low, and had to keep bending down to hear when it was over.

I knew a young lady of wealthy parents who ran away from home and was driving a taxi in New York City, living in Greenwich Village in squalor and misery. She said, "Well, I wanted to be free." I was able to show her that she was not free, she was only trying to be independent, which means

she was still dependent since she was fighting against her parents by
driving a taxi and living in poverty. That's not freedom, it's a struggle for
independence, which is a state of dependency.
—Thomas Hora, *Existential Metapsychiatry*

The Child as a Model for Freedom

Jesus said: "Except ye be converted, and become as little children, ye shall
not enter into the kingdom of heaven."
—Matthew 18:3

Jesus didn't say that children were getting into heaven, but he
seems to have been suggesting that there is something about the
way children are which if we could learn it might free *us* to get into
heaven. What is it? Are children free? In a way, no; but in a way,
yes.

On the surface, there could hardly be anything less free than
an infant. He appears to be a very self-centered, body-oriented,
tyrannical, and limited creature. He is helpless, weak, dependent
on others in every way. Yet, within a few short years, he has realized so much freedom that we can simply be amazed. From a
weak, nearly blind, pleasure/pain-bound, ignorant, uncomprehending, powerless, speechless little thing, he becomes in no time
a running, dancing, singing, questioning, understanding, delighting wonder. And talk about chaos! What could be more chaotic
than the crazy quilt of meaningless sensations that bombard the
uncomprehending newborn? Yet in an unbelievably short time he
has found in all that chaos order and meaning and a way of orienting himself so that he can move freely about and have some consid-
erable dominion over his experience. For all that he still doesn't
know, and can't do, for all that he remains dependent on others,
before he even enters school he has demonstrated a freedom to
become free that is mind-boggling. Of course, he has almost no
realization of true freedom. And before long—already in fact—it
is inevitable for him to experience conflict between what his Me,
Inc. wants and what the world of other Me, Incs. seems to require.
But as, initially, he transcends one limitation after another with

such incredible speed, he offers an astonishing demonstration of how it is that freedom is realized.

What is the child's secret? It is a secret from himself, and it is, in fact, the secret *of* himself. He doesn't *have* the secret of freedom, but he *manifests* it. Like a messenger with an unopened envelope, he brings it to us, hands it to us—whereupon if we can read the message insides it becomes ours.

> *In inexperienced infancy*
> *Many a sweet mistake doth lie:*
> *Mistake, though false, intending true;*
> *A seeming somewhat more than view,*
> *That doth instruct the mind*
> *In things that lie behind*
> *And many secrets to us show*
> *Which afterwards we come to know.*
> —Thomas Traherne, from "Shadows in the Water," in *Poems of Felicity*

Briefly then, children exhibit a freedom to become free that we seem to lack. They also lack something that we seem to have: self-consciousness. There are several things people universally envy and admire in children—one is purity, another is innocence, and still another is their *freedom—freedom to enjoy* life as it comes, naturally, honestly, *free of concern* about what others think. The tendency to glorify children for these qualities is a silly sentimentality, for they don't possess any of them. It is only that for a time they lack self-consciousness. And it is during that brief unselfconscious period that they demonstrate this seeming purity, innocence, and *freedom* we so admire.

Is there a connection between the child's striking lack of self-consciousness and his striking freedom to find freedom so efficiently? It certainly seems so.

If you observe a group of young children at play you will see that the freest child is the least self-conscious one. You can see that his freedom to grow freer by leaps and bounds comes with his ability to look at life for what it can teach him, an ability that is directly proportionate to his lack of preoccupation with self (and other). He is not distracted by thoughts of how he is doing and what others think of him; he is not distracted by how he feels; he is focused. Through his undivided attention to *what is, what is* ultimately gets its way with him and becomes a freedom. Self-consciousness seeks (and fails to obtain), strives for (and fails to achieve) freedom through exertion of the will. Consciousness seeks (and finds) freedom through constant awareness of the law.

Zen and the Art of Throwing a Ball

Once I heard a father marvel: "How did he learn to throw that ball so far? I didn't teach him! When did he learn to do this? I didn't even see him do it! Why did he do it? No one in our family is particularly interested in baseball."

Everything that father thought was missing might have been a hindrance had it been present. Somewhere along the way in the throwing of a ball, the child had conceived of a possibility of freedom. Perhaps it first came through watching someone else. Perhaps once in flinging a ball he had let it fly and surprised himself. At any rate, some freedom had been encountered and was now a possibility in consciousness. After that, as long as he remained unselfconscious (undivided) he was able to give his undivided attention to the possibility of which he had conceived. Through his pure desire for freedom (and the sense of possibility) certain laws were given the opportunity to gain power over the child. Aiming himself toward a conscious possibility, he became subservient to it. And then through the child's receptive and devoted consciousness, the underlying force of being itself organized and energized and utilized and coordinated everything in the child to express *it*self in the form of the freedom to throw a ball so beautifully.

He must have practiced for hours on end, expending tremendous effort but little strain, because his interest in seeing what was possible carried him along. Confident that what he could conceive of was possible and could be realized, he went at it. Sometimes the ball fell short, but he did not infer that he lacked power. Sometimes the ball went wild, but he did not infer that the thing was impossible or that there was no predictability (chaos). Whatever seemed too hard only showed him that he had not yet discovered the knack. Whatever appeared chaotic only suggested that the order and his oneness with it had not yet been discerned. Sometimes his shoulder hurt, but the very hurt became a guide, directing him into better alignment with the hidden force he did not doubt. He looked at everything for *what is* and *what isn't,* so everything taught him, until he could throw the ball—far, fast, accurately, and with remarkable ease. And he wasn't proud, he was pleased; and he didn't feel triumphant, he felt grateful; and he didn't feel powerful, he felt surer; and he felt and was freer.

It was never that he had his way with the ball. Rather through his undistracted, absolutely focused unselfconscious consciousness the invisible laws of physics had their way with him. Through the total submission of himself to the invisible laws he found both dominion and spontaneity which he rightfully experienced as freedom and joy.

Me, Inc. knows that freedom has something to do with law and order, but thinks order must be brought about by will power. The child shows us that, on the contrary, freedom comes through subservience to existing order—through conscious alignment with it. Me, Inc. knows freedom has something to do with pleasure, but thinks it means feeling good and being above the law. The child shows us that this pleasure is really spontaneity and that it, too, is a by-product of absolute compliance with, obedience to, the law.

Once we give the hidden laws of physics complete sway over us, we become free to navigate a bicycle creatively—no hands, standing on our heads, riding on only one wheel, almost anything we can think of—with a minimum of effort. To Me, Inc. it seems that such feats are a matter of personal pleasure and power; we do not usually attribute lack of freedom to ignorance. So we do not customarily expect to find freedom through spiritual consciousness. But the boy with the ball shows us again: we are seeing beings and seeing is being. Whatever we can (truly) see, we can be. He shows us that life is after all fundamentally orderly, which is the same as to say that it is intelligent, which is the same as to say that it is intelligible. He demonstrates that in any endeavor maximum freedom depends on maximum obedience to the fundamental order of being. Obedience means oneness—we do not oppose ourselves, we are not divided against it. Oneness with a fundamental intelligence is consciousness. Therefore he shows us that *seeing is freeing.*

And ye shall know the truth, and the truth shall make you free.
—John 8:32

The Parent as a Freeing Agent

"I didn't teach him." "No one in our family is . . . interested in baseball." We need not conclude that the way to raise a free child is to leave him alone or be permissive. Indeed, it seems that neglect is often better than what we imagine is necessary—power, ambition, pleasure, praise, intellectual understanding, reward, punishment, a forceful parent—all things that might call the child's attention to himself and distract him from what is. But even better than a parent who merely doesn't distract is a parent who exemplifies, recognizes, trusts, facilitates, and fosters awareness of the fundamental intelligent order of life.

1. The Free Parent looks at everything with such questions as *"What is being shown? What is really going on here? What is there for me to learn in this?"* The more we recognize that the only obstacles to our freedom are our own limited and limiting ideas (rather than outside constraints of circumstance or others' expectations), the more we reinforce our children's innate sense that seeing is freeing, the less they will be enslaved by the idea of having to fight against "outside" constraints.

2. The Parent as Beholder of the Free Child. The child's freedom depends on her confidence—in herself as a "see-worthy" individual, in life as based on a fundamentally intelligible order. The more we recognize that seeing is being, the more eager we are to let our children see for themselves. The more we recognize that all life is meaningful, the easier it is to entrust our children to life as a gentle instructor which teaches rather than harms.

The freeing parent is above all the seeing parent. As such we do not view our children (or ourselves) in terms of virtues and faults, but in terms of what is true and what is false. This way we are continuously setting free the true, good child, rather than tethering our children (or ourselves) to the false with cords of guilt or shame or blame.

3. The Parent as Paver of the Free Way. By understanding that the basis of freedom is fundamental, intelligent order, we are freed from confusions about strict versus permissive and license versus freedom. Whenever we are guided by awareness of what *idea* is being expressed and what the child is ready to *see,* it becomes clear from moment to moment when "laying down the law" fosters security rather than tyranny or dependency and when "letting be" fosters confidence and learning rather than insecurity or self-indulgence.

4. The Parent as Preparer and Maintainer of the Freeing Environment. The substance of freedom is order. Thoughtful orderliness is one way that we make way for the free child. Intelligent freeing order is sought in the management of household, time, behavior, and in the setting of all priorities on a "first things first" basis. (See pages 136, 179 and 326.)

> When her children were small, a well-known American illustrator bought a playpen—for herself! She did her artwork in the playpen, thereby protecting her work from the children and allowing them freedom for their own more physical and active work nearby. A novel approach that wouldn't suit everyone—but the underlying thought makes sense.

5. The Parent as Guide and Fellow Seeker. As freeing parents we make the least of ourselves, factoring ourselves out as much as possible according to the child's readiness. So we often ask before telling and, even then, more often show than tell how something can be done. The essential value of any instruction is to awaken the child to a possibility for himself (not his dependency on a superior parent). The value of any regulation is to bring the child a new encounter with freedom or to protect some existing freedom. We are fellow seekers of freedom with our children. All the attention we give to considering what is really freeing for the child enhances our own realization of freedom.

6. The Parent as Supplier of Opportunities for Freedom. The value of any activity is its potential to increase the child's awareness of freedom or of her potential to be free. Her interest in an activity depends on her sense that some order will be revealed (and thus free her) or that some freedom will be achieved and thus help her discover some underlying order. Animals wild and tame, gym sets, vehicles, trees and woods, indoor and outdoor activities, everything can be approached with freedom in mind.

A Model for the Freeing Parent

The parent is like the conductor of an orchestra. The conductor is not a powerful person. It appears so, but it is not so. On the surface it seems that the music is produced by the power of the conductor to tell everyone what to do and when to do it. He may have to do that, but it is not what makes the music. A good conductor does not merely tell everyone what to do; rather he helps everyone to hear what is so. For this he is not primarily a telling but a listening individual: even while the orchestra is performing loudly he is listening inwardly to silent music. He is not so much commanding as he is obedient. The conductor conducts by being conducted. He first hears, feels, loses himself in the silent music; then when he knows what it is he finds a way to help others hear it too. He knows that music is not made by people playing instruments, but rather by music playing people. How does music play people? Through consciousness. So the conductor reveres the individual consciousnesses of the members of the orchestra as the precious instruments that music plays.

By any and all means he endeavors to conduct his orchestra into a consciousness of what the music is. For this he is at once absolutely subservient to the music and absolutely respectful of the artists' consciousness as musical instruments. And he is always trying to factor himself out so that nothing whatsoever comes between the music and its instruments, the artists' consciousnesses. The conductor knows that music makes the music.

In *From Mao to Mozart,* the documentary of violinist/conductor Isaac Stern's visit to China, these ideas are beautifully demonstrated. After years of being forbidden to play or listen to Western music, Chinese musicians have little understanding of what it is. So they asked Stern to help. In the film we attend the rehearsal of a professional orchestra. The musicians play accurately, flawlessly, energetically. Meticulously, with masterful skill, they comply with the written notes. And yet it is not music, because they don't hear or feel it. They cannot make heard outwardly what they have not heard inwardly.

Stern cannot make them make music by telling them what to do. In fact, through sheer will and hard work, the Chinese have all the necessary technique; but it is still not music. Music is so subtle, so spiritual, that only a true understanding of what it is—only music itself present in individual consciousness—can coordinate and temper and vitalize and aim all that skill in such a way that music occurs.

So how does Stern conduct? How does he teach? In a master class he provides us with a model for parenthood. Is he strict? Is he permissive? Praising? Severe? Is he tender? Is he demanding? Does he *teach* at all or does he let them find their own way? At different times he responds in different ways. There is a time to be firm and a time to be gentle; a time to interfere and a time to let be; there is a time to demonstrate and a time to refrain from demonstrating; a time to appreciate and a time to criticize; a time to encourage and a time even to chastise; a time to permit, a time to forbid, a time to tell and a time to keep silent. How does he know what and when? Evidently he is guided by a keen discernment of what the music is saying, and of what each musician is ready to hear. And he is never personal—either about what he knows or about what the musicians do not yet know. In front of an enormous audience, a student performs for him. She has practiced for years; she is trying so hard and doing so well. "No! No!" he says. "That is not it." Your heart goes out to her as he interrupts only moments into her long piece. *How could he?* we think. *Poor thing! She'll feel so discouraged. She'll be so embarrassed.* But as harsh as it seems, his interruption is loving; it is not personal (he does not say, "You have that wrong"), so she is not overly embarrassed. In a way it is a musical interruption. Music has forbidden what is not music to go on. Stern's very refusal to let her go on playing what isn't music expresses his confidence in her ability to recognize what the music really is. He cannot speak Chinese, nor she English. There is an interpreter. But now Stern speaks a universal language. Picking up his violin, he plays the passage over, speaking in music. What was merely skillfully played a moment before becomes in his hands something beautiful. Before it was correct; now it is alive. *Oh,* you say to yourself. *Is that what it is! I didn't know. I didn't even know that I didn't know!* "Ah!" says the girl.

Later he interrupts another student. "Yes, yes," he says. "That is quite good. But now sing it, will you?" The student sings the melody. It is sweet and fluid. "Yes," he says. "You see, when you sing it is beautiful, because you are listening to the music. That is how we play the violin. We listen to the music and then we find a way to make it sound like that."

Mostly he listens, seeing through what he hears. Only occasionally does he explain a technique and even then it is to bring about a firsthand encounter with music. He shows how to free and relax the hand on the neck of the violin. The suggestion is tried —suddenly the music is richer and freer and the face of the student lights up in surprise. He had not known!

Everything Stern does or says is to help the student become conscious of what the music is. His power as a conductor is the power of music over him. He knows that everyone has the potential to become conscious of the music and everything he does is designed to liberate that potential. Sometimes he helps us discover it for ourselves. Sometimes he helps us encounter it through a demonstration. He is never personal; we are never insulted.

To the children he says nothing, only listening with evident appreciation. These children are growing up with Western music, and so they hear it. Stern sees this. Their teachers will show them technique. Music is teaching them music. So he keeps silent.

The conductor is always ruling himself out, replacing himself as conductor and teacher through elevating the consciousness of the musician to a point of direct contact with the music itself. The conductor is conducted by the music. The love-intelligent parent is conducted by love-intelligence.

A true Master according to the Eastern tradition embodies truth for the disciple and transmits it directly as a lit candle can light another. He represents the reality which is present, but as yet imperfectly released, in the disciple, and his purpose is to help the disciple to realize, in the Indian phrase, the eternal Guru and Teacher in himself. When he has succeeded in doing this, the need of external Master and mediator is over. In short, the

aim of the Master is to prove himself superfluous, since what he essentially is, the disciple is too.
—Hugh l'Anson Fausset, *The Flame and the Light*

Freed to Go

They shall mount up with wings as eagles; they shall run, and not be weary; and they shall walk and not faint.
—Isaiah 40:31

"Whither, oh whither, oh whither so high?"
"To sweep the cobwebs from the sky."
—Traditional nursery rhyme

As parents of active children how can we apply and recognize the idea that seeing is freeing? Our small children's most obvious frontiers are physical. They want to overcome all limitations and their first, most perceptible ones are physical. They want to get up, then to go, then to go higher and faster and farther and upside-downer and arounder. If we keep sight of the spiritual motivation behind our children's physical activity, we can be waymakers and guides rather than impeders of their growth.

At first their motives are so pure. They do not climb to compete, or to be physically fit. And, experience notwithstanding, neither do they climb to put gray hairs on our heads or to knock over our favorite lamps. They climb to see; they see to be free. This is the only value and motive behind their activity—until others are introduced.

We have considered two ways that we tend to use our children: for our own pleasure and for our own ambition. If we are not alert to these temptations we become hinderers rather than helpers in our children's growth toward freedom. The only possible way of being freedom enhancers rather than hinderers is: (1) to recognize and relinquish the tendency to use the child and his physical activity for selfish motives and (2) to behold all of his activity in the light of the idea that seeing is freeing.

Safety and Freedom: The Parent as Roadblocker

"Mother, may I go out to swim?"
"Yes, my darling daughter.
Just hang your clothes on a hickory limb,
But don't go near the water."
—Traditional nursery rhyme

The inclination to use our children for our own pleasure places roadblocks in the way of their freedom. With regard to their physical activity, it shows up in the imposition on the child of such ideas as: daring/fearing ("Don't be such a chicken." "Oh, my God, watch out! You're going to fall!"), pleasure/pain ("It'll feel so good/bad, comfortable/uncomfortable."), pleasing/displeasing ("Don't you want your father to be proud of you?"), wanting/not wanting ("He doesn't *want* to walk [do you, Baby?]. I think you should carry him." "But I don't want to carry him. I want him to learn to do as he's told."), sickly/healthy ("Wouldn't you like to be as strong as . . . ?" "Are you *sure* you feel all right? Let me feel your head. Aren't you afraid you'll get sick from doing that? Aren't you tired after all that running?").

Since none of these concerns has anything to do with the essential value or motive behind our children's physical activity, each is simply a way of changing the subject and effectively stopping them in their tracks. If we are inclined to use our children for personal pleasure (an idea of love as feeling good), we are likely to view them as fragile, physical beings and to impose on their physical activity the fear of injury. Or we may opt for the reverse: that the child should exercise to build a healthy, pleasing body. The parallel for psychologically minded parents and parents of older children is fear of the child's getting "hurt feelings," and having traumatic psychological experiences. It is neither necessary nor possible to consider all the many variations. But one experience worth extra attention is that of safety in relation to freedom.

New parents in particular are likely to feel afraid as their children begin to run and climb. Parents of older children face the same temptation when their children begin to want to drive a car, go off on their own, and undertake new challenges.

How can the parent as a freeing agent be a responsive custodian of the child's safety and freedom simultaneously? We need to be careful about "Be careful!" Almost against our will this cry dominates our parental vocabulary. When our children returned from visiting relatives in Holland, we found that although they hadn't learned much of the language, they did know many ways to say *be careful* (think of your . . . mind your . . . watch out . . . beware . . . look out . . .). Of course, this is unavoidable. The child is backing off the bed, standing up in his highchair, teetering heedlessly at the top of the ladder to the slide. . . . We have to warn him. But some parents are so fearful that they virtually keep their children chained up. I have seen children over two years old sitting harnessed in strollers *next* to sandboxes *watching* other children play! Others allow their children to play but are so terrified by precarious moments and imagined disasters that they even become angry, shouting, "What's the matter with you? Do you want to get killed? See? It's your fault that you got hurt. I told you to be careful."

Such children are likely to become reckless or awkward and clumsy, or timid and hypochondriacal, or, worst of all, apathetic—just waiting for the next meal. Most parents are not so extreme, but we all worry. We want our children to be safe from harm, but not *full of care!* How can we teach safety without teaching fear and curtailing freedom?

The more we see our children as seeing beings, the more intelligent order we will recognize in their impulse to seek greater freedom, and the more it becomes possible to entrust them to life. Even as the baby crawls toward the open fireplace, he is not trying to destroy himself. He is purely and rightfully interested in learning, which is life-fulfilling and even life-saving rather than life-destroying. Once he knows what *hot* means and that the fire is hot, he will not try to crawl into the fireplace. We do not have to teach safety so much as we must protect him from his ignorance and at the same time foster the awareness needed to exercise better judgment. (*Yes, ooh—it's hot! Ouch. Hot! Not for touching!*) There is a place for prohibition and prevention, but not for fear.

While we don't want to belittle or be negligent, it is good to help our children let go of pain. Most hurts arise in the process of learning. What hurts most is the interruption of the learning tha the child is trying to do, and she is glad to be released from this experience so that she can go on learning. Without arousing fear or self-pity, we can gently help her let go and carry on. While comfort may be needed, it is not helpful to worry her with excessive poking and checking and asking if it hurts. Usually a comforting kiss or hug, coupled with a quick change of subject, is the best medicine. The younger the child, often the quicker the cure (long suffering is a learned attitude).

One family refers to small injuries as minor mishaps. Their crying two-year-old receives a quick check and a generous hug, and then the parent says, "Did you have a minor mishap?" The child finds this a fascinating idea—more interesting than the hurt. "Yes!" he says, running off to play. "I had a minor mishap with the stairs!"

Because he cleaves to me in love,
I will deliver him;
I will protect him because he knows my name.
When he calls to me, I will answer him;
I will be with him in trouble,
I will rescue him. . . .
—Psalm 91:14–15

While we have to protect children from the violent consequences of ignorant violation of fundamental law, so-called bad experiences (pain, failure, conflict) as well as so-called positive experiences are teachers. Both can be freeing. *While positive experiences can deepen our awareness of the fundamental order of being, negative ones show us how we are misaligned with the fundamental order of being.* Therefore, as necessarily we protect our children from harm, we are nevertheless not too quick to come between them and a negative experience from which they can safely learn something on their own. The freeing parent asks: What is she trying to see? What is she able to see? What is she ready to see? What will help her see it? What will this experience show her? Is there really any serious danger? Sometimes the laying down of a strict, clear rule frees the child from distraction. Sometimes allowing the child to fumble through something and learn by trial and error is freeing. As freeing parents we recognize that while sometimes comfort is freeing, sometimes no-nonsense dismissal is freeing. (See also pages 112 and 123.)

The Boy and the Sponge

After ninety-three patient mop-up operations she found herself screaming, "Watch out! Why don't you look what you're doing?" Then she hissed, "I said don't *cry* about it!" so venomously that the crying grew louder. Nervous spills were becoming more frequent, and she was having self-hate headaches from suppressed fury and rampant guilt.

Then, one day she visited a Montessori classroom and encountered for the first time the idea of the child-wielded sponge. Each child was carefully shown how to dampen and squeeze one out, how to sponge up a spill with light circular motions, squeezing out the sponge and wiping again. A chore? No, a freedom. Later she had an opportunity to try it herself. "He had just spilled his paints for the fourth time in half an hour. I knew better than to get mad, but I felt angry and he was looking worried because he knew I was not happy. I considered putting the paints away just to avoid another accident. Then I remembered about the sponge. I gave him one and said, 'How would you like to clean it up yourself this time?' He looked as if I had just given him a present. He was so relieved. 'Oh, Mommy, I love you!' he said. I didn't know whether to be sad or happy—it takes so little, but most of the time you just don't see it. Now whenever he is doing something in which spilling is a possibility I make sure that he has a sponge nearby. He still needs my help, but he is learning."

Freedom and Competition: The Parent as Sidetracker

The inclination to use our children to fulfill our own ambitions through competition can be a way of sidetracking them. Competition is so much the American way that we do not recognize many of the accompanying problems. Even if we do, we certainly cannot avoid it—and neither should we. It is not to be feared more than desired. But with freedom as the central concern it is possible for children to compete without being overly competitive and to not compete without feeling out of it.

What is wrong with competition? Competition is a sidetrack, because it changes the subject of an activity from freedom to the false issue of selves against one another. Whereas children at first run and jump for the joy of freedom, when competition and comparison are introduced the subject gets changed. With the pleasure-seeking motive the subject gets changed to the material self and how we feel; with the competitive motive the subject is changed to how powerful the self is compared to others. Winning/losing, succeeding/failing, trying/not trying, rather then freedom and joy may become the major experience and central issue. Physical activity, sports, and recreation are associated in many people's minds with both freedom and competition. We equate being athletic with being competitive, and almost do not recognize other possibilities. But they do exist.

In Holland, sometimes, young boys and girls spontaneously sing and dance together; a beautiful sight. Because Holland is so small, most children know dozens of the same singing and dancing games which they delight in playing together. This is a perfect example of how order is basic to freedom and demonstrates nicely one possibility of noncompetitive shared activity. I have also observed Dutch children playing together energetically without songs and games, just frolicking, dancing, running, and jumping—perhaps with a simple piece of rope around which to organize.

Certainly this happens in the United States, too. But there is an extraordinary emphasis on competition here—on winning and losing and succeeding and failing—which all too often leads to difficulty. Some parents pit their children against one another like fighting cocks. Addiction to competition is so great that when grade school children, boys particularly, face free time, many of the most sports-minded find it difficult simply to play. If they can't agree upon a game and its rules, they either become bored or begin to fight.

> On one school camping trip most of the children simply ran about, exploring rocks, climbing trees, hiding in the grass. But two highly competitive children were restless and bored until they found each other. While the others hunted for frogs by the pond, these two played catch—back and forth, back and forth. They were not free to find the new fun, to make the discoveries that lay in wait in this new situation.

Whatever happened to tree climbing, fort building, exploring? Of course many still do these things. But as parents it is well to be aware of the tendency to equate energetic activity with contest. Our children's worth does not depend on their ability to trounce one another. And surely we can find ways of frolicking and being healthy and active together in some joyful, free way that is not an adversary relationship. (See *Co-operative Sports and Games,* page 142.)

The most freeing contributions we can make to our children are mental ones. By constantly calling to mind the child's ideal self, his essential perfection, we keep him free to pursue true freedom. True freedom is not freedom from anything, but there is much bondage to be avoided along the way. While there is a need for protection and comfort, there must be freedom from fear. At the same time that there is a need for guidance and teaching, there must be freedom from domination. At the same time that there is a need for reproof and correction, there must be freedom from guilt and blame. At the same time that there is discernment, there must be freedom from classification and comparison.

So we proceed, fellow freedom-seekers, endeavoring not to neglect, neither to hinder nor to overly direct our children. The main thing is to remain cognizant of the fact that freedom *is* an issue. Then as we help, and refrain from helping, our children, we can study for ourselves what freedom really is, where it comes from, who finds it, and how.

Pennant
Come up here, bard, bard;
Come up here, soul, soul;
Come up here, dear little child
To fly in the clouds and winds with me, and play
*   with the measureless light.*

Child
Father, what is that in the sky beckoning to me
*   with long finger?*
And what does it say to me all the while?

Father
Nothing, my babe, you see the sky;

*And nothing at all to you it says. But look you, my
        babe,*
*Look at these dazzling things in the houses, and see
        you the money-shops opening;*
*And see you the vehicles preparing to crawl along
        the streets with goods;*
These! ah, these! how valued and toil'd for, these!
How envied by all the earth. . . .

Child

*O father, it is alive—it is full of people—it has
        children!*
O now it seems to me it is talking to its children!
I hear it—it talks to me—O it is wonderful!
*O it stretches—it spreads and runs so fast! O my
        father,*
It is so broad, it covers the whole sky!

Father

Cease, cease, my foolish babe,
*What you are saying is sorrowful to me—much it
        displeases me;*
*Behold with the rest, again I say—behold not
        banners and pennants aloft;*
*But the well-prepared pavements behold—and mark
        the solid wall'd houses. . . .*

Child

O my father, I like not the houses;
*They will never to me be anything—nor do I like
        money;*
*But to mount up there I would like, O father dear—
        that banner I like;*
That pennant I would be, and must be. . . .
—Walt Whitman, "Song of the Banner at Day-Break"

Animals and the Freedom to Be Loving

Watch a baby the first time he sees an animal—total delight, recognition, almost a look of *hey, I know you!* Children seem to sense their kinship with whatever is alert and alive. So they are very interested in what animals can do, how they live, how they treat each other. The child's first concern with animals is really a matter of self-discovery. Can a deer run so fast? Then to run is a possibility for me. Can a bird fly? Then to be so free is a possibility for me. Can a beaver build such a dam? Then such a dam and a pond, perhaps even better ones, can be built.

Freedom is assumed until sooner or later some contrary information intrudes. Conflict, tyranny, the struggle for mastery between man and beast, between beast and beast, come as a shock. It may be a frightening encounter with a big dog or the witnessing of a fight between two animals. Or the fierce mastery of a pet owner over his pet. An animal's fear of the child's touch. Or the child's sensing of a parent's fear. Such problems always come as news to the child. *Can and do they fight and hurt each other? Would they hurt me? Must we fight for power over each other? Are we not free to be together?*

Whatever confronts the child, he approaches with such existential interest. He classifies every experience into categories of *what is* and *what isn't,* and finds his freedom increased or diminished accordingly. And so he will come to wonder as mankind has always wondered: Which is true? Freedom and love? Or fang and claw?

And, behold, I, even I, do bring a flood of waters upon the earth, to destroy all flesh, wherein is the breath of life, from under heaven; and every thing that is in the earth shall die.
—Genesis 6:17

The story of Noah's Ark is often the child's first exposure to the Bible and the idea of God. It is usually presented as a fang-and-claw story. Because man and the animals were bad, God killed them. God seems to have been made in the image of man, just bigger and stronger.

But this story can be viewed another way. In the beginning we are told, God made man in his own image, to have dominion over the earth and over earth's creatures. A state of harmony is described—not dominancy, not man dominating animals through power, but a state where freedom and love have dominion. It is only when man (Adam) sets himself apart to be "like God" that the knowledge of good *and* evil and the need of *one* to dominate *the other* occurs. This is when the idea of fang-and-claw, of enmity between man and animals occurs. Even the flood is not punishment from God, but only the by product of the belief that to be free one must impinge on the freedom of others. The flood is a universal expression of this universal belief.

> *But Noah found grace in the eyes of God . . . and Noah walked with God . . . and Noah did according unto all that the Lord commanded him.*
> —Genesis 6:8, 9 and 7:5

Noah is described as a man of God, who sees life from God's viewpoint, goes about life God's way, and lives according to God's wisdom. He is protected from violence and flood through being at one with the fundamental order of being. Noah is inspired to build the needed boat, and the animals who board it two by two are able to live peaceably *as one* under his roof, which is his consciousness of love-intelligence above all.

As our children encounter animals, and people with animals, and people who behave like animals, love-intelligence can remain the central issue.

> *Child:* When you meet someone you can usually tell right away whether or not you're going to like them.
>
> *Parent:* Maybe it's better to say that sometimes you can see people the way God sees them right away, and sometimes you know you'll have to look harder.
>
> *Child:* Yeah. Right. I remember I couldn't stand Kate the first time I met her—and now she's one of my best friends. I guess sometimes you have to see people the way God does even when they don't see it themselves.

While our children will meet people and animals who reflect love and understanding, they will also see people (even their parents) and animals responding cruelly to each other out of fear and power madness. We cannot prevent our children from being so confronted, but we can help them to see love-intelligence where it is revealed, to see the need for love-intelligence where it is hidden, to express love-intelligence where it is welcomed, and to perceive that it is love-intelligence, not fang-and-claw, that ultimately has dominion over the earth. A child can understand that when people do not know how to be loving they are flooded with troubles. A child can be inspired by the power of love in the life of Noah—when all the animals that "normally" fight and eat each other were free to live together, safe from the flood.

> *And the Spirit of the Lord shall rest upon him, the spirit of wisdom and understanding, the spirit of counsel and might, the spirit of knowledge and the fear of the Lord. And shall make him quick of understanding in the fear of the Lord. He shall not judge by what his eyes see, or decide by what his ears hear, but with righteousness shall he judge the poor, and decide with equity for the meek of the earth; and he shall smite the earth with the rod of his mouth, and with the breath of his lips shall he slay the wicked. Righteousness shall be the girdle of his waist, and faithfulness the girdle of his loins.*
> *The wolf shall dwell with the lamb, and the leopard shall lie down with the kid; and the calf and the young lion and the fatling together; and a little child shall lead them. And the cow and the bear shall feed; their young shall lie down together; and the lion shall eat straw like the ox. The sucking child shall play on the hole of the asp, and the weaned child shall put his hand on the adder's den. They shall not hurt nor destroy on all my holy mountain; for the earth shall be full of the knowledge of the Lord, as the waters cover the sea.*
> —Isaiah 11:2–9

Humility

"We were overanxious and overbearing . . . we tried too hard . . . smothered her . . . corrected her constantly . . . expected much too much . . . didn't let her be a child . . ." Parents often feel guilty about hard times they have given their children—things said and unsaid, done and not done—all later recognized and regretted. Often it's the first child with overzealous but inexperienced parents. But sometimes it's the second child. ("The first was a breeze. We didn't know a thing. We didn't even really care. It was so easy.") Is it worse to care and to try too hard? Maybe—passingly. But the answer is not to remain ignorant or even to back off fearfully. Some problems come with progress. They can't all be avoided, prevented or circumvented. Some have to be passed through. Humility helps. It annihilates guilt. It hastens understanding.

When a child begins to learn to walk, she succeeds in fits and starts, sometimes falling flat out, sometimes momentarily teetering upright. If she knew more, she might think it impossible and unfair. Had she heard of the law of gravity, she would seriously doubt it. Were she told of the beneficiality of the laws of physics to her, she would be incredulous. And yet, we know physical laws to be both reliable and, at least for walking, necessary and beneficial. We hardly think of the laws that enable us to walk, but we are aware of and count on them just the same. Without them, walking would be impossible. When the first docking of ships in space was attempted, the astronauts had a difficult time. They had detailed, accurate instructions; they knew what was supposed to happen and how to go about it; but without gravity, they were disoriented. They had not encountered the laws as they apply in outer space —no realization of their oneness with them had taken place. So it was very difficult.

The laws of classical mechanics that make walking possible are extremely complicated to master intellectually. Yet, without having even heard of them, we walk. As the prewalking child shows us, with total ignorance of the laws no walking is possible. As the astronauts demonstrate, intellectual mastery isn't enough. In walking we are not as ignorant as the baby of the laws, nor as knowing as the astronaut. Though we don't understand the laws, may never even have heard of them, we do know them. How did we master them? We didn't. Before we even conceived of them, they mastered us. It is a different kind of knowing in which we trust the laws and allow them to guide us. Through our senses, in consciousness, from moment to moment, we give them mastery over us.

Partly through the suffering that accompanies ignorant violation of the laws, partly from seeing others, mainly through his innate desire for freedom, the child slowly awakens to the nature and reliability of the laws and comes into harmony with them. Contrary to appearance and to his initial experience, he now finds the laws that seemed at first no laws and that seemed to work against him are after all orderly and work for him. And he can walk.

And he made from one every nation of men to live on all the face of the earth, having determined allotted periods and the boundaries of their

*habitation, that they should seek God, in the hope that they might feel after
him and find him. Yet he is not far from each one of us, for*
　　"In him we live and move and have our being";
as even some of your poets have said,
　　"For we are indeed his offspring."
—Acts 17:26–28

If freedom is spiritual, the only obstacles to our freedom must
be cognitive. What makes it possible for the child with no understanding to learn to walk, when everything in his experience is
suggesting to him that there are no laws and that they are neither
consistent nor beneficial? "Except ye become as a little child. . . ."
Jesus' statement quoted earlier comes to mind again. He didn't
mean *cute,* or *little* or *helpless* or *ignorant* or *good;* he was talking
about the child's most outstanding ability, the ability to learn. As
we have seen, the child is tremendously receptive. He expects to
learn, doesn't think there is anything better to do, and he assumes
that life is indeed learnable. Without self-consciousness the child
is comfortably ignorant. He isn't scared of his ignorance. He isn't
ashamed of it. He just knows that he doesn't know.

As clear as it may be that the child's receptivity is an effect of
his lack of self-consciousness, as adults we cannot simply go back
to the time when we didn't know that we existed. But we can go
forward to where we consciously know that we don't exist—that is
as separate selves, apart from the law and on our own. From
observing our children we can learn to seek a state of attentiveness
in which self-consciousness is lost in our desire to see what is.
Recognizing like the child that we do not of our own selves know
anything, realizing like the astronaut that knowing is not enough,
we can learn to give our consciousnesses over to that which is
revealing itself and so "lose our lives to find them." The effective
quality most needed for this is humility. What we most need to give
up for this to take place is pride.

One aspect of the tremendous teachability of the child is his
lack of pridefulness. Though he may be tearful when he falls, he
is not embarrassed. His disappointment is that *this* experiment in
walking didn't work, not that he is personally a failure. His disappointment is more a reflection of enthusiasm than discourage-

ment. Nor does he assume from his momentary failure that the possibility of walking is unreal or doesn't apply to him. He is neither insulted nor despairing. He is not egotistical enough to take either success or failure personally. In short, effectively at least, he is humble. The urge to walk and the conviction that walking is a possibility remain stronger than self-concern. In the child they govern the self. Hence, after only a moment of tearfulness, he tries again.

Humble and motivated, children thus fall a lot but learn quickly to walk. This is a fact really worth considering. The child does not begin to fall until she becomes seriously interested in walking, until she actually begins learning. Falling is thus more an indication of learning than a sign of failure. Also worth noticing is that once the child has learned to walk in the house, she can walk more or less anywhere. The physical laws remain consistent, and her new-found harmony with them will work for her almost anywhere. What a wonderful freedom! The falls along the way are nothing compared to it. Thus the child's receptivity, especially the aspect called humility, is life-transforming, the secret to freedom. There are many important freedoms, but the most fundamental one of all is the freedom to learn.

For us it is more difficult, partly because we must learn higher laws, partly because we have grown so prideful. Mostly we are not even aware that learning is the issue. Whereas our preconceptions about parenthood may have been filled with images of ourselves and our children being loving together, we may find ourselves more subject than ever to momentary irritation and outbursts of anger. We did not know love was a freedom, but now we find out because we don't seem to be free to love. Depending on whether we interpret this as a flaw in life or in ourselves, we feel either angry or guilty. It scarcely crosses our minds that we simply lack sufficient understanding of what love is. Love? Of course we know —the question is why doesn't it (or don't I as a loving parent) work?

How much easier it is when we view increased disharmony in our lives as a double sign of what we need to learn and what, in fact, we are ready to learn—just as the child's first tumbles indicate his readiness to learn to walk. As parents, many of us are suddenly more highly motivated and urgent about love than we have ever been before, ready to sacrifice anything—perhaps even our illusions—for our children's sake. We want to be effectively loving. No wonder we run into such difficulty—we have never tried so hard before. If we can keep from getting sidetracked by self-conscious concerns—success or failure, guilt or anger, pleasure or pain—we may struggle and suffer a bit like the child just learning to walk, but then finally discover what is really worth knowing, i.e., what love is, that it is, and that we are in it and of it. Just as the child who learns to walk in his living room can thereafter walk anywhere, once we learn to be loving with our children it is easier to be loving and to find love everywhere.

Meanwhile, let's be humble about disharmony in our lives. Without humility we become bitter. Sometimes we become discouraged because we are not the patient parents we thought we would be or because things do not go as smoothly as anticipated. We may feel discouraged or fearful, angry or guilty; but such feelings are stepping stones to bitterness, stumbling blocks to learning.

Sometimes a child becomes afraid of falling or angry with his momentary failure to learn to walk. Then briefly he ceases to try and to learn, until his natural need to walk becomes more urgent than the fear or anger. And it will become urgent; he must learn to walk. Likewise since it is our nature to need to understand, and since bitterness is effectively the refusal to seek further understanding, it is clear that bitterness is at least a painful and unnecessary indulgence in self-concern. Furthermore, if all the discord we suffer is only ignorance and if bitterness is the refusal to learn, it becomes excruciatingly clear that this is a cognitive mistake we cannot afford. Humility is easier and wiser.

The experience of parenthood and of human existence altogether is for the sake of our awakening. So we need not become discouraged if our experiences indicate that we have not yet understood. Of course we haven't. Nor do these experiences signify that there is no truth to the idea that reality is ultimately harmonious and fulfilling. We do not seek understanding for the sake of solving life's problems; rather we live that we may learn to understand. The fact that problems fall away as we understand is certainly a benefit, but it is not the ultimate point. The child does not learn to walk so that he may stop falling, but rather that he may be increasingly free.

Problems themselves do not reflect the nature of reality. They only reveal our specific ignorances of reality. As we do now and then reach clearer understanding, we will not find our problems solved, but rather *dissolved*. In the light of truth they never were the substantial problems we thought they were any more than the toddler ever really had a problem with the floor leaping up and hitting him in the face.

> *Problems are lessons designed for our edification. . . . The understanding*
> *of what really is abolishes all that seems to be.*
> —Thomas Hora, *Dialogues in Metapsychiatry*

In seeming contrast to Jesus' recommendation—"And ye shall know the truth and the truth shall make you free," it is written in Zen literature, "Search not for the truth; only cease to cherish opinions." But these statements do not really contradict each other. Both suggest that the most basic freedom of all is the freedom to learn, to understand. Jesus' statement calls us specifically to that aspect of receptivity which may be called gratitude (appreciation of the truth as valuable) or prayer. The Zen calls us to humility or fasting. If we value the truth and set our hearts on it as Jesus says, and if we are willing to give up our personal minds as the Zen says, then the truth which is the one mind becomes ours, is what we are. Then, already, we are free.

> *Be a lamp to your self,*
> *be like an island.*
> *Struggle hard, be wise.*
> *Cleansed of weakness, you will find freedom*
> *from birth and old age.*
> —Buddha, in *The Dhammapada,* trans. by P. Lal

> *In clearness comes freedom from all pains; in those whose minds are free of*
> *all pains, understanding is utterly steadfast.*
> —*The Bhagavad-Gita*

Practical Information for New Parents

This "Practical Information" section includes child-proofing the home, walks travel, travel equipment, trip tips, gym equipment, animals and pets—all loosely related to the issue of freedom. Parents of older children may also find the remarks about pets (page 190) of interest. Otherwise they may wish to turn directly to page 193, where the next chapter begins.

Child-Proofing the Home

To some extent, safety can be dealt with in a preventative way. It is certainly intelligent to take some precautions; but there's no need to go to fearful extremes. Freedom is a pretty good idea to be guided by when considering what safety measures to take. The more hazards that can be removed, the more freedom (from injury and scolding) can be enjoyed.

Baby-proofing is a breeze: you just don't put the baby down where she might fall or where anyone might step or anything fall on her. But toddler-proofing is another matter. You have to protect both the toddler and the house while maintaining the freedom of both—the right of the home to be lovely and pleasant for everyone and the right of the child to learn and grow.

Most safety measures are obvious, and numerous books go into them in greater detail than is appropriate here, but for starters: Put things that might get broken or hurt the child out of reach. Close off places where she might fall. Plug or cover up places where she might get shocked or burned. Indoors you will find *safety latches* for cupboards and drawers an indispensable way to keep small children from getting at dangerous or breakable things. But try to have one or two low cupboards and drawers that are all right for the child to explore. The pulling-out-and-dumping-all-over-the-place stage doesn't last long, and evidently something is learned from it. *Socket caps* are a must for closing off open electric sockets which small children cannot otherwise resist poking things into or trying to open with metal keys.

Good child-proofing frees the child to learn, the parent from worrying and nagging, and the home from destruction and disarray. But there's no need to go overboard and revise the entire home to suit the unsteady and not-very-wise toddler, no need to change your whole life for what is only a momentary stage. And while it is sensible to make some adjustments and take a few precautions, there's no substitute for the vigilance of a watchful adult. It may seem endless, but it really won't last long. At nine months she may bruise her head on the coffee table when trying to stand up, but at one and a half she can already open the door and dash out!

Practicing Freedom

After hours of struggling, a restless, wakeful baby falls instantly asleep when put in the carriage and wheeled out the door. The motion? The hum of outdoor sounds and the carriage rolling? The lulling effect of passing sights and the carriage rocking? No explanation seems adequate. But what is the difference between the parent who is trying to put the child to bed and the one who is taking a walk? The first says, "He won't even let me leave the room!" But who's not letting whom? The parent who is putting the child to bed is paying attention to and experiencing the child. The parent who is going on a walk is looking where she is going and experiencing the view. If the child falls asleep or lies contentedly in the carriage, is the child letting the parent take a walk or is it that in taking a walk the parent lets go of the child? Over and over new parents report: *So I finally gave up and decided to take him for a walk. You know what happened? I put on my coat and went to get the carriage out, and when I went back there he was, fast asleep!*

Long before the child experiences any conscious need for freedom from the parent, the new parent is certain to experience a need for freedom from the child and from the overwhelming (real or imagined) demands of parenthood. We get completely taken in by the child's early physical dependency on us and may experience bondage, to the child, both physical and mental, stronger than we have ever encountered before. So the experience of parenthood suddenly renders the longstanding existential yearning for freedom acute. Life is no good alone; but it is no good only together either. We cannot *get* along together unless we *go* along together. Take a walk. Quit running in circles. Shove off. Get the show on the road. Let the road take charge.

> *Trust in the Lord with all thine heart and lean not unto thine own understanding; in all thy ways acknowledge him, and he will direct thy paths.*
> —Proverbs 3:5–6
>
> *A man's mind plans his way, but the Lord directs his steps.*
> —Proverbs 16:9

Without a rightful perception of freedom on the part of the parent, the child's growing need for freedom (even so small a thing as the freedom to sleep) is frustrated.

> The first time we took our baby out for a walk, I thought she would be annihilated—by the sound of a jackhammer, the fumes from passing cars. Greasy dirt fell from the air onto her beautiful, clean cheek. I tried to wipe it away, but it turned into a black smear. I wanted to send her back somewhere where she would be safe. I pushed the carriage across the street. Faces streamed by—mothers, storekeepers, drivers, teenagers, policemen, thousands and thousands of city dwellers who had actually survived babyhood.

Different parents have different illusions, but walks are good for most of them.

Baby Carriers

A baby carrier is a wonderful way for a parent and baby to be together without revolving around each other. Sometimes a baby and a parent seem to be holding each other captive. The child cries the minute he is put down, and yet the parent suspects that his very efforts to put him down are precisely what are keeping him up. A carrier of some sort can help to break this vicious circle, releasing parents to carry on with their work while allowing the baby to be close but unfussed with. Usually what happens is that the baby falls asleep as soon as he is put in the carrier.

Back or front infant carrier. In Japan and Taiwan, this type of carrier is used everywhere all the time. It is worn on the back with the straps crossed in front and sometimes twisted into a rope that crosses between the mother's breasts. The straps are then divided again and tied behind the back. Used constantly until the child is two or three years old, it thus replaces the carriage and the frame-type back carrier, the stroller, and usually even the babysitter. It folds to a purse-size nothing and is considered almost as indispensable as diapers.

In the United States we insist on wearing such carriers in the front. Though this is less comfortable physically for the parent, it makes it possible to see how the baby is doing. But however you wear the infant carrier, it can be a handy problem-solver if you happen to live in a walk-up apartment, or if you're trying to house-clean when the baby is fretful, or for shopping in stores. And it is very useful for hiking and cycling families until the baby is old enough to set in a frame-type back carrier. Several versions are commercially available in the U.S.

Back carrier with frame. For carrying on without a lot of carrying on, in the woods, at the zoo, on a bicycle, on an escalator, in a store, at the beach, to the laundromat, in a museum, on the stairs of a walk-up apartment, and in the home, or backyard, there is nothing like a back carrier with a light metal frame. The big advantage, and the best proof of its worth, is that babies and toddlers are so happy up there. You can tell two ways. In the first place, they smile and laugh all the time they are awake, and second, they fall asleep there without a peep—suddenly, anywhere, anytime, whenever they are sleepy.

For some families the carrier indoors simply brings order back into their lives. When the baby is too tired to be happy on the floor but not ready to sleep, you *can* quickly get the dinner dishes (or the ironing, or vacuuming, or leaf raking or lawn mowing) out of the way with him on your back. When you are finished he will probably already be asleep, and you can snuggle him into bed without an hour of ritualistic nursing or bottle feeding. It's such a nice way for both of you to go about your individual business together, without interfering with each other. When the guests are hungry and dinner is ready (at your house or at someone else's), you can wear him to the table. He will enjoy it and be enjoyed, and again probably conk out in no time flat.

Like any backpacking, this *does* take getting used to. But if you have to use a carrier, you do get used to it. And once you discover the possibilities, the freedoms, you will find it difficult to imagine toddlering without one. A five-month-old is about ready for backpacking; you can start a month earlier if you sandwich the baby in with a pillow for a little extra support. The carrier may be used as long as you can stand it—most people find one and a half years or about 25 pounds the limit.

One mother's favorite early parenthood memory is two under one umbrella, three hands on the shaft. She can't say which version is better—being one of the two under the one umbrella, or looking from under a separate umbrella at father and son—saturated, rainy day colors, sunny day laughter. The three of them so private and safe somehow, traveling dry and warm and cozy along the wet city sidewalks, the rain pat-patting. You can hear snow falling on an umbrella, too.

Walks

For children and parents, walking can be a wonderful exercise in freedom—a way of setting each other free, and finding freedom together. But, especially if you have always liked walking yourself, it may take some new understanding before walking with your lagging ("Carry me") toddler seems anything like freedom. For many parents and very young children walks are pure hassle because the children keep stopping, hunkering down to look up— while the parents are dying to keep moving. Some parents drag their children; others manipulate, baiting them with promises of what they might see around the next corner or what they will eat when they get home. Thus freedom to go walking together can feel a lot like a restriction.

Around two and a half or three years old the child, too, will probably suddenly get the idea that a walk is a way of going somewhere. Quite spontaneously, he will begin taking your hand and walking down the street with you, viewing things as he passes them instead of stopping to study each cellar door, each fuel intake, and every different balustrade. But first he simply must examine these things.

In the meantime, before you set forth, decide which kind of a walk it's going to be. If it's a walk-walk for *him*, prepare to stand around a lot. His walk may be very short in distance and fairly long in time. It may take an hour and a half to go around the block at his pace. So if you want it to be short in time, don't plan to go far. On the other hand, if you are really trying to go somewhere, plan to take a stroller or carrier and be quite clear and firm about it. It's good to take both kinds of walks, and learning to appreciate both kinds is freeing.

Trip Tips

1. *Leave shortly before a nap time* or even when the nap is slightly overdue.

2. Will it be a long trip? Then *see if there is some place to stop off that will be of interest to the children.* With a toddler a picnic at a playground may be better than a greasy lunch and a wrestling match in a roadside restaurant. Twenty minutes in sandbox and on swings with a little snack will refresh and settle much better than his first milkshake and French fries in a restaurant where he doesn't know how to behave.

3. Plan to *take some things along* to entertain the child and expedite maintenance.

• A roll of paper towels (should be standard equipment in a car).

• A sopping-wet washcloth in a plastic bag and a clean hand towel. Or some prepackaged wash-ups. Or both.

• A few Colorforms (flexible, reusable vinyl shapes that adhere to smooth surfaces) to work with on the window.

• Any toy that is currently especially interesting to your child.

• A magic drawing board—those gray ones with acetate sheets on top. You draw with a wooden stick, and then erase the drawing by lifting the acetate.

• A story anthology which you can read or tell stories from.

• A book of ideas for activities to do with children on trips.

- Diapers. (Yeah, well, sometimes they get forgotten.)
- Disposable (or not) spoons, cups, and plates. If you have these in the car, you can shop for lunch in any supermarket instead of taking a picnic or going through the treasure hunt for a suitable restaurant.
- Snack food. Individual boxes of raisins are excellent.
- Bib. Even for the older toddler a bib is handy for car-seat meals.
- Pop-a-matic Bingo. Instead of cards and loose markers that slide off and get lost in the car, this set has reversible plastic "cards" with buttons to press down when each number is called. Not for babies, of course, but great on car trips with older toddlers and children.

Set Free

From gymsets to pets, from climbing themselves like monkeys, to capturing and releasing wild animals, our children seek to find and understand freedom. The question of when to provide what equipment or experience is best settled the usual way—by watching the child.

At first a few things to learn to see and reach for will satisfy any gymnastic needs not met by the baby's incessant kicking, waving, and playing with her parents. Next comes the desire to get up and get going, perhaps in a jumper or walker, and very soon on her own. Then there's running and jumping and swinging and climbing and the sky is the limit.

Jumper. A supportive seat/harness that hangs from a thick piece of rubber and in which the pre-walking child can jump up and down. Some find this too much trouble. But those who like it love it. We used it a lot with our first child; less with the second. Before our first son was born we were against this on the general principle that it was a contraption and he could learn to walk without it. We also feared that any such device might become a crutch and thereby a deterrent. Nevertheless, at about four months —when his desire to be vertical became a passion—we tried it, and we had to be grateful for all the squeal-happy hours it gave him. He could see better and turn around on his own. And he jumped and jumped and jumped for joy for about three months, until stricken with the desire to go forward as well as up and down.

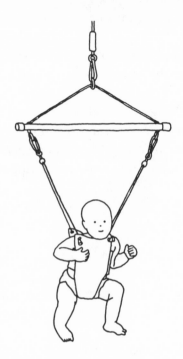

The first few tries last only a minute or so (less time than it takes to saddle up). The child just hangs there fascinated, drooling on his toes, until he begins to discover the possibilities of turning and jumping. Once he really gets going, the jumper is good for about two or three months, two or three times a day. It will last longer each time if he has something to do with his hands—a toy tied to the jumper perhaps, but never from so long a string that he can choke himself.

A jumper is not a place to put a child away. Be with him as much while he's jumping as if you were holding his hands to help him stand. Hang it in the kitchen doorway while you fix supper. Play music; sing. And he'll think it's wonderfully funny if once in a while you will jump with him.

Walker. This is no necessity either, but again, those who like them swear by them. There is no full-time substitute for walking around holding onto our hands, but like the jumper, this contraption brings pleasure and added freedom to the prewalking/sitting child and her parent. Walkers offer the child the experience of mobility and thus an early appreciation of the possibility and value of walking by herself. Round ones are best because they are less likely to get hooked or stuck. Make sure you get one that is very hard to tip over. Don't substitute a walker for all finger-holding practice, and never keep the child in a walker against her will or you will teach her to associate walking with confinement and isolation from you instead of with freedom and independence. Dependency on either walker or parent will not occur if we have a full appreciation of mobility as a freedom for the child rather than a hazard for her or an inconvenience to us.

Indoor swing. One whole category of equipment often overlooked for preschoolers is indoor gym equipment. Especially for city children who must often wait so long so often before being taken outside and who are too young to go to the park alone, a good piece of gym equipment may replace yearsful of toys and, to some extent, make up for the lack of a backyard.

Doorway swings are ideal. Unlike park swings, which must be used by children of all ages, and heights, the indoor swing can be hung low enough for even a one-and-a-half-year-old to experiment with alone. He will do lots of things on a low swing that he can't attempt on a standard swing. The most popular position for preschoolers is the flying position—hanging by his tummy, watching how the floor goes by. Dangling like that sure beats hanging around waiting to be taken to the park and pushed. The more space around your indoor swing the better. But if there's no rafter handy a doorway is fine. If the door frame is wooden the swing can hang from heavy eye-hooks. If the frame is metal a doorway gym bar will do. You can make your own swing with a board and rope or buy a rubber belt swing seat, trapeze bar, or combination. (See pages 145–147.)

Mattresses. Old ones that are free are cheaper than real tumbling mats and just as much fun—even more fun if they happen to be springy. Cover with a rug or fitted sheet.

Indoor climbing gyms. The small indoor toddler gym/slide combinations available from most preschool suppliers are outgrown too quickly to be of much value. More useful and for longer is a real climbing gym of some sort. Again, this is especially worthwhile for children with limited access to the outdoors. Many wonderful gym/playhouse/slide combinations are available. A horizontal or folding ladder climber takes up less space and can also be used with a slide or as a playhouse scaffolding. Space, budget, and personal preferences are the determining factors.

Impromptu and homemade equipment. Boxes, crates, and cartons can do the trick, too. Especially if you live in an apartment, you need and can find good stuff for temporary energetic fun indoors. If you are handy with a hammer and saw, you can build things. There are books for building and improvising play equipment. Besides, you probably have some good ideas of your own. For example, we built a sliding board that hooked over one stair of the bunkbed. It was put to an astonishing variety of uses. Children have ideas, too! There are so many ways—as many ways as days, as many different possibilities as snowflakes. But there is only one time to do them—now. And again now. And now again.

Outdoor swing sets. You can drive through miles and miles of suburbia and see hundreds and hundreds of used-to-be-bright metal gym set combinations in well-kept backyards and *nary a child* on one of them. If you look into the bushes and behind garages or in culverts and empty lots and up in trees with a very sharp eye, you will begin to spot the children. Except for the lovely big wooden jungle gyms and the expensive galvanized ones on playgrounds, most backyard gym sets are ugly to begin with and become eyesores as the chains break and the metal rusts. The swings are too short to be fun for long. And somehow these bare pipe structures in full view of the kitchen window just don't measure up to a kid's idea of freedom.

Swing. Anyway, since flying is the thing, how much nicer to hang the swing from a tree. The better the view the better the swing. The longer the rope the farther she swings. If you have the right tree and maybe a piece of board and some tire rubber to protect the tree limb, you don't need to buy anything but rope. If there isn't a good swing branch available, you can find other types of swing mounts (even one that attaches to a tree trunk) in some play equipment catalogs. Even if you haven't got a backyard you can still have a tree swing, any time you take a picnic somewhere. Just stick a good long length of clothesline in the picnic basket. Sling it over a tree branch and tie it (with the knot just above your head) close enough to the ground so that the child can step into the loop. Any two-year-old can learn to stand in this loop on one foot. Tell him to reach as high as he can before stepping up. If there's enough extra rope dangling from the knot you can pull the end of the line to give a nice ride. Remind your child not to step off unless the swing is still. And take it easy—let *him* tell *you* when he wants to go higher.

> *How do you like to go up in a swing*
> *Up in the air so blue?*
> *Oh, I do think it the pleasantest thing*
> *Ever a child can do!*
> *Up in the air and over the wall*
> *Till I can see so wide,*
> *Rivers and trees and cattle and all*
> *Over the countryside—*
> *Till I look down on the garden green,*
> *Down on the roof so brown—*
> *Up in the air I go flying again,*
> *Up in the air and down!*
> —Robert Louis Stevenson, "The Swing"

Climbing gym. Outdoors such a thing is probably more a luxury than a necessity—especially if you have a tree swing. But if you are going to have such a thing, a real climbing apparatus is much better than the usual combination metal swing/slide/seesaw set. Get nothing or get a real jungle gym of some sort. The big wooden ones are nice, and some include ladders, rope nets, movable platforms, and assorted swinging devices. Available from various play equipment suppliers (see catalog list in Chapter 3).

Animals and Pets

Oh, a hunting we will go
And a hunting we will go
We'll catch a fox
And put him in a box
And then we'll let him go.
—Folk song

Beastly books. Although many wonderful books about animals and their habits are too difficult for preschoolers, it is surprising how attentive young children are when the toad is in the hand or the wog is in the jar. There are too many excellent animal books to presume to make a best selection, but do support each creaturely interest with a trip to the library or bookstore. Especially helpful when keeping creatures are three books by Caroline O'Hagan: *It's Easy to Have a Worm* (*a Snail, a Caterpillar*) *Visit You* (Lothrop).

Pets. Children of all ages can benefit from opportunities to have and care for some creatures. Preschoolers are too young to care for a pet alone. Neither is it feasible for any household to maintain permanently all the wild catchables and patables that capture the child's interest. Nor, alas, can many creatures long endure the tender, loving ignorance inflicted upon them. But, whether or not we have permanent family pets, brief visitations—of school pets on vacation, pets of vacationing neighbors, and wild foundlings—can be a happy way to satisfy a child's interest and develop a love-intelligent reverence for life and freedom.

Whether the child watches actual creatures or reads about them in books, the study of animals and their habits and habitats provides startling revelations of the fact of intelligence at large. It is wonderful to observe and share with our children how meticulously it is given to each animal to know what marvelously to do. Don't belittle this intelligence by calling it instinct (we do not need to condescend); don't attribute it to the hidden genius of the creatures themselves (a fantasy that obscures its relevance to the child's own existence). The point is this: *love-intelligence is always available, providing the needed idea and the needed skill in the needed moment.* Share in the marvel of it and let its significance live in the

Captivating Captives

Creature	*In what?*	*How long?*
Caterpillar	in a jar with holes in the top, and inside a twig and fresh greenery of the proper sort (some caterpillars are very particular) sprinkled with water each day until the cocoon is built. Then keep some wet sand in the bottom of the jar for moisture.	until there is a butterfly or moth—if possible release before it is ready to fly
frog or fish or insect or any waterborn insects' eggs	gather with a jarful of the water in which you find them. From time to time scoop out a cupful of water and put in a cupful of new water from wherever you found them.	until they hatch—then release or else do a lot of research on what is needed by a growing, captive whatever-you-have.
fishlings	catch in a bath towel and keep in a jarful of their own lake, brook, or sea water. Baby fish are wonderfully transparent; significantly, they are little more than eyes with locomotive ability.	an hour of daylight.
fireflies	in a jar with a little greenery to perch on inside, and holes in the top.	an hour of darkness.
ants (about 2 dozen from the same colony) the bigger the better	in a thin plastic box (with tiny holes made with a pin heated red hot on the stove) or a jar with an upside down jar inside (to make a narrow space so you can see tunnels). Fill with sand. Cover side with dark paper when you aren't looking so the ants won't be sneaky. Put in a drop or two of honey or syrup once or twice a week. If ants get through the holes (the advantage of having big ones), stand your ant house in a little bit of water; then they will go back through the holes.	if you don't catch a queen, release in about a week and a half.
any insect or animal you run into	in a jar with holes in the top or in a creature cage.	just for a close look—see, she can fly! She needs more space to move around in.
a baby bird that has fallen out of its nest	nothing; just lift it gently off the ground and place it in a nearby tree just out of cat range.	only as long as it takes to put it in a tree. Now be very still and watch its parents come to it.

191

child as a sense of security and confidence and sufficiency.

In watching a captive creature, the true object of attention is not the animal itself, but the intelligence reflected in it. Intelligence governs each life. Intelligence has dominion. Guided by the same governing intelligence we can try to see what each creature needs while in our care: a suitable environment, food, and, ultimately, to be set free, released to the care of the governing intelligence at large. A key emphasis needs to be on letting be. Letting be free. Letting be so. Beautifully, the young child (still unpossessive of property or power) is spontaneously almost more overjoyed with setting free than with capturing. To let it come—to let it go —to let it be. Each temporary visitor presents an opportunity to explore the freedom that comes with subservience to divine love-intelligence. Catch a flying star. Put it in a jar. Watch it glow. Let it go!

> *A little light is going by,*
> *Is going up to see the sky,*
> *A little light with wings.*
>
> *I never could have thought of it,*
> *To have a little bug all lit*
> *And made to go on wings.*
> —Elizabeth Madox Roberts, "Firefly"

A well-balanced *fish tank* is something even a baby can appreciate. Vinyl ones are available for hanging over cribs, but they seem cruel and the fish do not survive in them for long. A 5- or 10-gallon tank outfitted with a light, air bubbler, and a filter system seems a good investment. It is especially nice if you can have a lighted tank in the child's bedroom where she can watch the fish in the dark at bedtime, free of other distractions. Watch how they swim perpetually, randomly, not in squares or in circles or straight back and forth within the confines of the tank, but as if freely, and never bumping into one another.

> *In him we live and move and have our being.*
> —Acts 17:28

5
Unity

One in all,
All in One—
If only this is realized,
No more worry about your not being perfect.
—*Buddhist Scriptures,* selected and translated by
Edward Conze

Hear, O Israel: The Lord our God is one Lord.
—Deuteronomy 6:4

For many people the least obvious aspects of reality are its underlying unity and reliability. We experience life as chaotic, unreliable, fragmentary, precarious, chancy, even meaningless. What order we do perceive seems worrisome, for we are sure it will bring us a mixture of bad and good. Yet as living beings, as seeing beings, it is unity we yearn for and, in an endless variety of mistaken ways, it is unity we seek.

We wish to find unity in life and become one with it. Not finding it, Me, Inc. tries to take life in all its apparent pieces and make it one. Believing ourselves to be separate—un- or dis-united from goodness—we take the seeming elements of reality—self, other, and circumstance—and try personally to arrange them so as to bring about unity ("get it together") and have only good experiences. We try to cause unity, assuming that it isn't there in the first place. In families, whether trying to organize our lives and households or to bring about desired family togetherness, our efforts are analogous to and about as successful as the very young child's first attempts to assemble a puzzle.

There are two elements in our picture of family unity. On the loving side we look for family unity as mutual support, comfort, enjoyment, friendliness, warmth, and coziness. On the intelligent side we look for reasonableness, cooperation, agreement, thoughtful consideration, and dialogue. Yet we experience bewildering difficulty when we try to bring about these two seemingly basic elements of love and intelligence in the form of family unity. There are more pieces to the puzzle than we can count—and they keep multiplying and compounding and changing and moving around unpredictably. As most of us can admit, the harder we try to bring about unity, the more disunity—disharmony, dissent, disagreeableness, disaffection, dissatisfaction, and distance—takes place among us.

Are we to conclude that unity is not possible in families? and that it is impossible to lead lives that are both loving and intelligent? that we cannot live unique lives as individuals and still be one with each other? Frustration and disillusionment drive us toward such conclusions. But inwardly we find them unacceptable. And even if we part company (storm out of the house, run away from home, separate, get divorced) we cannot get away from our desire for unity. We have sensed, conceived, and do not finally doubt that unity is possible. At least we recognize that it is necessary.

If we live in families, we need not abandon the idea of a lovingly warm, cozy, supportive family. Neither must we give up hope of being wisely cooperative and reasonable with one another. But before either of these expressions of unity can find shape, we have to abandon the fundamentally disunifying conception that each of us is a separate self enclosed in a separate body: Me, Inc. The "family picture" conforms to whatever underlying concept we entertain. So, for a unified, love-intelligent family picture we have to abandon our sense of separate selfhood and become one with the underlying love-intelligent force of being. This essential force alone unifies all of its expressions—self, other, and their proper relation to each other from moment to moment. This force alone can bring about the order and harmony we finally recognize as love.

Love and intelligence. These are no more separate from each other than we are from God. The outside of a glass gets its smooth curved beauty by conforming to the essential raison d'être (reason for *being*) of the inside as a vessel. The outside is defined by the inside. So, after all, is love the effect of the fundamentally intelligent order of being. Intelligence is the basic universal force which has as effects freedom, spontaneity, grace, harmony, beauty, peace, each of which includes the others, all of which can be summed up with the word *love*.

Intelligence is the one and only universal force; love its universal effect. *Universal* and *unique* have the same root: ONE. Like the wave on the ocean, the *unique* individual is a place where universal love-intelligence takes specific perceivable shape, comes to a peak (where we can take a peek at it). And that's all there is to it, and it's all we need to know, and it's the only thing we can know that can ever bring about anything and everything we need.

Without this awareness and the full identification of ourselves with it, life is a complete muddle. Proceeding in accordance with the sensation of separate selfhood, we try to impose love and intelligence on each other and succeed only in bringing disunity into expression as friction, conflict, discomfort, and all that pains and saddens us. *On our own* we cannot do otherwise; our efforts to bring unity to our children cannot help being perverted with the selfish, exploitative counterfeits of love as hedonism and intelligence as ambition. Conversely, however, conscious spiritual awareness of our individual oneness with fundamental love-intelligence is the only way that force can have its unifying effect; both as individual love that is truly intelligent and as individual intelligence that is truly loving.

> *In the beginning was the Word, and the Word was with God, and the Word was God . . . and the Word became flesh and dwelt among us.*
> —John 1:1, 14

The word is primary. It is an idea. The way to be one with an idea is to be conscious of it. So the Word is the number one idea and must be our number one interest.

> *Jesus said: "I and my father are one."*
> —John 10:30.

Through Jesus' conscious oneness with the primary and universal reality of love-intelligence, this primary reality gained full unique expression both as and through him. Likewise, as parents, if we wish to be unifying factors in our families, our primary task and ongoing first priority must be to maintain a constant, nonpersonal awareness of love-intelligence. Then in an infinite variety of unique ways everything will be uni-formed by love-intelligence itself.

Falling into Place

> As the truly parently parent is the childlike parent,
> as the truly nourishing parent is the nursing parent,
> as the truly teaching parent is the learning parent,
> as the truly freeing parent is the obedient parent,
> so is the truly unifying parent the unified parent.
>
> All things are done by love-intelligence, and apart from love-intelligence is not anything done that is really done.

One love-intelligent moment leads to another.

Some realization of or at least devotion to these ideas already helps us in many ways. In the first place, as seeing beings we behold the activity of our children in such a way that we can see the one love-intelligent mind at work, both as the child and in the child's life. Second, we become enabled to respond to our children in ways that enhance their discovery of the fact and value of unity and their oneness with it. So the one mind guides and governs—the parent through the child, and the child through the parent, both of us unique seeing beings in a unified and self-revealing universe of love-intelligence.

As long as the child is not self-conscious he continues to be himself a place where the one mind is expressed in the growing awareness of unity. For example, in their simple puzzle-solving our youngest children demonstrate how the discovery of unity is possible in the midst of seeming chaos.

If you present a child of less than a year with a knobbed wooden puzzle, he will probably lift out the pieces, his attention first attracted by the protruding knobs. The simple fact that what initially appears to be a whole can become parts is a revelation to him. He is not at all concerned with trying to put the puzzle together again, perhaps instead trying to stack or stand the pieces while totally ignoring the puzzle tray. When he does awaken to the possibility of putting the piece back into the puzzle, he will try to push them in anywhere. He is oblivious of the fact that each piece has its own hole or that there is any relationship between the outer edge of a particular piece and the inner edge of its particular hole. Only gradually does he discover the secret that he needs only to align the pieces with the holes for the fitting together, the unifying, to occur by itself.

With parenthood as with the child's puzzle—indeed with every aspect of our lives—there is the same discovery to be made: if you align the parts with the holes the parts become whole and the whole becomes evident. What the child is discovering on a material plane with his puzzle we must discover on a spiritual plane. Unity is a fundamental spiritual fact of life which can come into our experience not by pushing or manipulating everything or everyone into position, but by aligning our thoughts and ourselves with what truly is.

For adults, puzzles are often only a sort of intellectual activity, a fantasy confirmation of the sense of personal mental power —in this case, as a unifier. But the child's unconscious motivation is considerably different. Not yet having learned to believe in disunity, he proceeds according to an unconscious assumption that unity is. He is receptively delighted with all demonstrations of unity, and they all have existential import for him. He not only rejoices to see the many puzzle pieces transformed into one whole, but also rightfully experiences his part in fitting them together as an encounter with the unity of himself with life. A Playskool advertisement nicely pointed up this key issue in puzzles: "Puzzles reinforce a conviction necessary to learning: that things make sense." The child's joy in his puzzles goes even further: he enjoys being part of (united with) the underlying sense of things.

The Parent as a Unifying Factor

1. The Parent as a Rock.

Everyone then who hears these words of mine and does them will be like a wise man who built his house upon the rock; and the rain fell, and the floods came, and the winds blew and beat upon that house, but it did not fall, because it had been founded on the rock.
—Matthew 7:24–25

The unifying parent is the unified parent. The more we are one with the father, the less likely we are to be at odds with each other or to set each other at odds with God. Being at one with the father means being at one with love-intelligence. We bring every thought, word, action, the quality of our being, and our way of looking at everything into full and perfect alignment with what is love-intelligent. In this way we allow love-intelligence to take charge of us and we leave it in charge of everyone else. What is *both* loving *and* intelligent is true. Everything else is not bad, but false. Seeing everything in terms of what is and isn't rather than what should or shouldn't be or what we want or don't want makes us evener, surer, firmer, more reassuring and understanding. Our whole being demonstrates to the child that life can be counted on.

> . . . look to the rock from which you were hewn, and to the quarry from which you were digged.
> —Isaiah 51:1

> So we being many are one body in Christ.
> —Romans 12:15

> Let this mind be in you which was also in Christ Jesus.
> —Philippians 2:5

> Jesus answered, "The first [commandment] is, 'Hear O Israel, the Lord our God, the Lord is One; and you shall love the Lord your God with all your heart and with all your soul, and with all your strength. This is the first and great commandment."
> —Matthew 22:37–38

2. The One-Seeing Parent as Beholder.

> And the second is like unto it; thou shalt love thy neighbor as thyself.
> —Matthew 22:39

The more we are able to see each other as one with God, the more we are able to respond to each other love-intelligently. So it is that we behold each child as a point where the universal comes to a unique peak. We trust she is and respect her as an expression of love-intelligence, a fully endowed consciousness becoming conscious. Whatever appears bad is regarded as false and treated as having nothing to do with the essential child. Whatever is good is regarded as true and appreciated as an expression of God. Free, thereby, of parent-introduced self-centeredness, the child proceeds undistracted, a seeing being in the process of seeing what is.

> One is one and all alone
> and evermore shall be it so.
> —from "Green Grow the Rushes," traditional folk song

3. The One-Knowing Parent as One Waymaker. Recognizing life as a journey toward conscious oneness with God, we constantly release and entrust the child to love-intelligence at large, thereby expressing our confidence that through both lesson and revelation life will bear him up and bring about the full reunion.

> *Wist ye not that I must be about my Father's business?*
> —Luke 2:49

> *How like an angel came I down!*
>   *How bright are all things here!*
> *When first among his works I did appear*
>   *Oh, how their glory did me crown!*
> *The world resembled his eternity,*
>   *In which my soul did walk;*
> *And everything that I did see*
>   *Did with me talk. . . .*
>
> *A native health and innocence*
>   *Within my bones did grow,*
> *And while my God did all his glories show,*
>   *I felt a vigour in my sense*
> *That all was spirit: I within did flow*
>   *With seas of life like wine;*
> *I nothing in the world did know,*
>   *But 'twas divine. . . .*
> —Thomas Traherne, "Poems of Felicity"

4. The One-Centered Parent as Custodian of the God-Centered Environment. Long before the child can conceive of unity she can encounter and appreciate its value. Every aspect of the home, every task and activity, can be approached with the idea of making the fact of one love-intelligent force appreciable, discernible, and expressible by each unique individual. Order, simplicity, efficiency, respect, peace, and privacy emerge as outstanding qualities of the God-centered home. Whenever we sincerely ask what best expresses love-intelligence? what is love-intelligent? in the light of love-intelligence what's next? we will be guided by love-intelligence.

And ye shall hear a voice behind you saying, "This is the way; walk ye in it."
—Isaiah 30:21

5. The One-Pointing Parent as Teacher and Guide. The parent is a finger God points at God. We do not point to ourselves; we do not point at the child; we do not shake our finger in the child's face. Because he is of one mind with love-intelligence the child is taught most important things by the one mind itself, both through inspiration and by our example. But when we must teach or guide or explain or lay down rules, we are always focused on the one underlying and overriding love-intelligence and the child's ability to become aware of it. It is as if we sit beside one another in the sun with a book. We may point to the words as our children read, but it is the sun that really does most of the work. And it is seeing the light that is the real nature of the task.

Thus enlightened it becomes possible for us to discern and firmly insist on certain love-intelligent standards of conduct and maintenance within the home. Without becoming personal or overly interfering, we can set and insist that our children abide by such standards, knowing that they are necessary and true. By the same token we are able to discern when our children need to and can better discover the true value of love-intelligence through experiencing the false as consequence. There is a time to pick up the child's room for her; there is a time to require that she do so; there is a time to do it together; there is a time to tell her how; there is a time to close the door and let her live with it until she tires of the mess.

Let your light so shine that men may see your good works and glorify your Father which is in heaven.
—Matthew 5:16

6. The Parent as One Giving Hand. The parent is one hand of God. Through this hand God gives the child many good gifts that are one gift. Through the inspired, love-intelligent parent God gives himself. The parent who is aware of unity as a primary issue in life is able to select toys, lessons, equipment, and introduce them to the child in such a way that the child's awareness of fundamental love-intelligence and her oneness with it grows. Besides teaching necessary skills and providing pleasant experiences, the toys and materials presented at the end of this chapter are all things that help children encounter unity. In working with any of them (blocks, puzzles, sand) the undistracted child also has the experience of making the transition from apparent disunity to unity, from unreliability to reliability. He learns the impossibility of trying to force seemingly conflicting puzzle pieces together and instead to let go, gently easing, effortlessly allowing them to fit into place through proper alignment. He learns that the water in which he sinks while struggling fearfully after all supports him once he can give up his struggling to go it alone and rely on his oneness with the water, which is buoyancy.

Of course the child is not yet conscious of the significance of these experiences, so they do not yet become generalized in his life as understanding. But they are happy times that foster positive expectancy and the development of adaptability and steadfastness. As he becomes more conscious such experiences become his evidence that unity and reliability are facts of life, that contrary experiences are only belief, that it is possible and worthwhile to make the transition from one to the other, that the way to do this is through understanding, and that understanding is the whole point.

> *Do not be deceived, my beloved brethren. Every good endowment and every perfect gift is from above, coming down from the Father of Lights, with whom there is no variableness, neither shadow of turning.*
> —James 1:16–17

Science

> *O Shiva, what is your reality?*
> *What is this wonder-filled universe?*
> *What constitutes seed?*
> *Who centers the universal wheel?*
> *What is this life beyond form pervading forms?*
> *How may we enter it fully, above space and time,*
> *names and descriptions?*
> *Let my doubts be cleared!*
> —*Zen Flesh, Zen Bones,* compiled by Paul Reps

To drink milk will be the least absorbing activity in connection with the cup, while he is conducting research on the nature of the cup. He examines the outer surface of the cup, explores the inner surface, discoveres its hollowness, bangs it on the tray for its sound effects. Rivers of milk, orange juice and water cascade from cup to tray to kitchen floor, adding joy to the experiment.
—Selma Fraiberg, *The Magic Years*

Science means knowledge. Our children's scientific interest is an aspect of their quest to know love—not as a feeling, but as the by-product of a reliable underlying intelligence. Children are all scientists in the manner of the ancients, for whom science and philosophy were one discipline. They are supremely interested in how it is, this life around them, all these amazing goings on. Is life good? Is it a loving circumstance in which to be?

On the surface, the evidence is conflicting at best. You certainly can't just look around and say that life is love. But it is equally false to stop with the contrary evidence. The conflict and confusion at the surface are just that—surface confusion; it can be straightened out and harmonized by—and only by—deeper understanding. So whenever we foster our children's natural interest in getting to the bottom of things, we augment their ability to recognize love. Because love and truth are aspects of one reality.

So the most important thing about our children's scientific explorations is not the acquisition of information, but the discovery of life's fundamental intelligibility: that it exists, is perceivable, and that we, as perceivers, are not apart from it. Consciousness *is* spiritual oneness. When we are aware (intelligent) of fundamental intelligence we are one with it! So the important thing to see is that there *is* order and intelligence and that every event or phenomenon, even the self itself, signifies some aspect of this intelligence *when perceived aright*. This is the one sure premise upon which the discovery of love can be based.

Our children's growing scientific awareness not only equips them with skills and knowledge for living in the world. More important is their developing sense that truth is and that they, as understanding, seeing beings are one with it. One-mindedness overcomes tribulations in life just as consciousness of the whole resolves the seeming complexity of heaps of puzzle pieces into a lovely coherent picture. There is no orientation that can better help them transcend the troubles of this world and benefit mankind.

In this world ye shall have tribulation: but be of good cheer; I have overcome the world.
—John 16:33

At first our children's unconscious but rightful motive for wanting to know what is so is the desire to be reunited with the One Mind through awareness; with goodness through awareness of good; with love through awareness that love-intelligence is. They are spontaneously drawn toward this reunion. Each revelation that intelligence is underscores their secret yearning and hunch that they belong to, are one with what is—and that it is fundamentally good; i.e. that love is.

But today's constant academic testing and competition can intimidate us into pushing our children academically, thereby retarding and distracting them in their learning. It helps to remember that to know the details of *how* things work is not so important as to understand *that* they do—according to certain laws, according to what is so. Our perception of the facts constantly changes in the light of new understandings, ways of seeing. So, in our time it has become possible to hear a distinguished physicist (David Bohm) and a distinguished neurophysiologist (Karl Pribram) agreeing publicly that after all, "In the beginning was the Word!" (New York, 1979, at the Conference on "The Coevolution of Science and Spirit.")

Insofar as we stress personal knowledge, we chain the child to the idea of having a personal mind and drive him apart from the one mind. When knowing lots of facts is thought important, learning is difficult because what is already known must be clung to whether or not it is erroneous. When the child is placed constantly in the position of having to prove himself as a superior knower, loving encounters also become increasingly difficult as he pits himself against those who would otherwise be his friends.

This does not mean that "facts" need not be learned, only

that, for example, we memorize the multiplication tables not for their own sake but to be enabled to learn multiplication, to understand the principles of mathematics. Where discovering fundamental intelligence is the central concern it is easier for our children to remain open to new understanding. Incidentally this improves their effectiveness as scientists or scholars since new discoveries can be made only as old "facts" are relinquished. And at the same time they are freed to participate in life together with assurance and receptivity, their selfhood defined in the light of truth rather than in contrast to others whom they must constantly best in order to feel secure. One-mindedness enhances the possibility of our children fulfilling their potential to be both intelligent and loving. By maintaining truth as the central concern we leave open the possibility of our children continuing to assume that life is harmoniously ordered in favor of good. And only when life is discerned as being basically intelligent is it possible to discover that love, love-intelligence, is its underlying force and nature.

Our main role in our children's explorations is attentive noninterference. We can provide materials and opportunities while simultaneously getting out of the way to let be (seen) what will be (revealed). This letting be is the best testimony we can offer to the fact that truth is and that the child as an understander is part of it. In thought and *when called for* in word and action we regard our children as seeing beings rather than as doers and knowers. Recognizing that their most important task is not to know things but to develop their faculty of perceiving, we are better guided in what to say and do and provide that fosters learning. We are less inclined to correct wrong answers or to do over what their unskilled hands can do only awkwardly. And we are better able to point out and joyfully appreciate discovery of principle rather than acquired fact.

Instead of	*It will occur to us to say*
That is very good (or bad).	It doesn't work very well that way.
You are very good (very bad).	Now you can see that thus and such is so. (E.g., Glasses break when they fall on the hard floor.)

Oh, what a stupid (smart) child you are.	You have discovered . . . or, Isn't it wonderful, this shows us . . . or, What good pouring! or, That pouring was a little unsteady; perhaps it would be easier with two hands.
Don't (do) you know how to do that yet (already)?	You are learning. That was only a mistake. (see how smoothly it goes!)
Oh, what a lot you know! (You can say the whole alphabet!)	How wonderful! (The whole alphabet! That is the beginning of learning to read!) I see that you are finding out . . .
You can't (can) do that very well.	It is still a little difficult to manage such a . . . It's getting easier and easier to . . .
What a lucky girl you are!	Isn't it wonderful to see that such a thing can happen!

It's hard to say what's science and what's not for children. If nothing else, young children are certainly physical scientists. How does it feel? How does it taste? What does it smell like and sound like and do? Where did it come from? Where will it go? How did it happen? How does it work and what happens next? Everything they do, every mess they make, every toy they break, every tumble and every stumble is for the sake of learning. So the question isn't what's a good scientific toy or activity for a preschooler. What isn't? To begin with, all that's needed is a certain amount of scientific license and some enlightened appreciation on the part of the parent that science is what's going on. The cracking of an egg, the peeling of an apple are scientific revelations! Let the child play once with the peels, crack one egg and crumble the shell, squash a few round peas. It is a little hard to get started because we don't remember so well that we *learned* what we know now. But once it's clear that science is what is happening, it becomes a happy, easy thing to jump in and find out more with our children.

A child less than two years old went for a winter walk in a carrier on his father's back. Somewhere along the way the father made for the child his first snowball. So beautiful it was, scooped clean and white from beneath the surface and molded gently into a perfectly round, firm ball, that just fit into the child's cupped and mittened hands. On the way home he slept on his father's back, still clinging to the snowball. The father tried to remove the snowball, but the child woke up and cried. So they brought the snowball inside, put it in the freezer, and the child finished his nap. That evening when the child was having his bath, the parents brought him his snowball. "It will melt," they explained. "Put it in the water and watch it melt. Snow is made of water. In the warm water the snow will become water again." This time he was not sad when his snowball went away. He was amazed.

Some things that seem to turn to nothing still exist. Some things that seem to be really aren't. And some things that seem not to be really are. Telling what's what and what isn't makes life interesting. Is air nothing? You can blow up a paper bag with it, or a balloon. You can put out a candle by depriving it of air. When you try to hold your breath, what happens? You can blow bubbles under water—of nothing? Moving air cools things, and dries things, and moves things, and can help things fly. When I was a child I thought that if you flew a kite near a tree it would fly better; I thought there was more wind near the trees because that's where I could see it. Sail a boat. Blow up a bunch of balloons and see how light and easy they are to keep aloft. What's what? And what isn't? And who says so?

> Who has seen the wind?
>   Neither I nor you;
> But when the leaves hang trembling,
>   The wind is passing through.
> Who has seen the wind?
>   Neither you nor I;
> But when the trees bow down their heads,
>   The wind is passing by.
> —Christina Rossetti, "Who Has Seen the Wind?"

When helping our children with their scientific discoveries, we are often asked the question of why? It is fine to answer this question and we must, but it is not of ultimate importance. While giving answers to why questions, also give your child this question: *What is the meaning?* What does it mean that we can see the work of the wind but never the wind at all?

> *The wind bloweth where it listeth, and thou hearest the sound thereof, but canst not tell whence it cometh, and whither it goeth; so is everyone that is born of the Spirit.*
> —John 3:8

> *For we look not upon the things that are seen, but upon the things which are not seen . . .*
> —2 Corinthians 4:18

There was hardly any toy he loved so much as his father's flashlight. Brighter than the light from any flashlight was the light in his face whenever he held one. One day, at two, he was "helping" by holding the flashlight while his father did some work in a semi-dark corner of the house. "Okay," his father called. "Would you please come back and give me a little light now?" The child ran happily to his father's side, shook the flashlight like a salt shaker or a watering can over the work and then ran off to play again, clearly believing that his sprinkled light would continue to enable his father to see. How like the child we are, flicking little bits of love, little partial understandings at dark corners, and then being bewildered and disappointed at the lingering darkness.

Discipline

Neither children nor adults are greatly distressed by the tumbling of sand castles and block towers, or the failure of water to remain in a leaky or overturned vessel. Over and over the castles are built, gradually better and better, until the properties of sand and the laws governing its behavior are at least partially understood. For the most part progress is made harmoniously and the sandbox remains a pleasant place to play.

The secret of this harmonious unfoldment is our lack of personal sense regarding material laws. We understand that sand behaves according to reliable physical principles, so we do not teach our children to take this behavior personally, neither do we too often take personally our children's ignorance of these laws. From the start we say "that's how it is" and "that's what happens when," and the child does not develop the notion that through exertion of his personal will he can somehow successfully take exception to physical law if he so desires.

We are not so enlightened regarding the less tangible but higher laws of being. As Me, Inc., we do take life in general, our children in particular, and ourselves above all, very personally. It is for this reason that most of us have difficulty with our children in the area we call discipline. We have a whole battery of techniques, which we fire at our children "for their own good," ranging from old-fashioned, punitive insistence, through all the more subtle forms of manipulation, coercion, and bribery, to hands-off permissiveness. Results vary accordingly from fearful compliance and passivity through anxious uncertainty to broad anarchy and rebellion, often moving from one extreme to the other, especially in adolescence.

As none of our various approaches proves successful, most of us wind up trying a little of everything. The reason none of them works is that each is false. Less obvious is that they are also all the same. Each of those disciplinary techniques is based on the idea that personal mind is the basic issue and primary reality. We believe we are personally and causally responsible for the existence of our children and for the way they behave. We also believe that life and living are matters of personal opinion.

In the sandbox we express a certain degree of faith in the sand as teacher and the child as learner, but we assume full personal responsibility for just about everything else. In fact, the less we know about something the more personal responsibility we assume. In ignorance we constantly violate higher laws of being and thus invite experiences of disharmony that reinforce our belief in lawlessness. Misinterpreting our own ignorance of higher law as the fact that there is no higher law, that reality is lawless, we undertake the awesome responsibility of personally authoring and enforcing law. When it comes to our children (whom we also believe we have authored), we even believe we *must* take this personal responsibility. But in adhering to this misconception, the biggest lesson we are teaching our children is that personal will (be it compliant or defiant) is the basic issue. And this places us and our children in immediate conflict with life and therefore with each other.

In reality, of course, we too are but children in the sandbox. Our children and the situations in which we find ourselves are like the sand, relentlessly—but not maliciously—manifesting certain principles of existence as law. We are to each other both sand and fellow diggers in the sandbox. As diggers we are responsible only for reflecting or expressing those laws in our lives. But in neither case are we *personally* responsible. We do not create the laws, nor can we vary them, nor force anyone to live by them. We are responsible only in the sense that we are *able* to respond to the laws both in understanding and in our mode of being in the world. These laws are the truth about us; we do not make them true.

What does this mean regarding our role as parents? How can we avoid the years of struggling, frustration, anger, disappointment, and even tragedy that plague so many wholeheartedly well-meaning families in this area called discipline?

Silent Knowing

It is important to remember that it is what we know (in principle, in truth) that makes the difference, not what we do or say. Sand castles will tumble one day and tower the next in a bewildering fashion unless the builder is aware of the difference between wet and dry sand. Though from a material standpoint sand is characteristically shifting, in ideal terms it is constant; it is reliably shifty. It always expresses the laws of its being. So it is most important to make a continuous effort in consciousness to discern the truth that is being revealed in any situation—not the facts or details or cause but the underlying principle.

For this we must maintain an unceasing vigil over our thoughts, distinguishing with relentless honesty between our ignorant personal moods and whims and what is a matter of genuine law or truth. This is especially true with regard to our little children, who are so easy to push around. Insofar as we understand the truth of any situation it will be possible for us to remain as constant as sand in our loyalty to those principles without making it seem a matter of personal will. For example, knowing the properties of sand to the extent that we do, we are not tempted to interfere overmuch in our children's experimental struggles in the sandbox. Nor do we feel impelled to make them accept our word for it that this is what will happen.

Best of all it seems that *what we truly know is somehow transmitted to the children through consciousness and does not have to be spoken of or enforced at all.* Insofar as we can see that law, one law, is operating for us and for our children we can more easily let each other live and learn without being swayed (through false fears and personal responsibility) by the ups and downs of our inadvertent compliance with and violation of these laws. Our assured noninterference is conveyed to the child as a sense of confidence in both himself and reality—confidence that, despite all appearances and experiences to the contrary, reality is reliable, and he can know this too.

So the first answer to the problem of personal mind is silent seeking and knowing. This involves letting go of our misconceptions and exaggerated personal sense, and receptively turning our attention toward the revelation of principle.

Demonstration

The second answer to the problem of personal mind is the demonstration in our lives of those principles we understand, our appreciation of their value and validity, and above all our confidence in the fact of their existence.

On the one hand this means simply practicing what we preach —an easy matter if we really know what we're talking about, otherwise more difficult. We have dominion over our children much as we have dominion over the sand, not through domination but through understanding the dominion of principles. For the most part our children will behave in accordance with our values, reflecting positively or negatively the ideas we cherish most. Any truths we fully understand, and thus demonstrate in daily living, will be picked up by our children. This means that although the child is not yet conscious enough to understand the principles per se (we are only beginning to discover them for ourselves), he will nevertheless be drawn to them, and live in accordance with them, and thus experience their fruits. This is a happy way to grow up and a joyful way to be a parent.

Sometimes, however, we do not know the law ourselves, much

less the principle behind the law. In such instances, both for our own sake and for the sake of our children, affirmation in the face of uncertainty is called for in order that learning may occur; we affirm that truth *is,* that the sand does behave according to law even though it is not immediately clear to us why this particular sand castle has just caved in or why at this particular moment our child seems to be having a tantrum. In fact it is not possible for us to have any personal difficulty with our children any more than we truly have difficulty with the sand. The only difficulty we can ever have is with error, the ignorance of truth.

If we do not understand the laws behind the behavior of sand we may try to force it to behave in accordance with our erroneous preconceptions, quite against its own nature, or fling it about in frustration. As long as we continue to cling to our error and believe that the problem is with the sand, the sand will only be able to manifest our error. It will be shifty, unreliable, hurtful to the eyes. Likewise, when we run into difficulty with our children, we are often inclined to try to change them rather than our thoughts. As with the sand, we are thus keeping them in bondage to our errors, contrary to the truth of their own as yet unconscious being. At best it is a bewildering experience for both parent and child. At worst, since the child, unlike the sand, is growing in consciousness, he not only manifests the error, but sooner or later he will begin to adopt it in the form of a conscious, but false, belief.

So it can be seen that the acknowledgment of discord as error or ignorance of truth is a vital first step toward relinquishing error and its accompanying problems. For the child just this one small step already means tremendous release from the false lessons of personal badness and conflict. There is little worse that we could hope to spare our children. Affirmation that truth exists, whether we yet know it or not, is called faith. In our children it will be expressed as confidence, enthusiasm, and happy expectancy, the freedom to live and learn. In our own lives the practice of known or acknowledged principles will be accompanied by our firsthand discovery of their validity.

So with regard to discipline, the removal of personal sense from parenthood means first of all the silent seeking and knowing of principle in consciousness and, second, the practice and exemplification of principle in experience as law. But is this enough? Do knowing and exemplifying substitute altogether for teaching? Of course not.

Spelling Out the Law

Much, if not most, of the intruding and interfering and bullying that passes for what has been called discipline is done away with in silent knowing and demonstrating. But there remains for the parent a very important role as guardian and teacher, a very constructive one once the error of personal sense is removed. With children, by and large this is the setting forth of certain precepts or laws.

Whatever is not communicated through silent knowing and example must be reduced to laws. Laws are a temporary measure necessitated by the imperfection of our understanding of principle and by the fact that our children, who are by definition largely unconscious, cannot receive principles, which by definition can be understood only in consciousness.

As consistently as possible we must try to see that the laws we set forth are based on principles that we consciously understand. This will help us to avoid the problems of personal sense and the accumulation of an excessive number of mutually conflicting laws. At the same time we need to keep in mind that such laws are at best an imperfect reflection of principle and often even a temporary substitute for the awareness of principle. We will thus be ready to revise or relinquish any law in the light of greater understanding or the growing readiness of our children to move from regulation toward principle. Once we begin to appreciate that the apparent destructiveness of the toddler in taking apart a flower or knocking down sand castles is in fact a constructive effort to understand unity, we are able to revise our view of the situation, moving from reprimand and prohibition to the intelligent channeling of his efforts and the fostering of discovery. Perhaps instead of "don't touch," we may now be inspired to give him one flower from the centerpiece to examine. Or we may offer to rebuild (demonstration) the same sand castle several times in a row, allowing the child the freedom to knock it down and find out.

Likewise, we are ready to revise or relinquish any of our laws as the child himself grows in understanding. At first we protect our children and our property from each other by not allowing any hazardous opportunities to arise. Dangerous and breakable things are kept out of reach and our babies are kept physically out of danger. But as the child grows, a progression occurs from protection and prevention to admonition and advice. More and more the child is allowed to discover and prove things for himself through trial and error (depending, of course, on the possible danger of any given situation).

This does not mean that the formulation of laws as principles is never called for. As we have seen, it is not in the definition of the child to become conscious of principles as principles. That is the task of maturity. It is true that we can and should verbally express from time to time in front of our children the few principles we genuinely understand as principles, but only as sowers, letting the ideas fall as seeds in consciousness, to sprout and bloom later when he is ready. But we cannot expect the child to infer anything about his behavior on the basis of principle. Therefore, *it is important for all laws to be formulated in the most concrete terms possible.*

Initially this means not even using words, as in the physical protection of the physical baby from physical harm. Later it means expressing laws as do's and don'ts. For example, when children first begin to play with each other they have great difficulty sharing. They do not, they even cannot, understand what sharing is or its possible value. Yet somehow we have to help them overcome the problem of fighting over cherished toys if they are to have a happy social experience and ultimately discover the joy of sharing. A helpful and effective law that can be set forth at such times is, "No one may take anything out of anyone else's hands." With older children such a law may only reduce sharing to competitive snatching and conflict, but for the youngest children it is wonderful. It is concrete, comprehensible, and it works. At the right time such a principle-based concrete law is a tool with which the child can encounter for himself the underlying principle.

It is also wise in formulating laws to express them as positively as possible. For example, it is almost universally known that, on a nonverbal level, it is easier to stop a child from repeatedly heading for an electric socket or banging the glass coffee table with his xylophone if something more interesting is presented to take his attention away. The same thing is true on a verbal level. While there is certainly a place for taking a firm, stern stand against error as error, in most instances it is wise to express laws in positive terms. One incident that comes to mind has to do with kicking. Like most children, one little boy used to kick his legs while his diaper was being changed. As he grew bigger and stronger, the kicking became painful and also playfully purposeful. Saying "Don't kick" and "Stop it!" only fixed the idea in the forefront of his thoughts and made it impossible for him to turn to anything else. Then another idea occurred to the parents. "Kick leaves," they said, "not people." The idea itself was a distraction and also suggested an additional possibility. The kicking stopped.

But there is more than technique working in this illustration. The principle behind the effectiveness of the technique is that true behavior is always to our good. Sacrificing error does not mean loss, but rather fulfillment. The living child cannot be concerned with how not to live, but only with living.

Finally, *in formulating laws for our children the most important thing to keep in mind is the removal of personal sense.* It is truth that is at issue, not personal will or mind. There isn't anything more important that we could do for ourselves than to realize this, and there is nothing more important that we could do for our children than to spare them a too-persuasive indoctrination into the personal point of view. Bad and good behavior does not imply badness or goodness on the part of the child, nor is it bad or good because we say so or because we do or do not like it. In fact, there is not good or bad behavior at all. There is only that which works existentially and that which doesn't, that which is valid and that which isn't, that which is harmony-accompanied and that which is discord-accompanied. The opposite of true isn't bad; it isn't even really false; it is only ignorant. Both in order that we may truly realize this and in order that our children may not come to think otherwise with too strong a conviction, it is helpful to delete the misleading personal words of "I" and "you" as much as possible when setting forth laws or instructions for our children.

This means first of all casting all discordant behavior into the category of mistake—error—irrelevant. It has nothing to do with the true child and nothing to do with the truth of life. It is no way to be. It is nothing. Another name for this realization is forgiveness. Instead of "Why did you do that?" or "You shouldn't do that" or "You are a bad girl!" or "I told you not to do that" or "Don't you ever let me see you do that again!" we say, "That was a mistake" or, more concretely, "Hitting is a mistake—it doesn't work." This way the issue is understood to be ignorance, and the assumption is that the child would not do such a thing if she genuinely knew better. This leaves open the possibility of learning. It is even possible in many instances to spell out positively the lesson that, say, "Hitting breaks things. Now the glass is broken." (See also pages 112 and 287.)

Likewise, it is a good idea to *delete "I" and "you" from all commands and positive rules and regulations.* At first this seems awkward, for we rightfully realize that we do not know the principle behind the laws we are setting forth. It may be clear to us what must be done even though we don't clearly see the underlying principle that makes this so. We know that the sand must be wet if there is to be a tunnel, but we do not have a precise understanding of the principle that makes this so. So, to our personal way of thinking, it seems presumptuous to set forth anything as a law. Trying hard to be realistic and democratic, we struggle to choose between "You have to do this because I said so, don't ask me why," and long, drawn-out, incoherent explanations that are mostly incorrect and don't mean anything to the child anyway. It is hard to say which of these two approaches is more tyrannical and irrelevant. But since truth *is,* an immediate here-and-now reality revealing itself here and now, we can most truthfully say, "This is not a good time or place for" thus and such, or "Now is the time for putting on coats," or "Right now it seems best to go home for supper." Even if it remains necessary to pick up the child and bodily cart him off, the issue will not become a matter of personal dominance. Such phrasing is not better because it is less offensive; it is less offensive because it is more truthful.

Perhaps at first it seems stilted and cumbersome to speak in this manner, but the fruits are well worth the effort. By making such a conscious effort to speak in precisely truthful terms, we are keeping the quest for truth as the central issue. It *is* the central issue. This most valid of all existential orientations will transform our lives and the lives of our children.

The True Disciplinarian

Behind the laws there stands the Law, which is greater and more perfect than the laws and which the laws must serve. Behind the Law there stands principle or truth, which is purer and more perfect than the Law and which the Law must serve. Only truth is ultimately redemptive. Even though redemption in our lives depends upon our conscious, individual realization of truth, truth is not personal. Neither is it impersonal. It is transpersonal. The best way to reach the realization of truth for ourselves, and as parents to foster our children's growth toward this realization, is through silent knowing, exemplification, and teaching.

The highest of these is silent knowing, which is the pure concern in consciousness with pure principle. Its fruits in our lives are revelation and redemption. Its fruit in the lives of our children is the maintenance of a wholesome and happy environment for growth. Another name for silent knowing is prayer.

The second way to reach realization is through exemplification, the affirmation, practice, and demonstration of principle in daily life. In our lives its fruit is the discovery and validation of principle in experience as Law. In our children's lives this is the providence of healthy models of being in the world and the maintenance of the desire and freedom to be healthy. Another name for exemplification is witness.

Finally there is teaching. On the highest level this means voicing realized truth in the presence of anyone sincerely interested, but as parents it is mostly the concern with what to do or say *in the meantime*—until we know, until our children are ready to seek to know. This is the most confusing of all because it is the farthest from the truth, the most human and temporary. It is made much easier by the removal of personal sense, and it is largely replaced by silent knowing and exemplification. In our lives the fruit of teaching is learning. In our children's lives, it is easier growth.

So the true disciplinarian of us all is truth. The true discipline is the following after or seeking of truth. The best way for us to discipline our children is not to discipline them at all, but rather to be ourselves disciples of truth. The true answer to the problems of discipline is thus discipleship.

> *Mountains and rivers, the whole earth—*
> *All manifest forth the essence of being.*
> —*The Gospel According to Zen,* ed. by Sohl and Carr

> *So we, being many, are one body in Christ, and every one members one of another.*
> —Romans 12:5

> *Kabir said: Behold but One in all things; it is the second that leads you astray.*
> —Lao Tzu, *The Way of Life,* trans. by R. B. Blakney

> *The One is none other than the All, the All none other than the One.*
> *Take your stand on this, and the rest will follow of its accord;*
> *To trust in the Heart is the "Not Two," the "Not*
>   *Two" is to trust in the Heart.*
> *I have spoken, but in vain; for what can words tell*
> *Of things that have no yesterday, tomorrow, or today?*
> —Seng Ts'an, in *The Religions of Man,* by Huston Smith

Practical Information for New Parents

The toys and materials covered here offer children material demonstrations and encounters with unity. They are presented roughly in progression from the most specific to the most general, the most concrete to the most open-ended and potentially abstract. Included are baby toys, puzzles and pre-puzzles, blocks, construction sets, carpentry, gardening, play with water and sand, and science books —all things through which a child can make discoveries about fundamental unity and order. Parents of older children may be interested in the "Gardening" (page 231) and "Science Books" (page 234) sections, before going on to Chapter 6 (page 237).

Parts and Wholes

Among small unity toys a rattle is a whole composed of parts. Any infant hand toy with parts that do not come off demonstrates the parts/whole idea (*It is apart from me, but I can pick it up.*) Anything with moving parts also demonstrates the parts/whole idea (*It has parts, but it is one thing.*) Stack and nesting toys, puzzles, and pegboards are all wholes that can become parts, all parts that can become wholes. Blocks and construction sets are parts that can express the infinitude of the possibilities of unity (*With the same set of parts I can make many different things*). Tools implement the parts/whole idea. Mud, sand, and water are the most amorphous materials of all and are thus of the longest-lasting usefulness and the best teachers of both the fact and the infinitude of unity and reliability.

For Babies

It's almost silly to speak about what makes a good rattle or other hand toy for a little baby, and yet even on this level there are toys that work and toys that don't. As with anything else, you have to pay attention to the baby—what she can do and what she's *trying* to do. To help her learn to grasp things, choose something that's easy for a tiny hand to hold. Little dumbbell-type rattles are best for tiny babies—they can hold them before they know about holding. It is often the sound of a rattle in her hand that seems to call the baby's attention to the fact that the hand and rattle are there in the first place.

Obviously a baby's toy must be safe—not small enough to swallow, not sharp or breakable or soluble in the mouth.

Less obviously, if you're buying a few toys you don't want them to be redundant. Look for variety. Buy or make something that will help the baby learn to grasp and pick up, something bright-colored to help her learn to use her eyes, something with a pleasant sound to help her learn to use her ears. Find something with moving parts, something that rocks, something that slides, something that rolls, things of different shapes. Find something hard and something soft in hand or mouth. Most toys do/are several of these things; see if they do/are them differently.

And remember, you *really* don't have to buy anything, because your house is full of inspiring things already:

● An *empty film can* with some split peas inside.

● Some *big buttons* or *wooden spools* on a ring of nylon string.

● A *homemade cloth book* with four pages of bright shapes sewn on by machine. Use various textured materials (fake fur, wool, satin, corduroy, oilcloth).

● A *shape sheet.* Sew a few wonderful things like enormous round shiny buttons or a plastic costume jewelry bracelet onto a small piece of sturdy cloth for the baby to hold. Or do the same thing around the edge of a larger quilt or blanket for her to lie on. Nothing small enough to choke on, of course.

Once you start, where can you stop? The possibilities are endless.

Pre-puzzles, Parquetry, and Then Some

Gradually the child becomes ready for parts/whole toys that really come apart and can be put together. On the way to puzzles the following may be useful.

Pole and rings. Most children find the stacking of disks or doughnut-shaped rings around a centerpole interesting at some point (one year old, more or less), though not for very long. Fewer rings are better (less trouble to pick up) than more. A straight center shaft is better than a tapered shaft. Tapered shafts are designed to force the child to discover seriation (the big one goes on first, the smallest one last). But simply removing and replacing the rings appeals to children long before they are ready to select for size. The tapered pole only baffles and frustrates the one- to two-year-old.

Stackable/nestable cups or boxes. Seriation comes more effortlessly with these than with stacking rings. And besides stacking and nesting, the cups and boxes are good for putting (things) in, out, on, and under, all activities of interest considerably earlier than stacking. Games can be played with them, such as hiding an object beneath an overturned box or cup and then guessing which one it is under. Don't fall for an expensive set of beautiful nesting boxes made of cardboard or wood covered with marrable, chewable, soak-offable paper. Two breeze-easy ideas for homemade versions are as follows.

A three-can *silver tuna tower* can be easily made from 3½-, 7-, and 13-ounce cans of tuna. Throw away the tops, eat the tuna, and wash and save the cans. Check the inside of the cans and pound down any sharp edges. No need to decorate unless you want to; they look very pretty in natural silver, and some are gold inside. Box, gift-wrap, and present them to her when she wakes up from her nap.

A *super tower* several feet high can be made from stackable cat food cans. Put strips of red, orange, yellow, blue, green, and purple contact paper around enough of them and you have a beautiful striped tower taller than an adult. For a sturdier base and an even taller tower, try nailing a can with its bottom intact to a board. Or make a puzzle column by depicting a clown or other figure on a stack of four or five cans to be scrambled and reassembled. For the older preschooler, these cans also make perfect units for basic math exercises: build a one, build a two, build a three, build a stairway up to ten.

Many kinds of *shape sorters*—boxes or containers with geometrically shaped holes that admit only objects of the same shape—are available. We saw one designed to look like a mailbox which turned out to be frustrating because, unless the door was closed, the objects fell to the floor and made the door impossible to close. Some have too many holes and surfaces to work with. Try before buying to be certain of how hard or easy it is likely to be for your child at the time.

With tiny, tweezerlike fingers and surprising strength, the baby begins tweaking tiny patches of skin on your neck. Smile while you wince; he's developing dexterity. He is also checking things out. Do they come apart? Do you? *Pegboards* and pegs are for older preschoolers, but if you're willing to supervise (no swallowing and no scattering) you may want one earlier. Briefly, well before a year, he will find simply picking out the pegs an absorbing challenge. When he is one and a half or so he will again become briefly interested, this time in trying to maneuver the peg into position in his hands and then fit it into a hole. It's fascinating to watch. It looks the way it feels to unbutton a coat with freezing hands.

A *pincushion* does as well as a pegboard at one and a half and offers the advantage of not being an extra thing around the house. But if you want a pegboard, a plain one with regularly spaced holes and colored pegs is most useful and will come in handy later for math, color, and design work. When your child is older he will enjoy having a design to follow. Copy the board on paper, drawing one circle for each hole. Photocopy and then make various designs by coloring in the circles to match the different-colored pegs.

Knobbed wooden puzzles are ideal first puzzles for children. Made of plywood, they include a number of different cutouts of geometric shapes or realistically painted animals or objects. They can be introduced soon after the baby can sit up alone and will continue to be of interest for a long time, both as puzzles and as sort of first books from which to learn to talk.

A farm animal puzzle such as the one pictured here is fine to start with. For several months the newly sitting child will be concerned with simply trying to lift out the pieces. He will also enjoy learning to recognize the animals' names and the sounds they make. For a while the puzzle may cease to be a challenge—but in a month or so the idea of fitting the pieces back into the puzzle will dawn. At the end of a meal, help him with the puzzle in his highchair. (Turn it! Turn it! There it goes!)

You can also eventually use the animals as play figures, making up stories about them or using them for simple hide-and-seek games. You can even act out little stories:

Once upon a time the duck and the hen went for a walk on a sunny day. [Child takes these pieces away from the puzzle and walks them.] Dum—teedum—teedum—teedum [a good strolling noise]. After a while they sat down to rest in the shade of a tree. [Child puts pieces down somewhere.] Next the cow and the crow decided to take a walk. Dum—teedum—teedum—teedum. Pretty soon they came to the tree where the duck and the hen were sitting. What a surprise! They were very glad to see each other. So they all sat together in the shade. [This goes on until the child has seated all the animals under the "tree."] "Well," they said, "what a nice surprise! If only we had known we could have brought a picnic." For indeed by now the animals were all very hungry. Just then the hen looked up. "What do you know!" she said. "We do not need a picnic, for the tree we are sitting under is an apple tree and it is full of apples!" So the duck and the hen and the cow and the crow and the dog and the pig and the lamb and the sheep and the rooster and the cat and the goat and the goose and the rabbit all had an apple picnic party under the apple tree on the sunny day. Then very happy and very full they all went home.

Simple wooden picture puzzles, in which each piece is a whole shape in the picture, are the next step after the knobbed whole-object puzzles just described. Lots are available but not all are equally suitable. It is desirable that anything which is going to be worked over and looked at as much as these first picture puzzles should be lovely in appearance. You do not need many, for they will be quite satisfying for some time if introduced soon enough.

First jigsaw puzzles. Difficulty depends on the size, number, and distinctive shape of the pieces. Start with puzzles that have only a few large pieces, all easily distinguishable from one another in shape. Work up gradually to smaller, more similar pieces, depending on the child's developing ability and continuing interest.

Good wooden puzzles are always nice, but cardboard jigsaws are more available and perfectly adequate. The child will no longer work the same puzzle so many times if he no longer learns anything from doing so. So once some facility is developed, a whole boxful of cardboard puzzles is probably worth more than one or two wooden ones. Cardboard puzzles will be more easily managed if they include a frame and backing, and, of course, it is still desirable to select puzzles that are handsome.

Homemade jigsaw puzzles. With your child, select a pretty and interesting picture from a magazine. Or use a favorite photograph or children's poster. A puzzle will be more successful with a preschooler if it has a tray, or at least a frame, around it, so take two pieces of cardboard that are sufficiently larger than the picture to allow for a ¾- to 1-inch margin. With rubber cement glue the picture to one of the pieces of cardboard, leaving straight margins all the way around. With a single-edge razor blade or mat knife cut around the picture, leaving the remaining cardboard frame intact. Glue the frame to the other piece of cardboard. Cut the mounted picture into pieces that are appropriate in number, size, and shape for your child. For durability, you may also give the surface a coat of spray varnish.

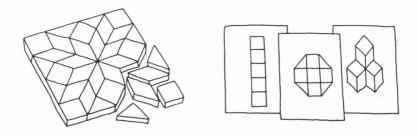

Parquetry. The official verb that describes this type of activity is "to tessellate," that is, "to form of small squares or blocks, as floors, pavements, etc.; form or arrange in a checkered or mosaic pattern." Many sets of lovely, wooden, colored tiles are available, from giant size for working on the floor, to almost pocket size for working anywhere, to basic medium size. Parquetry tiles are enjoyably used for everything from simple random arrangements to sophisticated studies of symmetry and optical illusion. Beautiful colored design cards of varying degrees of sophistication can be purchased from some educational suppliers. (See list of direct mail sources in Chapter 3.) But with or without these cards, parquetry is an excellent activity in which unity becomes apparent and reveals itself as beauty. It is well worth it to buy a set or two of these tiles, which cannot be easily duplicated in the home.

Pangrams. Every child should have a set of these ancient Chinese puzzle tiles that combine parquetry and puzzling in a remarkably versatile way.

Construction

Blocks

The youngest block-builders are, of course, entirely unconscious of motive, and almost completely without skill. It takes understanding to view their crude buildings as models of truth and beauty. Nevertheless, as builders they are themselves models for us. They build without preconception—not to prove anything, not to please anyone, but to find out. With such a motive revelation is automatic—understanding (on however primitive and material a plane) rushes in.

The child is not yet conscious enough to benefit from her own demonstrations of creativity. It is almost inevitable that she must first become as intellectual and self-conscious as the rest of us before one day she will consciously seek the purity of motive she manifested spontaneously as a child. But we can foster or discourage this growth as we sit beside her on the floor or in the sandbox. In every way we must ourselves cultivate appreciation of the revelation of principle rather than human achievement.

If we teach our children to build towers for praise or a sense of power, we have led them astray. But we can rejoice with them in their small revelations of balance, stability, order, line!

Practically, this suggests a few don'ts. Don't channel, don't instruct, and at first don't even build anything very spectacular to "show the possibilities." If you build spectacularly, he may respond appropriately by becoming a spectator. Watch what he tries to do with his blocks. Many children first "draw" with them, making long lines of blocks placed end to end. Help if you will, but don't change course.

Once the interest in building is established, here is a nice game to help the child discover new building techniques. The whole family can sit down and enjoy doing this together. Decide in advance how many blocks each individual may place at one time —two or three are about right. Then take turns working on the same building, with each member of the family adding the prescribed number of blocks to the construction any way he likes. It's a surprisingly pleasant activity of equal enjoyment for a variety of ages at once. Also provides a good first experience in taking turns.

Here are some worthwhile blocks and building toys:

Bright-colored 1-inch wooden cubes designed for teaching math to three- and four-year-olds are also perfectly delightful for one- and two-year-olds to use in tabletop or highchair building and designing experiments. Little babies love them, too, so they can be bought early and used a long time.

One four-year-old we know uses these cubes to invent and play wonderful games with his two-year-old sibling. Same/different: "You build what I build" (or the other way around), so patiently, block by block. "Is this the same? Is this? No, that's different. Which one looks like this?" Colors: "Can you find another *red* one?" Numbers: "Now let's count them. Hey, let's build a stair!" Relationships: "Let's make a pattern: Here's a blue one, here's a red one, blue one, red one—can you find the one that goes next?"

If you have space for them, corrugated *cardboard blocks* are lots of fun. They are large enough so that a stack of three is already rewarding. They are light enough to be managed easily, strong enough to be climbed on, and when they fall down nobody gets hurt. Cardboard blocks are available from a variety of places. Almost any educational mail order house has them.

Wooden block sets. The small cubes and large cardboard blocks are adequate for the preschool building days, but, as the child grows, almost nothing compares with *a good set of wooden blocks* from which more complicated structures can be built. There are a great many sets to choose from, so a little anticipation of what will ultimately prove most useful is helpful and can save you from buying several different sets as the child grows.

Basically the choice is between tabletop sets (small pieces which are good for the floor as well as tabletops) and floor sets (big pieces). The bigger pieces of the floor sets are significantly more satisfying to build with and are really not much more space-taking. Buy a starter set and then add to it as needed. Try to see the blocks before you buy—some are better finished (smooth-sanded, rounded or planed edges) than others. And do be sure to buy modular ones, with each block relating to the others in direct ratio. Among the toys you might buy, a set of good blocks is worth the extra money you have to pay.

Non-Block Construction Sets

The more open-ended a thing is the more you can do with it. Thus although a gaudy plastic toy may occupy the child intensely for a few hours once or twice, it is to plain blocks, or even better, to sand, clay, paints, hammer, and nails that he will return again and again. So one of the best things you can do for your pre-schooler is to let/help him learn to saw and hammer as he becomes able.

Wood scraps are more open-ended than blocks; blocks are more open-ended than construction sets. But in the whole hierarchy of toys, construction sets tend to be more interest-sustaining than most, and can contribute much to a child's pleasure, sense of spatial relationships, manipulative development, and repertoire of ideas about how things can fit together.

In buying a construction set, select the most open-ended one you can find while still taking your child's *present* skills into account. Recommended are: Crystal Climbers, Tinkertoys, Bristle Blocks (or Multi-Fit), Build-O-Fun, Thing-a-ma-Bobbin (from Learning Materials Workshop—see Chapter 3, Direct Mail), Legos . . . and more and more, by any and all means, Legos. Legos are extraordinarily wonderful for the oldest preschoolers and they last and last for years of quiet and shared exploration.

Real Tools and Carpentry

There's nothing so nice for preschoolers as the real thing and real skills. A *pounding bench* is one of the best toddler toys around, good for children around age one, but by the time they are three, most girls and boys are capable of using a hammer and saw and drill on soft wood. A bag of nails, a hammer, a drill, the kind with a crank on the side, and permission to go to work on the tree stump in the backyard is about all they need to be happy. Then, of course, there are perfectly gorgeous tool benches available which are lovely to have if you *know* you will provide a steady supply of wood and a fair amount of help and guidance. Most lumber yards have barrels of scrap wood to give away—choose only pieces of soft pine. Instead of buying a child's work bench you can just build a bench for her to stand on at your work bench. Or build a child-size one yourself.

All you really need, besides a small 12- to 18-inch *crosscut saw* and a medium-sized *hammer* and maybe a *drill,* is a *vise* to hold the wood. A vise makes a tremendous difference in the preschooler's sawing success. While an older, stronger child can manage fine without one, the preschooler needs two hands to saw and thus depends on something (or you) to hold the wood steady. Woodworking vises (the kind with plates) are rather costly and C-clamps will do. The main advantage of the vise over the C-clamp is that the preschool child can mount the wood in the vise by himself, which is not possible with the clamps.

Teaching the proper care of tools is important whether or not a tool kit is purchased. Be sure to set up a good place for her tools or for the ones you share with her.

Mostly the child will be happy just to pound in nails (hang up a "Bent Nail" original) and make cuts. Give him some wire or rubber bands to entwine and stretch into designs on a board of nails. And keep some glue available. When hammering and sawing become discouraging, gluing is glorious.

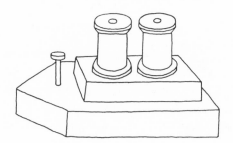

Besides all this it is encouraging and satisfying to complete a few "real" carpentry products. A bath boat that really floats is wonderful. Also a hook thing for neckties or kitchen utensils:

● The child cuts the board. (You may have to start the cut.)

● Together you sand it—perfectly (but make the sanding the issue, not the child's willingness to stay with it).

- Supervised waxing and polishing.
- What a beautiful, smooth piece of wood this has become!
- Screw in the hooks (L-shaped) after careful measuring. You start and finish; he gives a few turns in the middle.
- Give it (gift-wrapped) to someone, if possible someone who will really hang and use it.

Of course, it's like anything else—there's a time to help and a time to refrain from helping, a time to demonstrate and a time to refrain from demonstrating, a time for experimentation and (more rarely) a time for finished products. You have to be guided by the child to see what he is ready to learn. You also have to be ready for his idea of what a finished product is. For a whole bookful of truly do-able woodcraft ideas for children, see also *Easy Woodstuff for Kids,* page 142.

Mechanical Wonders

From small hardware items to tools and machines, mechanical things fascinate children and increase awareness of unity. Anything you can find that a child can safely work—*an eggbeater, a crank, a typewriter*—is happy and edifying for him. Hardware stores are full of toys for children. A great big nut and a bolt is a beautiful thing to a toddler.

Almost all children are fascinated by *keys.* They jingle nicely for babies and provide a growing challenge for the growing toddler who likes to fit things into things, and the older preschooler for whom opening and closing a padlock is a joy. Buy a good-size padlock and hide the extra key. Even better, also buy a latch and mount it on a board. Even better, cut a door out of the board and attach it with real hinges. But just a padlock and a key will do. A better gift than two dozen junky toys.

Never miss an opportunity with your youngster to dissect an *old machine*. An old toaster or clock that is ready for the junkyard is a whole afternoon of investigation, the perfect opportunity to see, first of all, that things work, a little bit of how, and to demonstrate and practice the use of screwdrivers, pliers, and other real tools.

Water, Sand, and Mud

The more amorphous the material, the more can be done with it, the longer it will sustain interest, and the more can be learned from it. There are no toys for sale to equal water, sand, and mud in entertainment and educational value, or in long-lasting appeal. Like everything else in the world, these simple materials are significant of ideas far beyond themselves. So even when we become old men and women, if we have grown at all wise we will still be able to contemplate and learn from these materials as symbols.

Sandbox. Buy or build a wooden one (1-by-8-inch boards are about right), or make one from a half-sunk tractor tire. And don't forget, just a washtub full of sand (or rice or corn meal) and a few small kitchen cups and spoons on the porch can be tremendously satisfying. Think about a sandbox in the basement for the winter.

Sandpile. You don't have to have a sandbox at all, you know. You don't even have to have sand. A mound/mountain of sand or soil in a corner of the yard may be even more fun to climb and work on. Just shovel it back together again from time to time to make it last a little longer.

Toy vehicles. While there are many beautiful wooden vehicles available, the most affordable and satisfying to children are the realistic metal ones (although they do corrode in salt water). Among model vehicles the earth movers are the most useful, especially in a sandbox or pile of dirt.

Splish splash. Children don't need to be bathed every day for cleanliness, though regular bathing may contribute to their appreciation of order and provide certain mental purification. But the bath is one of the best places for the very young child to enjoy some quiet and uniquely private play. One mother tells of living in an apartment in which the only bathroom was off the kitchen. It was totally inconvenient in every way except one. Strategically it was the best possible location for her toddler's bath. She could fix dinner while keeping an unobtrusive eye on her child, and she found that all the best bath toys came from the kitchen. "I want da colander, please!" her two-year-old would call. Given a simple trickle of running water to work with, the child played happily for nearly an hour each day before supper. Mother and child were equally refreshed by this period of quiet independence.

So take advantage of the bathtub, sink, a sand or water table, sandbox, the hose in that patch where the grass refuses to grow anyway, a rainy day, and the beach above all, amen.

Sticks and stones and leaves and Popsicle sticks are more than enough equipment to keep a child busy with sand and water, but here are a few toys you might make or buy and some activities you might set up.

Sponge boats. You make them with sponges and scissors.

Plastic tube. For blowing noisy bubbles in the bath. Buy 2 feet of fish tank tubing from any pet store.

Cups, colanders, ladles, funnels, and measuring cups. All such utensils from the kitchen are marvelous for sand or water.

Bubble bath. Many children are somewhat fearful of this at first, but after a time or two they all discover the fun of shoveling, modeling, land- and seascaping, and wearing the bubbles.

Boats. Most cheap plastic bathtub boats are not a bargain because they capsize or sink. If they fill up with water, they also mildew inside. So, as with any real boat, it matters that a toy boat be leakproof and buoyant. Buy a wooden one. Instructions for how to make rubber-band–powered paddle boats can be found in *American Folk Toys,* by Dick Schnacke.

Bubbles. To get a *giant soap bubble* rub a wet piece of soap along the side of your wet index finger and thumb. Close thumb tightly around index finger. Open slowly into a ring. Blow softly and steadily. If the ratio of water and soap is just right, you will now be able to softly blow a giant bubble, equaled in size only by the child's wide eyes.

Water machines. There are a number of toys available—suction-powered machines for the side of the bath, small pumps, and water wheels—that demonstrate the power of water.

Gardening

One of the finest activities we can do with our children is gardening. The activity of growing things is a prayer for the awareness of love that we and our children can participate in together. You begin by kneeling down and soon you will see love sprouting up all over the place. At one and a half or two years old a child can already begin to participate in, enjoy, and learn from numerous planting, transplanting, and tending experiments. It is not necessary to have a garden or even a window box. On any spring walk, seedlings can be found pushing up last fall's leaves beneath the budding trees. Discovering these beautiful little sprouts under the soggy old brown leaves is a delight. Choose one or two promising ones and dig them up with a good clump of dirt. Take them home in an ice cream cup or a pair of careful, small, bare hands. At home they can be planted in small pots and watered from time to time. Be sure to pot them tightly, pressing down the soil firmly around the roots.

In autumn, maple seeds, pine cones, and acorns can be harvested. The seeds can be planted indoors. Our most successful venture was with a seed from the honey locust tree. It grew nicely and each night its leaves folded up, each morning they opened. Such astonishing precision! Even indoors it had its autumn/spring cycle, complete with the falling and returning of leaves.

The important thing with both child and plant is not to insist on anything in particular happening. The object is simply to see what is revealed. Let the child help, but don't insist. It is good to keep in mind that growth of both the child and the plant is what is being fostered. If the plant appears to need water, you will give it water; if it appears too wet, you will refrain from watering it. Likewise, if the child appears interested, encourage him; if he becomes bored, let him move on to the next thing, and you carry on with the plant.

Again, let him help whenever he can and wants to, even if it's only in the finding of the sprout, the holding of it on the way home, the pressing down of the earth in the pot. From doing, his interest is sustained, and he learns a bit more dexterity. From watching the plant and listening to you, he gains botanical information. But he learns most of all from watching you. From this he begins to learn the nurturing point of view—the patient waiting, the faithful caring, the joyful appreciation of growth. The other name for this is love, which is, after all, what we are supposed to be learning, too.

Some Good Growing Projects

• Set an *onion*, pointed side up, in the top of a glass or jar of water. The bottom of the onion should just touch the water. In only a few days it will send roots down and, soon after, leaves up. It grows with almost visible speed!

• Cut the tops off a couple of *carrots and beets* and put the tops in a flat dish of water. A few pebbles will help to keep them in place. New leaves will grow like crazy. It's an interesting way to demonstrate that different leaves grow from different plants.

• *Nasturtiums* are very satisfying for little children to cultivate. The seeds are big and obvious for little fingers to push into the soil. They can be grown indoors if placed in a window with lots of sun. They take quite a while to bloom (over a month) but in the meanwhile they produce many pretty leaves. When the flowers do come, they are likely to be abundant. From 4 to 5 seeds you may have as many as 30 blossoms open at one time. Pick them and more will follow. Buy a package and just follow the directions on the package.

• Plant, tend, and harvest *something edible* from seed—basil or carrots, for example. Carrots take rather a long time to grow—up to two weeks just for germination. But there is no hurry and as a revelation of the miracle of growth and fruition they are particularly wonderful for children. From the slow-growing seed so tiny and brown come the feathery green leaves up and at last the secret carrot down—to be tugged up all at once, so startlingly orange and crunchy.

For a quicker response, try sprouting alfalfa seeds in a small, covered dish. Soak in lukewarm water overnight in a dark place. Then drain off the water and rinse with fresh, lukewarm water through a tea strainer or piece of cheesecloth stretched over the dish. Continue to keep the dish covered and in a dark place, rinsing this way once or twice a day. In two or three days, when the seeds have sprouted and the seed leaves have opened, place the dish in a light window for a few hours to turn the leaves green. Then harvest—which means eat—raw as a post-nap snack, in a liverwurst sandwich, in a salad or soup. They really are delicious and reputed to be highly nutritious as well. The seeds can be bought in any health food store.

● Experiment with *seeds from your child's plate*—watermelon, apple, grapefruit, grape, squash, pear. Beans and corn grow with gratifying speed but must be dried hard first. As for technique, you can either green-thumb your way, hoping, or do a little simple research at the library. Some seeds need wintering. A day or two in the freezer should be enough to fool Mother Nature.

● Gift-wrap a little package of ready-to-grow, paper-white *narcissus bulbs* for your own child or as a birthday gift for a playmate. It may be passed over for the moment but will soon prove itself a wonderful gift. Besides providing more fun, the gift wrapping says the truth so nicely—that the growing of a beautiful flower is a gift.

Place the bulbs on a bed of pebbles in a dish. Keep the pebbles in water up to the bottom of the bulbs. That's all! If possible, when the bulbs flower, keep them near the child's bed so he can enjoy their lovely scent in the darkness and their pure glory in the morning.

Science Books

The early scientist/philosopher had one primary interest: to understand the nature of being. The old sage wanted the facts, but then he also wanted to know what the facts meant. Nowadays we tend to think of philosophy and science as separate. The scientist wants the facts; the philosopher is the dreamer, the guy with his head in the clouds. They may follow completely different educational routes, and the fellow who keeps a foot in both camps is so unusual that he stands out—a genius: Einstein, Schweitzer.

Children constitute the only large group for whom science and philosophy have always remained united. When a baby meets other living things—dog, insect—an earthquake happens in him. Listen to his exploding laughter. "Eureka!" he is exclaiming. He has no words, but you can see the marvel in his eyes. Well, for goodness' sake *give* him the words! In school he may not get "science" until third or fourth grade, by which time the world is divided into fiction and fact and he may already be pegged as a math or science "type" or as a literature/history "type."

So it's up to us to help our children retain in consciousness what they already "know": that science and philosophy are just two sides of the same coin—being alive—and that learning is the way to spend it. Recognize her questions and help her find the words for them. Allow her to conduct her whole life as a scientific experiment. And books—above all *books!* There are so many terrific ones to show a child amazing things and to give her the words for her amazing questions. What books? Let her interests guide you. Try not to let any interest die of neglect; without forcing, help her follow each interest as far as it goes. The library is a perfect place to pursue momentary scientific interests—stars, worlds, insects, whatever—and here are some books that are well worth owning. (See also books on pages 142–145 and 316–317.)

> *Cooking Up Learning*, by Jackie Jundt and Lucy Rumpf. A wonderful cookbook for learning (science, math, social studies, life skills) and good times prepared by two nursery school teachers. Tested and found fabulous by scores of parents and children at home. Organized by season and perfectly tailored for the young child. A best must. Available for $5 from Jundt, 2340 St. Clair Ave., St. Louis, MO. 63144, or from Growing Child (see page 146).
>
> *The Children's Picture Atlas, The Children's Book of the Earth, The Children's Book of the Seas,* by Jenny Tyler and Lisa Watts. Though not specifically designed for preschoolers, these three titles are excellent for family reference. Highly graphic and inviting presentations of a wealth of information in captioned pictures. Together a veritable encyclopedia. Usborne, 5 years and up.
>
> *The Cloud Book,* by Tomie de Paola. ". . . if you could hop on a bird and fly way up, you would see the whole earth covered with clouds." As much fun as a story book. Increases a child's awareness and enjoyment of his environment. Scholastic, 4 years and up.
>
> *The Kids' Kitchen Takeover,* by Sara Bonnett Stein. There is nothing quite so happy as an 8–10-year-old alone in the kitchen with this book, unless it's a preschooler in the kitchen with this book and you. Includes science, craft, cooking, and nature projects that encourage freedom and creativity. For example, "stir in a little milk until it gets as thick or as thin and gooey as you like." Workman, 4 years and up.
>
> *Mickey's Magnet,* by Franklyn M. Branley and Eleanor K. Vaughan. The story of a small boy's discoveries with a magnet, including

how to make one. A small magnet is included with the book. Scholastic, 3–8 years.

Science Toys and Tricks, by Laurence B. White. From bubbles in the sink to straws in wrappers—an introduction to the world as a science lab. Really easy directions for really easy science-powered tricks and toys. All are fun, none too elaborate, and each teaches. Addison-Wesley, 3–8 years.

The Science Book, by Sara Stein. As the jacket says, this book is "a feast for young science explorers" from about 8 to 12 years. By the author of *The Kids' Kitchen Takeover,* who really knows how to talk to children about what interests them: about boys and girls and belly buttons, about people who can spread their toes apart, about molecules, and dog talk, and the shape of space. It's a book for older children—and for old children like me who want to bone up for their youngsters. Workman, 6 years and up.

Sharing Nature with Children, by Joseph Bharat Cornell. "A Parents' and Teachers' Nature Awareness Guidebook." If you're having a play group outdoors or if you just want your child to grow up with a reverence for nature, you may find the activities here helpful. Classified by age, type (e.g., calm or energetic), topic, equipment. Very thoughtfully prepared. Ananda, 2 years and up.

What Do People Do All Day? by Richard Scarry. Farming, mining, paper, electricity, the water cycle. This book full of busy animal folk is really an encyclopedia made fun and an indispensable introduction to the wider world. Random House, 2–6 years.

6
Beauty

i thank You God for this most amazing
day: for the leaping greenly spirits of trees
and a blue true dream of sky; and for everything
which is natural which is infinite which is yes

(i who have died am alive again today,
and this is the sun's birthday, this is the birth
day of life and of love and wings: and of the gay
great happening illimitably earth)

how should tasting touching hearing seeing
breathing any—lifted from the no
of all nothing—human merely being
doubt unimaginable You?

(now the ears of my ears awake and
now the eyes of my eyes are opened)
—e. e. cummings, *Poems 1923–1954*

When Moses came down from Mount Sinai,
with the two tables of the testimony in his
hand as he came down from the mountain, Moses
did not know that the skin of his face shone
because he had been talking with God. And when
Aaron and all the people of Israel saw Moses,
behold, the skin of his face shone. . . .
—Exodus 34:29–30

Beauty is universally associated with goodness. We speak of the "good things in life." Everybody wants a "good life." But as Me, Inc., we understand life only in terms of having pleasure (materialism) and exerting power—especially in relation to others (dualism).

So we are looking to have and do beauty. We want to have personal beauty and beautiful possessions, and we want to do beautiful things. We envy beautiful and creative people. We desire to be both, fear to be neither, and go to desperate lengths to achieve either. We associate beauty with visibility. We want to be visibly beautiful and to have visibility in the eyes of others. All of these motivations have an impact on our way of being parents.

Having and Doing Beauty

"Having" beauty translates into having things that look good and into looking good or having good looks (and beautiful feelings—the feeling that we are personally beautiful and good). So some of us spend fortunes to improve our appearance (and wind up looking worse than ever) or the appearance of our homes (and only wind up with clutter).

"Doing" beauty translates into efforts to gain recognition as creative persons. In these we suffer from such notions as "lacking talent" or "having bad breaks" or not gaining "deserved recognition." Failing to be personally creative, some of us seek recognition as connoisseurs of the arts, or attach ourselves to artists in order to be vicariously "beautiful people."

All attempts at having and doing beauty have an artificial and superficial quality because the concern is with the appearance of goodness rather than with goodness itself.

As parents we sometimes seek to use our children to have and do beauty for us. We want them to look good and to make us look good. They are our "little works of art," for which we expect to get credit and through which have vicarious pleasure. So we doll them up, straighten their teeth, fuss over their complexions, tell them to stand up straight and smile and be polite. In return they slouch and give limp handshakes and somehow manage to get their permanent front teeth knocked out or cut their own hair the night before

Aunt LaLa arrives. We want to show off children who are talented and at least cultured, who perform if possible and are noticeably creative somehow. So we give them lessons and drag them to concerts and museums. And they turn out to be "tone deaf" or are uninterested and rebellious.

> Someone commented that on hearing the news of his mother's death, his first thought was: now I don't have to take piano lessons anymore. In the second place he was sad about his mother, but first he was glad about the piano lessons.

We have all these mental pictures—fixed ideas of how it is that our families are supposed to express beauty—beautiful personal appearance, beautiful bodies, beautiful home, beautiful children, beautiful relationships. There is an American Dream—in Pepsi ads, for example—about how we should all be and act and how it should look. There is something wonderful about those ads—and something awful, too. Because what if our children aren't *that* kind of beautiful? What if for a while our relationships with each other aren't so beautiful? What if we aren't "beautiful"? Shame. Panic. Horror. Terror.

But, for crying out loud, who says what's beautiful? *Pepsi-Cola?* And who gives Pepsi-Cola the right to tell us what's beautiful anyway? (I have to admit it: I do. At least Me, Inc. does—unless we have a better idea.)

Actually, more ugliness comes from existentially pouting and fuming and fussing over not being able to have or bring about some preconceived beautiful mental picture than from any other source.

> The child runs up to her mother, with joy dancing in her eyes and news to share. And her mother stops her.
> "Your nose is running. First wipe your nose—and then tell me."
> So in a minute her nose is clean and her eyes have died down and her shoulders are slumping and her mouth is hanging open.
> "What was it you wanted to say, dear?"
> "I forgot."

By day, we nag our children about their appearance, about doing better work, and at night, when they are asleep and we sit quietly, their faces float before us like the afterview from a flashgun —so sweet and beautiful with little mustaches of chocolate milk and strawberry jam on. So the problem is not so much to bring about the beauty that should be but isn't. Or to deal with ugliness that shouldn't be but is. The bigger task is to recognize the beauty that is when we see it.

The most beautiful sights on earth are those that force us to see beyond the seen to the unseen. And true creativity is that sort of seeing. There is a man of vision who takes retarded people camping. In one such expedition a group of retarded adults camped and cooked out and rowed boats for the first time in their lives and had the most beautiful time—in the pouring rain. "I like camping," one retarded camper told a reporter . . .

> . . . and the sheets of rain that streamed down on the bonfire seemed to touch some great fund of inner amusement in him.
> What did he like most, he was asked, the boating, the fellowship?
> "To be alive," he said, grinning as the raindrops dripped from his nose.
> —Glenn Collins, in the New York Times

> How beautiful upon the mountains are the feet of him who brings good tidings, who publishes peace, who brings good tidings of good.
> —Isaiah 52:7

> For our light affliction, which is but a moment, worketh for us a far more exceeding and eternal weight of glory; while we look not at the things which are seen but at the things which are unseen: for the things which are seen are temporal; but the things which are not seen are eternal.
> —2 Corinthians 4:12–18

All Life as a Work of Art

A young child was looking at a picture book. At the edge of one page was an illustration showing only the tail and hind legs of a dog. The child frowned. "Oh, dear," he said. "He is broken." The picture was then explained to him. "But where is the front of him?" asked the child. "Is it lost? Did it get cut off? How did it get cut off? Did he get deaded?" He did not recognize that the dog was walking away.

* * *

One day a mother drew a picture of a child. She asked her two-and-a-half-year-old daughter, "Now, can you draw some clothes on this boy?" The child said, "I will draw a sweater for him." She took up her crayon and carefully drew a line around the whole drawing of the child.

It is important to learn to see beyond what seems to be. The second child was not yet able to do that. It is something we have to learn. To appreciate the first child's drawing we have to see beyond the crude lines of her drawing to their significance. Then we see how her drawing beautifully expresses her idea that *a sweater is warm and cozy and goes all around me.*

It is noteworthy that the study of the beauty of art and music is called art and music *appreciation. Appreciate* means much more than merely to like. It begins with valuing and is fulfilled in understanding. *Appreciation* is a synonym for *gratitude* which also does not mean merely liking or being happy with the way things seem on the surface.

It is often recommended that we take time to count our blessings, by which is meant the things we are glad about. But in true gratitude we appreciate the significance of whatever presents itself to us. Recognizing that spiritual realization is the ultimate and only real blessing, our uppermost interest is to see what is so and what is not. Now everything, good or bad, becomes a teacher and potential blessing, bringing to our attention further clarification of what is good and true—and what is not. Whether as hard lessons about what isn't or beautiful revelations of what is, both the good and bad bring us "blessons" for which we are grateful.

The prerequisite and partner to gratitude is humility. With humility even in the face of ugly appearances and discordant experience we are able to set aside our thoughts about what should and should not be and allow for the possibility that the only real problem may be ignorance. True gratitude is not possible without humility; true humility is not possible without gratitude. Another name for this combination is prayer (gratitude) and fasting (humility). They are not sentimental or religious; they are love-intelligent.

All apparent life is a work of art. And every work of art expresses an idea that the artist has in mind—in fact, it expresses an idea that the artist has of himself. Ugliness is also a work of art. It occurs when a false idea of who we are or what life is gains visible expression. At any moment each one's life is either his own work of art or God's. And at any moment we can choose which.

> *For my people have committed two evils; they have forsaken me, the*
> *fountain of living waters, and hewed them out cisterns, broken cisterns that*
> *can hold no water.*
> —Jeremiah 2:13

All ugliness (ugly experiences, ugly situations, ugly moods) is the self-expression of self as something broken, apart from God. What's ugly is this suggestion of brokenness. All beauty, on the other hand, expresses one universal good. It takes shape whenever an individual seeing being through conscious awareness (oneness with God's good) becomes a vehicle through which God is expressed.

There are two artists shaping our lives. One is a faker and one is the ultimate Old Master. The faker (who is of course, Me, Inc.) endeavors to paint a picture of itself as beautiful and brilliant in and of itself and by contrast to everyone else. But at best, this is never lasting and rarely is it convincing. Sometimes, at worst, the image proves false by coming out all wrong—misshapen, imperfect, malformed—and then it's too convincing. But either way, beautiful and brilliant or stupid and ugly, it is only a phony and cannot compare with or detract from the master work which lies, discoverable, beneath.

So it is that the seemingly retarded camper (seemingly strange, seemingly slow) nevertheless perceives and demonstrates the true good of his oneness with fundamental being, and in that moment is transformed into an unquestionably beautiful and creative individual—before which the beholder stands breathless as the counterfeit picture fades and flakes off, revealing the hidden master's perfect work.

As any amateur painter quickly learns, an ugly appearance cannot be changed just by working on the surface. Our failure to express beauty does not mean that we are uncreative or unbeautiful, only that our underlying idea of what beauty is and where it is to be had and how done—precisely the idea that Me, Inc. is itself a cause or possessor of beauty—is incorrect. As with every good that we yearn for but cannot seem to bring about, we need to reach a clear understanding of beauty—and its source. The secret to realizing beauty is not doing or having, but seeing. We are not here to look good or to do good, but to see *and thereby be* good.

The Single Eye

If my eye is to distinguish colors, it must first be free from any color impressions. If I see blue or white, the seeing of my eyes is identical with what is seen. The eye by which I see God, is the same as the eye by which God sees me.
—Meister Eckhart, trans. by R. B. Blakney

The five colors can blind,
The five tones deafen,
The five tastes cloy.
The race, the hunt, can drive men mad
And their booty leave them no peace.
Therefore a sensible man
Prefers the inner to the outer eye:
He has his yes—he has his no.
*—*Lao Tzu, in *The Way of Zen,* by Watts

Since "beauty is in the eye of the beholder," it is the eye that must be trained, first to see, then to see beauty. Ultimately there is another eye altogether with which to see. The primary objective in our quest for beauty is the discovery of this eye. To see anything clearly beyond the tip of one's nose, to see beyond the surface of a picture, beyond the difficult circumstances and seemingly ugly personalities, are all steps toward this objective.

". . . *the eye* of the beholder." The use of the singular—*eye* rather than *eyes*—is important. The eye that beholds beauty is the single eye, the inner spiritual one rather than the material two. Only the inner spiritual eye sees the beauty that is truthful, the truth that is so beautiful. What the spiritual eye sees is ideal, spiritual truth which, even in art and music, is entirely free of both sound and image. Spiritual truth consists of spiritual qualities—harmony, order, goodness, peace, grace, joy.

Even more important than what we see with the inner eye is what we become in the moment of inner seeing. In such a moment we become what we truly are—one with the One Mind, one with the infinite qualities of the One Mind, undivided from our source of being. When we perceive order we become orderly; when we perceive harmony, we become harmonious. Perceiving spiritual reality, our lives become spiritual, leaving no room for material limitation or discomfort. Perceiving oneness, we become one, leaving no room for conflict of any sort. Perceiving truth, we become truthful. Perceiving beauty, we become beautiful. Whatever is seen with the single eye finds expression in our lives.

How You Look Is How You Look

We are what we think
Having become what we thought
And joy follows a pure thought
Like a shadow faithfully tailing a man.
—*The Dhammapada,* trans. by P. Lal

The eye is the lamp of the body; if therefore thine eye is single, thy whole body shall be full of light.
—Matthew 6:22

I have never seen a spiritually alert individual who did not have beautiful eyes, with such spiritual qualities as kindness, merriment, and clarity. Evidently our eyes take on a look that conforms to our outlook. An individual of conventional beauty who lacks a loving, a lovely perspective may strike us as not beautiful; whereas another, less conventionally beautiful, but with a beauty-filled outlook, strikes us after all as being visibly beautiful as well. By the same token, how we regard our children is how they will come to perceive themselves. And how they perceive themselves is how they will appear.

Other People's Children

I had seen Bobby several times with his mother. She found him extremely difficult to control, trying, a great, embarrassing, unappealing burden—a fact blamed on his supposed brightness. Like his mother he was always impeccably groomed, with every hair in place. But he was demanding, brazen, and interrupted constantly—at once controlling and out of control. His eyes all the time sort of winced and flinched, evincing his own conviction that he was unacceptable.

Despite his exceptional physical handsomeness, at first I found him unattractive, too. It was hard to see the perfect child. Then one day I picked him up and gave him a lift home. "Nice day, isn't it, Bobby?" I said, secretly watching to see how love-intelligence was present in him—the unique spiritual qualities that had to be there. "Oh, boy, is it ever!" he said, and began to talk cheerfully about his love of the early spring morning—the birds, the little animals, the fresh smell of flowers and grass, the dew on the spider webs. His face was shining, and I was suddenly struck by what a wonderful, gorgeous, enthusiastic child he was. That, I thought, was a good place to begin.

The eye is not only the instrument of seeing, but also expresses and *calls forth* what is seen. Our lives can be entirely transformed by our perspective on life—and other lives blessed as well. There is, in fact, no other way for transformation to occur. In viewing both ourselves and our children we must learn to tell the difference between the work of the faker and the true old master —thereby bringing the true to light.

Realizing beauty means affirming the goodness of life. It means we are interested to see goodness expressed; and when we see beauty to try to understand what goodness it is expressing, what particular spiritual qualities. Always if we see something truly beautiful we can find God—good—behind it. It may appear in individuals or in homes or in our children or in works of art or in nature, but whenever we see real beauty it is some aspect of God, of love-intelligence coming to light.

To cultivate our ability to recognize and express and bring out beauty, we look at everything for what it signifies, to see what is of God and what is not. What are the qualities being expressed— divine spiritual ones? or not? And in seeking to express beauty ourselves we look to see what spiritual qualities need expression in which circumstances. Because then it becomes easy to recognize what will be lovely and beneficial.

> With three small children in a small apartment the family sometimes felt crowded and oppressed. It was clear that there was a need for peace and freedom. So they decorated their home around these qualities, emphasizing light and space with soft cool colors and white, with unmassive furniture—whatever contributed a sense of peace and freedom. The result was surprisingly lovely and refreshing; the whole atmosphere changed and people often commented on how spacious their apartment was.

What essential idea is being (needs to be) expressed? If peace in the bedroom, perhaps joy in the kitchen? Or, with clothing, *what spiritual qualities am I meant to express in the world? What spiritual qualities are most called for in this particular situation?* We cannot impose a good appearance on each other. We cannot get "good taste" from each other by copying. Recognizing the qualities expressed as beauty by another may indeed lead us to an equally beautiful appearance, but it will be a very different one. Because the universal has a unique way of being beautiful in each life. This is an inner thing that becomes outwardly visible through inner seeing—as an "outward and visible sign of an inward and spiritual grace." It is always original because it originates with the true origin of all beauty.

Creativity

> *Let your light so shine that men may see your good works and glorify your father which is in heaven.*
> —Matthew 5:16

> *I must be about my father's business.*
> —Luke 2:49

In seeking to fulfill our own creative potential and/or to help our children, it is good to remember that creativity is divine self-expression. This can protect us from apprenticing ourselves to the faker, and give us the privilege of watching and serving the old master at work.

Contrary to our usual impression that beauty is the artist's means of expressing himself, truly fine artists (composers, writers, dancers) are not interested in self-expression. It may start out that way as the personal ambition of child or parent, but along the way —probably over and over—that self-ish motivation has to die until the artist becomes himself the tool through which truth expresses itself as beauty. The musician must lose himself in his music. Otherwise he will never have the necessary discipline to learn his craft, nor the receptivity to be truly inspired, nor the peace of mind to present his gift to the world. Our task as seeing beings is to lose ourselves in love-intelligence.

A favorite toy of young children is the Play-Doh Fun Factory, an extruder through which amorphous modeling material is formed into a variety of shapes. Likewise when we are free of self-concern our consciousness becomes a channel through which universal love-intelligence takes unique shape. Whenever we perceive a divine quality in beautiful form it becomes ours and can take new and unique expression in our lives. If at the ballet we appreciate grace, then, without taking up ballet, we become more graceful, bringing grace into expression wherever we are, *and whatever we are doing*. We may go a long way in life without recognizing the unique shape that God is trying to take in our lives or the lives of our children. But we can be absolutely sure that as we commit ourselves unconditionally to seeing and expressing love-intelligence, our unique purpose in life will take shape as well. But first we must give up our fixed ideas, whether about our own creativity or our children's.

Two Music Lesson Lessons

For years the boy dutifully studied viola. As was expected of him, undoubting, he practiced and became quite skillful—good enough to play in a quartet and to impress as superior the audience of parents and children at recitals. Yet at fifteen, when his ability and need to make choices on his own was recognized, he surprised everyone by giving up the viola. Someone asked him why, and whether he ever expected to take it up again. "No," he replied, "I couldn't see the good of it."

* * *

Attempts were made at music lessons, but the child religiously forgot to practice or, when made to, practiced without improvement, didn't show up for band rehearsals, and lied and said that he had. Parental disappointment and childish guilt and failure hung like gloom where music was supposed to have been. Finally defeat was accepted—well, almost. For months after the lessons were abandoned, just as the child had not been able to face practicing, the mother somehow failed to find time to return the rented instrument —a shiny horn, sitting in the front hall in its dusty black case—silent, forlorn.

Meanwhile something else happened, in three parts: (1) a new car, (2) with a tape deck, (3) a commitment that placed mother and son together alone in the car each week—an hour each way. Otherwise, much of the time they were either apart with separate busy lives, or together as supervisor and supervisee, dealing with daily shoulds—homework, meals, clearing the table, wiping the counters. They had a nice, happy life, but it was a busy period. So, whereas the weekly trips might have seemed a nuisance, they proved after all to be an oasis between this and that and the other thing—and a very precious time together.

With eyes on the road, neither here nor there, moving right along, these were shouldless times, characterized by mutual regard, a sense of refuge from the world, ease, freedom, joy, peace, laughter, and love. There was an assortment of tapes from Beatles to Handel, according to the diverse tastes of the family. The mother drove the car, and the boy selected the tapes and ran the tape deck. And moving down the road, singing outrageously, he fell in love— with Pachelbel.

As the young ex-violist pointed out, the issue is to "see the good" of it. As the second child demonstrates, genuine recognition of the good cannot fail to bring about appreciation of its creative expression. We simply do not have to be concerned about what interest the child should pursue or what we are going to "make of ourselves" but only with seeing the good.

So if as seeing beings we attend a concert we are not looking enviously at what the other can do and wishing we could do it too. And if as seeing beings we compose or dance or paint we are not thinking of how we look or what others are thinking of us. Whether performing or creating or listening or looking, or mowing or cooking, our objective is the same: to see and become one with the good of God, or through wholeheartedly expressing the good of God to come to see it better.

Two Artists

My father used to tell of a newspaper vendor in Chicago's University Station. Commuters went out of their way to buy from him. As the hurrying buyer extended his hand to pay, the vendor would slap a folded paper under his arm. In this way each transaction was made without the commuter even breaking stride. I have forgotten what I saw in museums as a child—I think this story did more to help me understand true creativity than all the trips we made to art museums put together.

*   *   *

Soda jerk was hardly a grand enough name for the master he was. He even placed our orders with flair. "Ham on rye—keep off the grass" meant hold the lettuce. But his best act was to fix a Coke. Taking a glass in his left hand and scooping up a few ice cubes, he would then, with his right, pump in a little syrup, all of which was normal. The normality ceased and the marvel began as he threw the glass into the air in such a way that without spilling a drop, it turned full circle, coating the entire inside of the glass with syrup before landing right side up in his right hand—just as his left was ready to pull the soda water lever down.

The exaggerated elevation of music and art and writing and dancing as higher expressions of creativity and beauty is a by-product of Me, Inc.'s idea of doing beauty as power over others—to gain recognition and express oneself as superior. But in truth, the very act of moving a piano can be as moving as the playing of the piano.

My grandmother passed on to me her beautiful grand piano which then had to be transported across several states to my home. I did not expect to be transported in the process, but that is what happened. By phone I hired a recommended piano mover and arranged to meet him at my grandmother's house. He turned out to be a slight, 65-year-old man and arrived in a light pickup truck with an even older and slighter assistant. With all of us so far from home, there seemed no way of backing out of the deal and sending the men home, but I could not imagine these two unhefty men lifting the hefty piano. "I used to lift pianos," the fellow commented quietly. "But I gave that up years ago." With absolute understanding they obeyed and harnessed every physical law to maximum advantage. With only one brief exchange of words and no visible strain whatever the two men removed the legs, swaddled the piano, and without even the benefit of an hydraulic lift, guided and glided the enormous piano onto their truck and secured it for travel in less than fifteen minutes. It was a ballet! A masterwork. Pure love-intelligence did the job—and it was lovely to see. (Sometime later I witnessed three men, half as old and twice as strong, move the same piano by brain and brawn. They removed more pieces from the piano to make it light and, using twice as much equipment and six times the muscle, succeeded in loading the piano onto their truck in four times as long. The piano was slightly damaged in the process, and one of the men strained his back.)

Parenthood and Creativity

Sometimes we experience the demands of parenthood as an interruption in our "creative" lives. But parenthood is an unmatched opportunity for growing in beauty and creativity.

First of all, our children are models of how it is that beauty takes place. As long as they remain fairly unselfconscious they are drawn and driven by beauty; in this way they express it creatively and like Moses coming from the mountain are made radiantly beautiful by it. Even before they learn to speak in words, they talk in music; and dancing is not recreation for them, it's the only way to travel. Nothing is so beautiful as the way a child's face lights up at a sudden encounter with beauty.

Secondly, as we strive to bring goodness to our children we are forced to understand it ever more clearly and thus enabled to bring it into ever more creative expression. A special beauty comes of this and, whether or not we have previously identified them, our unique gifts are developed more and more.

A portrait-painter said, "I acquired most of the skill I needed years ago. But to be a real artist I had to come to see what makes a painting beautiful. Learning to love my children made all the difference."

Another spiritually alert artist was going to town on some errands with her three-and-a-half-year-old son along. She suggested to the child that they might look for beauty on their walk. "Perhaps you might collect some beautiful things and make a collage when we get home," she said.

It was autumn. There were many beautiful things everywhere. Leaves, acorns, and a crumpled red and white striped package caught the child's attention. As they trudged back up the hill toward home, the boy became increasingly awed by all the beauty-full things that lay on the ground for him to pick up.

"Look, Mommy," he cried as he scrambled back and forth across the path. "This is beautiful. And this is beautiful. And this is beautiful. And this is beautiful! Why I could pick up everything for my collage." Then suddenly his attention was lifted from the many beautiful things on the ground to an entire, outstandingly beautiful tree, aflame with autumn colors. He stood still and stared. "Oh, Mommy," he said softly. "The whole world is beautiful. There is nothing to be afraid of."

In an uplifted moment the child encounters, beyond the pleasing sights themselves, their deeper significance. Through beauty he encounters life as good, and the good is recognized as true, wiping away his fear that there is anything bad in reality.

Perfect love casteth out fear.
—John 4:18

As freedom is clearly related to fundamental intelligence, beauty is kindred to love. Freedom is a function of the fact that life is orderly; beauty expresses the fact that this order is good. Intelligence is cause, love its effect, beauty its aspect. Again consider the drinking glass, which gets its curved beauty through conforming to and expressing the inner purpose of the glass as a vessel. So does fundamental love-intelligence manifest itself beautifully and uniquely through each individual consciousness.

When old age shall this generation waste,
 Thou shalt remain, in midst of other woe
Than ours, a friend to man, to whom thou sayst,
"Beauty is truth, truth beauty,"—that is all
 Ye know on earth, and all ye need to know.
—John Keats, from "Ode on a Grecian Urn"

Beauty and Spiritual Growth

Beauty is the point at which seeing becomes being. Once beauty is understood as the good of God, expressing beauty becomes a nonpersonal way of changing the subject from ourselves to God. We do not have to know how to do beauty, only to be aware of and devoted to expressing spiritual qualities. The simple commitment to recognizing and expressing goodness for goodness' sake places us in the position where goodness itself can take charge and make itself plain. Beauty is the inevitable sign of an even greater blessing: the realization of our oneness with divine love-intelligence.

Daily, indeed moment by moment, we have the choice of expressing ourselves or God. Whatever we put in charge of one moment determines the quality of the next. If desire, feelings, ambition, and power are put in charge, dishevelment, ugliness, and no creative inspiration ensue. But if love-intelligence is put in charge of one moment, then beauty and creativity are inevitable. One beautiful love-intelligent moment leads to another.

The Parent as a Beautifying Influence

1. The Parent as a Model. The parent is a paintbrush through which God paints a picture of himself. For such a parent, beauty is a high priority as the evidence of God's goodness. As a seeing being he endeavors to be beautiful and to beautify the home through paying attention and calling attention to the spiritual qualities which are the good of God. Whether through personal appearance or creative activity or grateful enjoyment and appreciation, he expresses a constant love of beauty. He recognizes that expression of spiritual good is both the means and meaning of beauty. He is characteristically grateful, joyful, gracious, lovely, loving, graceful, and thoughtful.

2. The Parent as Beholder. Insofar as we behold our children as seeing beings rather than our own more or less pretty reflections and more or less talented creations, it becomes evident that each child is both uniquely beautiful and gifted. The essential spiritual goodness of the child is constantly kept in the forefront of our thoughts. Smiling to them readily, presenting them with beauty often, we assume, recognize, honor, and welcome forth this goodness, allowing it to take whatever surprising, unique, and beautiful shape it surely will.

3. The Parent as Preparer of the Lovely Way. Instead of being a slave to appearance or ambitious for creative recognition, the parent joins the child in recognizing and celebrating the good of God as it can be expressed in everyday activity. Nothing is regarded as more or less creative. Every activity is approached as an opportunity to see, rejoice in, and bring spiritual values into expression as beauty. So we look for and silently appreciate spiritual values in everything the child does and express our appreciation of them in everything we do with the child (not necessarily verbally).

4. The Parent as Landscaper of the Beautiful Environment. Everything in the home is arranged so as to bring spiritual goodness to light as beauty. Whether in laying out her clothes or decorating the house or arranging her toys or serving meals we bring the child opportunities to encounter and participate in spiritual values as beauty. Whenever possible, beauty is expressed not to impress others but to make God's love intelligible. Joy, simplicity, originality, variety, grace, order, peace, and love emerge as qualities of the home, setting the stage for all who enter within to exclaim, "Oh, how cheerful! How peaceful! What a lovely idea!"

5. The Parent as Teacher. "Creative activity" is introduced as a medium for seeing and celebrating spiritual good. Music and art, whether as lessons or projects or experiences, are approached not with the idea of making the child (or parent) look or do good, but with the idea of helping the child encounter and see and participate in the good of God. How to help and when to show what become clear. Also evident in this light is the fact that it is as well to avoid much praise as it is to avoid criticism.

In the beginning, at least, discovery is both the child's objective and her reward. The child does not seek *personal* praise at first; rather, all her activity is directed toward learning. Understanding is the reward that brings the child delight, and it is understanding alone that will most facilitate her existence.

Personal praise is a distraction. If we teach our children that praise is any reward at all, we are in fact impeding their learning progress by encouraging self-consciousness and the growth of Me, Inc. Through praise we may be able to get them to *do* more, but only at the costly expense of perverting their motive. Each time they turn *to* us for praise, they turn *from* their learning. And worst of all, in fostering a desire for self-acclaim, we have introduced the possibility of self-doubt. In this way an appetite for praise and self-acclaim develops that will be less and less easy to satisfy as the child grows. Sooner or later it is almost inescapable that some of both will creep into the child's motivation, but it is not necessary to introduce these elements prematurely, and it is possible to minimize them when they do come.

What then must we offer our children as they endeavor to learn (be it music, art, dressing themselves, or whatever)? Enthusiasm, love, gratitude! *Wonderful!* we can say. *How beautiful! What a nice thing to do! You must be so happy to see it turn out that way! How bright that picture is! How happy that looks! . . . Oh, see how nicely those lines go around together. . . . That is wonderfully straight! This picture is so graceful. Thank you for showing me!*

To the child, shared discovery and appreciation of what is beautiful is worth ten times more than personal praise and actually furthers creative growth where praise (by distracting) stunts it. (See also pages 124 and 205–206.)

6. The Parent as Art Supplier. The parent who is aware of the importance of beauty is able to supply the child with appropriate materials, equipment, and opportunities to help him grow in his ability to appreciate and express beauty. The two eyes and ears must be well trained before the true eye and the true ear can be awakened. "Practical Information for New Parents" at the end of this chapter is devoted to this process. Broken arbitrarily into separate sections on music and art, the main guidelines are invitation and letting be. There are not a lot of things to buy, though it is good for art supplies, records, and tapes to be abundant, since they are vehicles for invitation, education, and inspiration. Letting be is harder, but awareness of the child's quest for beauty helps to guide us in how to help and not help, and how not to interfere or deter.

Then I said, "I covet truth;
Beauty is unripe childhood's cheat;
I leave it behind with the games of youth";—
As I spoke, beneath my feet
The ground-pine curled its pretty wreath,
I inhaled the violet's breath;
Around me stood the oaks and firs;
Pine-cones and acorns lay on the ground;
Over me soared the eternal sky,
Full of light and of deity;
Again I say, again I heard,
The rolling river, the morning bird;—
Beauty through my senses stole;
I yielded myself to the perfect whole.
—Ralph Waldo Emerson, "Each and All"

I hearing get who had but ears,
   And sight, who had but eyes before,
I moments live who lived but years,
   And truth discern who knew but learning's lore.

I hear beyond the range of sound,
   I see beyond the range of sight,
New earths and skies and seas around,
   And in my day the sun doth pale his light.
—Henry David Thoreau, "Inspiration"

Practical Information for New Parents

This "Practical Information" section deals with art, music, and poetry for very young children. Parents of older children may be interested in "No Such Thing as Tone Deaf" (page 267), before proceeding to Chapter 7 (page 275).

Art: Dwelling in Loveliness

When Nancy, a beloved high-school babysitter, returned from a trip to the Far East, she brought one of her small charges a gift: an unusually beautiful, hand-made bamboo box with a lovely painting of a tiny bird on it. Every detail of the box was exquisite. It was even lined with a highly polished veneer of bamboo. What an unusual gift for such a young child! The parents were somewhat puzzled.

On Nancy's next visit she took the child on a long walk in a city park. Some time after she had gone home, the parents happened to look in the box. Inside were two beautiful heart-shaped leaves from a beech tree. Now the parents understood. The box had been given with the idea of helping the little boy to come to an early, conscious appreciation of beauty.

Be sure to hang something pretty and moving over the crib and changing table—a lightweight *mobile*, out of reach, suspended from a cloth-backed stick'em hook. Mobiles can be purchased in many places, or you can make them yourself. The more they move the better. And it's nice to change them from time to time. Be sure to give some thought to the baby's perspective. Most paper mobiles are nearly invisible when viewed from below. Either choose ones that are best viewed from below or else hang them to the side or over the foot of the crib rather than directly above the baby's face. To add mobility to any mobile, tie it to a small swivel clip (used in fishing tackle). In fact, if you have one of these hanging from the ceiling at a good height, it will be very easy to switch mobiles from time to time without the use of a ladder.

Transparent plastic envelopes with safe, rounded corners can be bought in most dime and office supply stores. These make excellent prebooks. Put bright pictures, postcards, wrapping paper, or photos inside and change them from time to time. With the youngest babies, high-contrast black-and-white designs seem to be most easily perceivable and interesting. Wonderful for the baby on his tummy. It won't roll out of reach, and it isn't uncomfortable if he gets tired of holding up his head and puts his face down on it.

Pictures on the wall: Some of the best windows to the world and beyond for wide, young eyes are the pictures hung on the nursery wall. It is here, during those most private moments on both ends of a nap, that little children may take their first solo flights, examining and memorizing every detail of each picture, stepping through the frame and traveling into the world and beyond.

Not all the pictures in a child's room should be childish. Besides the many prints and posters available specifically for children, we can be grateful for the availability of reproductions of great masterpieces. Choose nothing that might be scary, for the painting last viewed before the child's eyes fall closed must surely sometimes accompany him into his dreams. Peace, beauty, joy, harmony—again, these are what to look for in selecting a painting or reproduction for a child's room. The beauty he lives with will become the beauty he appreciates when he grows up. Landscapes seem particularly appropriate.

Except for a few really lovely pictures which may remain a permanent part of a child's room, most pictures should be changed fairly often, as the child learns all she can from them or moves to new interests. Keep her eye level in mind when hanging pictures. Hang some close to the floor in a hallway for the crawling baby.

Arts and Crafts

Though they sometimes require more parental supervision than toys, hardly anything is quite so fruitful, fulfilling, absorbing, and inexpensive as crayons, felt-tip pens, Play-Doh, watercolors, finger paints, etc. Crayons and Play-Doh can be introduced anytime beginning around one year, and the rest according to your child's readiness and your willingness to cope. Be willing. Set things up so that you don't have to be defensive about walls and furniture. This means either sticking close by or putting the child in some place where disasters are improbable. For the very youngest the highchair is good and augments concentration. Try the bathtub for finger-painting. As he grows, having his own table will be handy and an easel wonderful.

This section is not a complete guide on arts and crafts. Many more ideas and instructions can be found in the books on pages 142–145 (especially, *I Saw a Purple Cow and 100 Other Recipes for Learning; Making Things; What to Do When "There's Nothing to Do"; Three, Four, Open the Door*). Here are just a few ideas to get the ball rolling.

Crayons. Store these safely out of reach if you aren't fond of interior graffiti, but make them available any time after about one year. Don't make a big deal out of broken crayons or peeled ones or even eaten ones. One book suggests peeling and breaking in two all crayons before starting to use them, claiming that half of a peeled crayon is the most useful crayon in the first place.

Good old crayons are fine. A small set is as good as, if not better than, a big one. But for preschoolers you may also like the hexagonal ones that don't roll off the table, or extra-fat ones that make fat lines and can be fist-held.

Don't start by suggesting that the object is to draw something. Making a picture that represents something is a much later stage and will come (and perhaps also go) of its own accord. Just demonstrate things like dots! wiggles! lines! scribbles! If you take up a crayon at all, let it be to share with your child the discovery of *what happens when you do this with that*? Sometimes the child will be most interested in what he is doing with his hands; sometimes he will pay attention to the colors. After a while he will begin to *read* his pictures. "Hey!" said a two-year-old, "I drew many tiny fingers!" Try to see what he is trying to see and appreciate the discovery.

Felt-tip pens are highly satisfying for preschoolers because the colors flow onto the paper so easily and so brilliantly. Get the fat kind, and make sure the inks are washable. By the way, washable doesn't mean that it comes off with a quick sponging or hand washing, but it does come off "by tomorrow" (a couple of hand washings and a bath) and comes off clothes in a washing machine.

It's well to begin early to teach the idea of putting the tops back on, but since felt tips will dry out if left open for extended periods, be prepared to help a lot. If he is interested in his work, he will forget to put the tops on—be glad for the interest. And for the older preschool child indelible markers are wonderful for decorating Easter eggs or drawing on wood.

Finger painting. Recipes for finger paint are included in several of the books listed at the end of Chapter 3. Small finger-paint sets are generally not worth the money. You need a lot of paint to make one painting, and the small sets have a lot of box and very little paint. Maybe homemade paints are the answer, but large quart and pint jars of finger paint are available from most big art-supply stores for a good bit less than your time is probably worth.

Some very glossy paper is necessary, either special finger-painting paper or glossy freezer or shelf paper.

At first many children hesitate to put their hands in the goo.

Why, tell me, why? They are so willing to cover themselves with food! Anyway, don't insist. Just demonstrate the joys of finger painting yourself, put the paints away, and hang your painting up. You may even have to do this more than once before the child finally dares to dig in. Here's how:

- Wet the paper by dipping it in water or soaking both sides with a wet sponge.
- Place the paper on a large baking pan or edged cookie sheet to confine the mess.
- Spoon a tablespoon of paint, or lesser amounts of different colors, onto the paper.
- Spread the paint around with hands or forearms and then paint in it (you could say "unpaint") with fingers. That's the conventional way. Sometimes it's nicer and a little less messy to put a spoonful of each color on a plate or paint tray and dip and paint with single fingertips.

Tempera paints tend to be more successful than finger paints with preschoolers at home. (To be perfectly honest I found that nursery school was a better environment for finger painting than home.) This is another thing you can make yourself from dry pigments, but not very successfully unless you buy tempera medium and use a blender . . . once for each color—let's see now, that's— You figure it out. It may well be cheaper and easier to buy unbreakable plastic pints of premixed paint.

A good way to introduce tempera painting to a one-and-a-half or two-year-old is one color at a time. When more colors are used, it is well to have a separate brush for each. It is also advisable not to put big jars before the child until the idea of not mixing colors in the jars is fairly well understood. Use smaller jars (baby food, junior size, is perfect), lidded juice cans, muffin tins, or paint pans.

Watercolors. For sheer pleasure, ease, and inexpensiveness hardly any paints can equal a small cheap set of watercolors. It is surprising how early a child can learn to dip the brush in the water before touching it to a new cake of color. To make it easier, put a few drops of water on each color before the very young child starts to paint. During most paint sessions the temptation to run the brush across the whole box of colors, playing it like a xylophone, is irresistible. But no matter, the paints can be cleaned off (more economically with a damp paper towel than under running water), and it will soon be time to buy a new set anyway. We can afford to be generous regarding anything that offers so much quiet, constructive activity so inexpensively.

Paper. If possible, never be in a position in which you have to refuse a child a piece of paper. Keep a small pad or notebook and perhaps a set of colored mini-pencils in your purse, and have a big pad of newsprint and a stack of construction paper at home. A big roll of shelf paper is wonderful. Trace the whole child and let her decorate herself. Shelf paper makes good wrapping paper, adequate finger-painting paper, and a giant surface for all kinds of creative activity on the wall or floor. On a rainy afternoon invite another child over. Spread out enough shelf paper so that they can sit on it and make drawings all over the place. Draw a landscape for play: railroad tracks for a toy train, fences to keep in toy animals, roads for cars, airstrips for airplanes. Build houses out of blocks beside the roads. Hang a big sheet in the hall and let every member of the family who wants to add something to the mural. From smaller sheets of paper make books for your child to fill in. Use newsprint, note cards, shirt cards, paper bags; brown wrapping paper is beautiful to paint on. Just don't run out of paper.

Easels. A good easel is a worthwhile purchase, if only because it makes painting so much easier on the parent and therefore more available to the child. Some are also chalk boards. Painting on a back-to-back easel is a pleasant way for two not-yet-quite-socialized youngsters to be together happily and busily—also nice for siblings to share. Compact wall easels are also available. But you don't have to buy something expensive; you can improvise or buy a modified version, trying to meet as many of the qualifications listed as you conveniently can.

Chalk board. A chalk board is a must. The kitchen is a nice place for one—with a high stool beside it. It's easy enough to draw a picture or write a message for the child while you're waiting for something to come to a boil, and she will enjoy drawing and, in a minute, learning to form letters by your side. If you like, hang another one low down in a hall or on her bedroom wall.

Modeling materials. In the beginning (between one and two years) a soft play dough (commercially manufactured or home-made) is best, as most nonhardening clays are too stiff for young children to work with. Better not to insist that he make something (though it's perfectly all right for you to make things for him); just help him to find out what he can do with the clay—squeeze it, poke it, pinch it, stick Tinkertoys in it, cut it, scratch it. Make a slide for him that a bunch of little balls will roll down. Give him an egg slicer, dull knife, rolling pin, apple slicer, and some of the Play-Doh Shapemakers and the Play-Doh Fun Factory, an extruder for forcing modeling dough into various shapes.

When, at around three years old, he becomes interested in "making things," a slightly stiffer modeling material is nice, since dough models tend to slump and sag.

Printing with a pad. Printing with a real ink stamp pad is fun, though fairly indelible. A large office-size stamp pad is more satisfactory than a small one. Try brushing tempera paint onto the stamp. For stamps try anything. All kinds of vegetables are great (dry them with a paper towel first). Or try pressing a leaf to the pad and then on paper. To avoid fingerprints, use two index cards for this: one to press the leaf to the stamp pad, one to press the inked leaf to the paper. These cards are also very nice for printing on. If you use a big sheet of paper you tend to wind up with just a hodgepodge of stamped impressions, some good, some bad, but all in all not worth hanging up.

Printing with a brayer. One way is to take a still-very-wet painting and cover it with a clean piece of paper the same size but placed at a different angle. Roll the brayer back and forth to make a print. One picture may not be much, but (especially if the print is in a position on its piece of paper different from the original) the two mounted and hung together may look terrific.

An alternative method is to scratch a picture with a nail into a block of soap or very soft balsa wood. Roll the brayer in some water-base printing ink (from any art-supply store) on a smooth surface (a piece of glass or a metal tray). If you don't have printing ink, you can try thick paint. Roll the inked brayer over the etched surface of wood or soap. Make a print on the paper. Experiment. Usually it works best to put the paper onto the block, but you may find it better sometimes to work the other way around. Try rubbing the back of the paper with a spoon while it is in contact with the inked block. Thin ¼-inch sheets of balsa can often be purchased in art-supply stores; they are ideal for small children, even less than three years old.

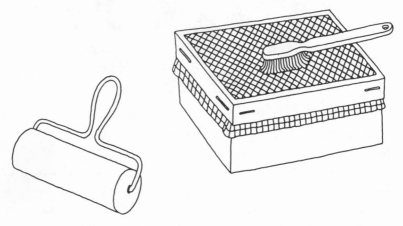

Printing with a screen. Cut the lid of a small cardboard box so that only the sides and a little bit of the top remain intact. Inside the box top place a piece of window screen (larger than the top) and staple it securely to the sides of the top. Place a piece of paper with a cutout or object on it in the bottom of the box and put the screened top on the box. Dip a toothbrush in paint and scrub it across the screen until the object has been silhouetted.

Rubbings. Go on a texture hunt with a piece of paper and a crayon or a pencil. Sidewalk, brick wall, wooden table, tree trunk, the bottom of a pair of rubber boots, leaf, the bathroom floor.

Skill building. An hour of cutting, folding, stapling, or punching holes in paper will prove to be of lasting value. To the child who is just ready to learn (in fact, even slightly before he can manage) scissoring is an activity in itself—not for making anything, just scissoring for the sake of scissoring. Partly it is the joy of simply using a tool, and this could therefore be listed under unity just as well as beauty. But of course the skill is one that will be useful in many art projects as the child grows.

Trashcan sculpture. Make trains, houses, boats, and free-form sculptures by gluing saved-up cardboard tubes and boxes together. As another activity, paint them.

Wooden sculpture. Buy a bag of wooden parts or some wood scraps from a lumber yard, and let the child glue them together into a structure or sculpture. The results are usually quite pretty. They may be left plain or, as another activity, painted. With a little extra parental help and some parts from a hardware store, a nice lamp for a child's bedside could be made this way.

Sand painting. Dye some sand with food coloring in paper cups. Spread the colored sand out on paper plates to dry in the sun (or plan to wait a little longer before actually sand painting). Draw or paint with glue on paper, and sprinkle the colored sand over the glue (one color at a time). Shake off the excess sand. Elmer's glue drawings result in Jackson Pollock-type pictures. Brushed-on glue or paste yields more surface-covered pictures (à la watercolor landscape). This is a perfectly wonderful activity, much nicer in many ways than finger painting. The results are beautiful. Children as young as a year and a half can begin to do it. It is such a satisfying activity for most children that it is worthwhile to dye enough sand in the summer to last through the winter.

Collage bin. Keep a bin of everything glueable—jar tops, beads, cartons, tree bark, etc. Collecting and sorting these can be as enjoyable as later working with them. Try to arrange it so that by age three, if he is interested, your child knows how and is allowed to work with these materials at will and without supervision. Only simple procedural experience and equipment are necessary.

- A table to work at and, if necessary, a covering to protect the table.
- An apron to protect clothing.
- A sponge for spills and some training in wetting, wiping, rinsing, and squeezing out.
- A place to put finished works for drying.
- A place for trash.
- The obvious: glue, paste, scissors, paper.

The Whole Point Anyway

While creative freedom in artwork is crucial and should even be counted sacred for children, it is important that sloppiness not become a factor. There is one basic principle that can help to avoid this: the valuing of beauty as it is sought and expressed in their work—not as accomplishment, not as pretty good for a little kid, but as beautiful. It isn't silly to say that the work of these little ones is beautiful. It is only necessary to develop an appreciation of ideal beauty to find beauty in children's art. Spontaneous motion, brilliance of light and color, and striking form are often clearly present in the drawings and paintings of unhindered children.

The fact that you value the work enough to hang it encourages the child regarding his ability to express beauty. Having truly seen what is lovely in a particular picture, you will rejoice to hang it—not just to make your child feel good, but because it is lovely and you would like to see it on your wall.

Mount the child's painting so as to set off the beauty as clearly as possible. (Since children are prolific, you may wish to have a frame or two in which to change pictures from time to time.) Some children's paintings also make nice gift wrapping. Use a finished painting or wrap a gift in white shelf paper and invite the child to decorate it with felt-tip pens. It looks nice, and children like to participate this way in the giving.

Sometimes after painting happily for a while, a child becomes aimless and sloppy in his work and begins obviously messing around. Perhaps all that is needed is a little companionship or a little help. See if he can tell you what he is trying to do, or just work beside him for a minute, focusing appreciatively on whatever beauty may be taking place.

If restlessness persists despite the arrival of a little helpful companionship, clean up immediately. He may be through, or it may be the wrong moment for this project. Whenever beauty isn't happening beautifully, it's time to stop. Always try to finish and thoroughly clean up while the spirit is happy.

When a craft project is being undertaken with specific results expected, make sure that the activity is something the child can do and that the end product will work. In a summer craft class for preschoolers the project for one day was to make hats out of paper plates. The children worked all morning gluing things to the plates and painting them and decorating them according to their individual inspirations. But when the strings attached to the hats were tied under the chins of the little milliners the hats fell off. Nothing short of glue could have made those hats stay aboard the silky heads.

Lots of things can be done with scraps and trash, but the results should never be trashy. The children in the above story would probably have been quite happy with the fruits of their work if they had understood that they were making something to hang rather than something to wear. It is one thing to make a pile of scraps while practicing how to use scissors, but when the objective is to make something or create something beautiful the end product should work (if that's what it's supposed to do) or be beautiful (if that's what it's supposed to be). With crafts this involves careful planning and paying attention to the readiness of the child to do the work required and to the prospects of getting a worthwhile result.

Music: Going Forth with Joy

For ye shall go out with joy, and be led forth in peace; the mountains and the hills before you shall break forth into singing and all the trees of the fields shall clap their hands.
—Isaiah 55:12

Just Listening In

Crib bell. One family had a bronze wind chime from Japan hanging over their son's crib almost from the first day they brought him home. He obviously loved its musical sound. The only thing they had found to hang it from was so low that the chime's paper sail was within reach of his foot. After a week or two he began accidentally ringing the bell, usually when he cried or was excited. This surprised and pleased him so much that he often stopped in mid-cry to listen. He came to notice that there was a connection between his excitement and the lovely sound. They could see him working on the problem. Gradually he discovered that general movement, and then specifically kicking, was what did the trick. Before long, as his vision sharpened, he began moving around and grabbing the sail with his hand. Then they had to change to a sturdier bell and cord. From then on he announced nearly all his wakings by ringing instead of by crying.

Music box. This is one of those things you will probably receive five of as gifts or not any. It is nice to have one to wind up and play for stilling moments. (String-operated ones tend to break.)

Tapes and records. These are invaluable and unsurpassed in the many contributions they make to children through music. A lively tune well performed inspires the child to dance, and it is through movement after all that the child can first really participate in and feel the music. Constant exposure to recorded songs not only helps develop musical skills and appreciation, but also aids in language and concept development. And through listening to records, parents and children easily learn songs together. You don't have to be musical, you don't even have to try; eventually you discover you know the songs. Recordings are more effective than television in eliciting active participation and, of course, with recordings you have the advantage of being able to select what your child hears, at least until he goes to school.

There are many musical toys and instruments to buy for very small children (drums, pianos, horns, etc.), all fine to introduce at some point. But for a start for a baby, a bell and a music box seem sufficient. Wait until the real singing and dancing begin before adding other things.

Children especially appreciate times of singing and dancing together when the harmony of music becomes the harmony of people together. It is a special kind of wealth to a small child to see his parents join with other adults and children to sing some of the songs he knows and even dance together. Sometimes you can see a child's face become positively radiant with happy amazement on witnessing such a wonder for the first time. Such things can't and mustn't be forced, but if they occur without too much self-consciousness they're nice—just one family or two, the children jumping for joy, the parents for love. Then you might want some rhythm instruments. Pots and pans, spoons and forks, sticks and stones, etc., ad infinitum, will be perfectly adequate, but, if you really get going, a selection of well-made rhythm instruments adds a lot.

Private concerts. Ask (hire? invite?) neighboring grade-school children who are learning to play musical instruments to come and show their instruments to your preschooler and play a little tune or a scale. Ask the older child if he will let your child touch his instrument and perhaps even try to play it. "Maybe you could blow, while she pushes down one of the keys?" Musicales are coming back, too. Several families can get together—take turns performing and then have dessert. A Christmas concert with carol singing too? Tape it and play it back each year to hear the progress!

Chiming In

No Such Thing as Tone Deaf

When the boy was small he was fascinated by music, especially songs. Folk songs, musical comedies captivated him. He listened so intently that he would memorize entire records within only a day or so. Yet he did not carry a tune. His mother did not believe in tone deafness. She thought, *There is no such thing as tone deaf. He is perfectly endowed with every gift that God is.* Then she thought, *But if there were such a thing as tone deaf he would be a perfect example of it.* One day he said, "How come when everyone else sings it sounds like singing; but when I sing it sounds like talking?" That settled it. There was nothing tone deaf about him. On the contrary he clearly heard and appreciated the notes perfectly. But because he could not exactly match what he heard he hadn't been trying. "Don't worry," she said. "You'll learn." Sure enough, very soon the tune "came in," and he has been singing and playing ever since. Too many people labeled tone deaf as children remain so all their lives, never developing the skill of matching heard tones, never realizing the joy of music. Such a waste! To label a child tone deaf is like labeling a baby speechless simply because he can only say "goo."

Everyone knows that there's nothing like a verse or a song and the will to sing for turning a gloomy, boring, or struggling moment into a cheerful one.

A song at bedtime, a rhyme to shake hands by, a tune with ten verses for long trips—all of these can have a cheering and harmonizing effect on our daily affairs with our children; and they all suggest to our children that life is something worth singing about. When a child hears words that both rhyme and make sense he is finding order and harmony in a world that often to his young eyes must seem pretty helter-skelter.

Repeated rhymes and songs aid a child in his speech and vocabulary development, and help train his ear for an earlier, fuller experience of music. Even more, they add to his impression that joy and harmony are real possibilities and important priorities in life. All that—just for a song!

Poetry Books

> Catch Me and Kiss Me and Say It Again, by Clyde Watson, illustrated by Wendy Watson. When you feed your child a snack, lift her down from a high place, pick her up from a tumble, a rhyme can always help to make light of it or make the most of it— whatever is called for. And this book is full of such rhymes, to celebrate your youngster's life with a little extra love and joy. One Mother Goose sounding rhyme for almost every ordinary thing a child might do. Indispensable. Collins, 0–4 years.

> A Child's Garden of Verses, by Robert Louis Stevenson, illustrated by Erik Blegvad. Twenty-four of Stevenson's most charming and beloved poems about childhood made accessible to the young child through Blegvad's illustrations. Random House, 4–6 years.

> Each Peach Pear Plum, by Janet and Allan Ahlberg. "Each peach pear plum. I spy Tom Thumb." And now you try to find Tom in the

lovely full-color illustration. Children love to search the pictures to find favorite nursery book characters. Simple rollicking verse also tumbles easily into memory and can provide the basis for many "I spy" games with young ones. At first glance a quick and simple book, *Each Peach Pear Plum* has layers of value for the preschooler. Scholastic, 2–4 years.

Father Fox's Pennyrhymes, By Clyde Watson, illustrated by Wendy Watson.

> *Let the fall leaves fall*
> *And the cold snow snow*
> *And the rain rain rain till April;*
> *Our coats are warm*
> *And the pantry's full*
> *And there's cake upon the table.*

Whacky, joyful, grateful rhymes accompany charming pictures to depict the country life of a huge fox family. Written and illustrated by two talented sisters, *Father Fox's Pennyrhymes* contagiously transmits the happy spirit of their Vermont childhood. Definitely a book to grow up with. The perfect sequel (although this one was written first) to *Catch Me and Kiss Me and Say It Again.* Crowell, 4 years and up.

Nibble Nibble, by Margaret Wise Brown, illustrated by Leonard Weisgard.

> *One by one the leaves fall down*
> *From the sky come falling one by one*
> *And leaf by leaf the summer is done*
> *One by one by one by one.*

> *If you go to the library for a poetry anthology you will find many good ones to choose from, but you might not happen to meet this little collection of poems by Margaret Wise Brown, that lady who knew almost better than anyone how to talk (in a whisper, of course) to little children. If you've ever been grateful for Goodnight Moon, The Sailor Dog, The Little Fur Family, or The Golden Egg Book, you may want to give this collection a try.* Young Scott, 4–6 years.

This Little Puffin, by Elizabeth Matterson.

> *Round and round the garden*
> *(Run your index finger round the baby's palm.)*
> *Went the Teddy Bear,*
> *One step,*
> *Two steps,*
> *(Jump your finger up his arm.)*

Tickly under there.
(Tickle him under his arm.)

Round and round the haystack
Went the little mouse,
One step,
Two steps,
In his little house.

(Repeat the same actions for the second verse.)

A good collection of musical games, action songs, and finger plays. The finger plays are especially useful with very young children and do not require musical skills on the part of the parent. Penguin Books.

William Blake's Inn, by Nancy Willard, illustrated by Alice and Martin Provensen. Having fallen in love with Blake's poetry as a child, Nancy Willard has written a book of poems about life at an imaginary inn run by Blake himself. With dragons that bake bread and a bear for a bed portrayed by the Provensens, *William Blake's Inn* is a world of its own, and a rich and cultured one, too. Though not really a book for preschoolers, it is that sort of rare, magical book that is good for a child to grow into and up with, beginning with whatever catches his fancy and going on forever. Harcourt Brace Jovanovich, all ages.

Song Books

If you have not learned to read music, don't buy song books that contain many unfamiliar songs. On the other hand, don't think you have to be able to play the piano or the guitar to use a song book with your child. Just sit down on the sofa with a nicely illustrated song book and sing. Even if you do play the piano, this sofa system is often much more harmonious with the littlest ones, who otherwise insist on helping you to play the piano. One mother found that using a back carrier made it possible to have some wonderful singing and playing times at the piano with her very young child. He was happy up there, where he could see and sit comfortably and rock to the music with his mother. Quite often that was how he fell asleep at night.

In buying a song book remember that size is not necessarily

an advantage and may even be a drawback if you have to spend five or ten minutes between songs hunting for another that you know. Look for singable songs, with (if you also play) arrangements that are at once musical and not more difficult than you can play and not too hopelessly out of your singing range. With traditional songs, be sure that most of the tunes in the book are the traditional ones.

A vast number of song books are available for young children. Some of the best are really better suited to group work than to the home; they contain songs that are just right for nursery schools but that you wouldn't be so inclined to sing around the house. Most of the books listed below have been selected partly on the basis of their usefulness in the home, where singing is more spontaneous.

> *The Fireside Book of Children's Songs,* compiled by Marie Winn, musical arrangements by Allan Miller, illustrated by John Alcorn. An excellent selection of songs that appeal to children—67 of them divided into chapters: Good Morning and Goodnight, Birds and Beasts, Nursery, Silly, and Singing Games and Rounds. The rather stylized art is less appealing to youngsters than the songs themselves. Guitar chords and easy piano arrangements. Simon & Schuster.
>
> *The Fireside Book of Folk Songs,* compiled by Margaret Bradford Boni, piano arrangements by Norman Lloyd, illustrated by Alice and Martin Provensen. This is the best book of folk songs for the whole family that we have seen. Includes traditional ballads, work songs, Christmas carols, marching songs, hymns, and spirituals. Easily playable, musical piano accompaniments and guitar chords. Simon & Schuster.
>
> *The Golden Song Book,* selected and arranged by Katharine Tyler Wessells, illustrated by Kathy Allert. All the best-loved nursery songs, with pleasantly simple yet musical piano arrangements plus guitar chords. Golden Press.
>
> *Jim Along, Josie,* compiled by Nancy and John Langstaff, illustrated by Jan Pienkowski. A perfectly superb selection of 81 singable, danceable, versatile folk songs and singing games for young children at home or in groups. Simple, *musical* piano arrangements by Seymour Barab. Guitar chords by Happy Traum. Lovely, unusual, black-and-white silhouette illustrations. Harcourt Brace Jovanovich.

> *Lullabies and Night Songs,* music by Alec Wilder, illustrated by Maurice
> Sendak. Some of Sendak's finest work illustrates this lovely
> book of new and rearranged traditional lullabies. Harper &
> Row.
> *Playtime with Music,* lyrics and text by Marion Abeson, music and
> arrangements by Charity Bailey, illustrated by Sally Michel.
> Sixteen fine songs that are just right for preschoolers to dance
> to and act out. Liveright.
> *Wee Sing,* by Pamela Conn Beall and Susan Hagen Nipp. Two former
> music teachers compiled this excellent collection of more than
> 70 children's songs and finger plays, together with the actions
> and music. Sing your way through a whole childhood of car
> trips, rainy days, birthday parties, and other happy times.
> Price/Stern/Sloan.

There are a number of picture books that are simply illustrated
editions of single children's songs. As a picture book editor I never
particularly appreciated the picture books that illustrate single
songs. But as a parent I discovered that they can be a source of
great delight to young children who have learned the songs but
often do not understand the lyrics and who, in any case, like to see
more about something already familiar. Some fine ones to look for
are:

> *The Erie Canal,* by Peter Spier, Doubleday.
> *The Foolish Frog,* by Pete Seeger and Charles Seeger, Macmillan.
> *The Fox Went Out on a Chilly Night,* by Peter Spier, Doubleday.
> *Frog Went A-Courtin',* introduction by John Langstaff, Harcourt Brace
> Jovanovich.
> *Hush Little Baby,* illustrated by Aliki, Prentice-Hall.
> *London Bridge Is Falling Down,* by Peter Spier, Doubleday.
> *Old Macdonald Had a Farm,* by Pam Adams, Child's Play.
> *People in My Family,* by Jeffrey Moss, Golden Press.
> *To Market, To Market,* by Peter Spier, Doubleday.
> *There Were Ten in the Bed,* by Pam Adams, Child's Play.

The very best songs are the ones that you and your child make
up together. Singing a song about anything, *especially* the most
routine activities, reinforces the child's experience of life as harmonious, flowing, joyful, orderly. The lyrics don't have to rhyme;
the tune can be different every time (or use an old tune). Narration

or nonsense, one-line repeater or long-drawn-outer, a song will relieve some situations and enhance others. But its real, invaluable contribution lies in the sharing of a sense of joy between you and your child.

One family's best song—from a winter walk:

Soft, soft snow is falling on my hair (face) (hand).
Soft, white snow is falling everywhere (every place) (on the land).
I hear the crow calling.
I hear the snow falling—soft, white snow.

7
Truth

In the beginning was the Word and the Word was with God, and the Word was God. He was in the beginning with God. All things were made by Him and without Him was not anything made that was made. In Him was life and the life was the light of men. And the light shineth in the darkness and the darkness comprehended it not. . . . That was the true Light which lighteth every man that cometh into the world. He was in the world, and the world knew him not. He came unto his own, and his own received him not. But as many as received him, to them gave he power to become children of God, even to them that believe on his name: which were born, not of blood, nor of the will of man, but of God. And the Word became flesh, and dwelt among us, and we beheld his glory, the glory as of the only begotten of the Father, full of grace and truth.
—John 1:1–4, 9–14

We all associate *truth, communication, ideas, language, speech, intelligence, understanding, reality,* and *word* with one another. *Word* is perhaps the most inclusive. *Word* includes both concept and expression; it is the transition between *idea* and *expression,* the point at which idea turns into event. *Idea* is the cause, *event* is the effect, and *word* is the transition between the two.

So we recognize that language is important. We define our uniqueness and superiority as a species by the sophistication of our language. We know language development is important in children, communication in families. We recognize that the printed word is powerful when we say that "the pen is mightier than the sword." Through both the written and the spoken word we seek to understand reality and change our lives for the better.

Bridges

Some words are bridges, and after the bridge is crossed you don't need these words any more. In this book, *Me, Inc., seeing being,* and *love-intelligence* are bridge words to help us cross from the false side of an idea to the true. I don't love these words. It's a bit awkward and presumptuous to go around using coined words, and I'll be glad when we can get rid of them—leave them behind. But crossing over is a life or death matter, so we can be grateful for bridges.

Me, Inc. and *seeing being* help us cross from who we aren't to who we are. *Love-intelligence* helps us with what is and what we are about and what the good of it all is. Why not just say *I?* Because that could mean either I/Me, haver and doer (the one all wrapped up in itself), or the I that sees (I and my Father are one—the one that is one with the Father).

There are synonyms for *Me, Inc.—devil, satan, ego, self*—but *Me, Inc.* implies a self *in corpus* (in a body), incorporated, and calls attention to the fact that it is always in business for itself, and that it is a nasty business. Me, Inc. is not a person, but it is a personal idea and a very tricky imposter. It goes around looking for a place to call its own, and convincing us that we are it—not only its place but *it,* itself. Why *love-intelligence?* Because *love, truth, God* have so many meanings. Because sometimes these are Me, Inc.'s key words, masterkeys for sneaking into our lives. Me, Inc. has a whole ringful of key words—want/will, have/do, think/feel, right/wrong—all of which get used in the name of love and truth until finally Me, Inc. succeeds in getting *us* to impersonate *it!* We even think we *are* it. This is a corporate takeover and it can ruin our lives if we don't watch out. We have to watch out. Whenever we are watching out, the seeing being which is what we really are is waking up. And whenever the seeing being is awake, Me, Inc. can't get a toe in the door or sit at the hearth, because we are no longer confused by all its confusions.

We have been observing Me, Inc. for some time now. So we are getting pretty familiar with its tricks; we are not surprised to find that Me, Inc., which approaches everything in terms of having and doing, looks to have and to do truth through using the word. Words are seen as vehicles of self-expression and are employed to bring about self-ish ends: what Me, Inc. wants and wills.

Having and Doing Truth

Me, Inc. the haver perceives words as experience producers, as sensational. Spoken words are sound effects. To Me, Inc. it feels good to talk. Words can give him good or bad, hurt or nice feelings. Silence is intolerable because then Me, Inc. is not having any sensation—and no sound effects, no Me, Inc.

To Me, Inc. the haver, communication is a way of exchanging and working out feelings. Whenever our talk revolves around what we like and don't like and how we feel—if we feel good when nice things are said about us and bad when bad things are said; if words arouse, bore, or sicken us—then we know Me, Inc. the haver is getting its way with us.

With regard to intelligence, Me, Inc. the haver considers words to be containers of facts. He wants to feel that he has a good mind, and so he is concerned with getting facts and storing them as information. He is a container corporation. He believes that his mind is in his head and that it is a receptacle. Words are fact capsules which are kept in his mind, which is his head. The more facts are stored the more Me, Inc. feels he has intelligence. He learns by rote. Sometimes he experiences not having a good memory, not grasping ideas. Sometimes he feels stupid.

With regard to communication, say within the family, Me, Inc. the haver wants to "have a say" and to "get a hearing"—to talk and be listened to by others. He uses speech to make demands for pleasure, whether directly as in "scratch my back" or indirectly as in paying compliments and hoping to receive a pleasantry in return. Whenever these are our thoughts, we know Me, Inc. is in charge.

Concerning truth (the Word of God), Me, Inc., the haver, regards truthful ideas either directly as experiences in and of themselves or indirectly as a means of bringing about pleasurable experience. Directly he may get "high" or have sensuous and emotional experiences from hearing "the Word." Indirectly he hopes to trade on the truth for pleasure. Viewing God as a potential source of pleasure, he may try to please God (meet God's demands) by giving up certain pleasures in the hope of receiving greater pleasures (having his own demands met). Me, Inc. is a believer. He believes in the power of belief. Just by believing "good" ideas, he expects to get good. He tries to incorporate the truth by rehearsing and repeating it. He tries to apply truth to improve his life experience by positive thinking and imaging. He expects thinking nice thoughts to produce nice experiences.

When Me, Inc. begins to suspect that his approach to life won't work the way he wants it to, he imagines he is going crazy.

Me, Inc. the doer perceives words as powerful. He uses them as instruments, tools, and weapons for bringing about what he thinks should be. Talking is a form of taking action and bringing about action. Me, Inc. talks to feel powerful and exercise power and often experiences the talk of others as exercising power over him.

For Me, Inc., the doer, communication may take the form of verbal combat. His talk revolves around what he thinks should or shouldn't be. More than feeling good or bad, Me, Inc., the doer, is overly concerned with being right. He feels strong and influential when people concur and comply with him. He feels great when people think he is right; he feels devastated when people think he is wrong. He feels threatened when challenged. Whether secretly or overtly, he tends toward (and experiences in others) bossiness, contention, argument, persuasion.

Me, Inc., the doer, wants to have a powerful mind. Whereas Me, Inc., the haver, views his mind as a receptacle, Me, Inc., the doer, views his mind as a generator or an arsenal or a tool shed. To Me, Inc., words are power cartridges and formulas. Me, Inc. works with thoughts, picking them up and turning them over and rearranging them constantly to flex his mind and have the illusion of producing thoughts. Me, Inc. learns by analyzing, interpreting, figuring, formulating, and calculating. Sometimes he appears clever and sure, but he is also subject to tremendous anxiety, doubt, dilemma, guilt, and indecisiveness, as by-products of the belief that his intelligence and what he says are powerful.

Me, Inc. the doer uses speech to issue commands either directly, as in "Do what I say is right," or indirectly, as wit, in the hope of commanding attention and gaining recognition of his mental power. With regard to truth and the Word of God, he seeks to master and gain command of the truth. He tries to master the truth by thinking about it. Then he tries to use it by doing right in order to exercise control and have greater command over his life. Me, Inc. may view God's Word in terms of commands or techniques. Directly, he uses God's commandments for personal power, by seeming to be "in the right" and have "God on his side." Indirectly, he hopes that if he does what God commands, then God will do what he commands. He tries to do what he should, so that what he thinks should come about will come about. He thinks that right makes might makes right.

Paul voiced the cry of Me, Inc., the doer of truth, when he said, "The good that I would I do not and the evil that I would not, that I do." When Me, Inc. is most discouraged, he experiences terrible feelings of powerlessness and the sense that life is meaningless. If this is our experience, Me, Inc. is to blame—and there is nothing more to it.

Truth and Communication

We speak of truth and communication. We believe we are interested in truthful communication. Yet often we experience difficulty. We don't agree about the truth. We say we "aren't communicating." Parents especially complain of finding it difficult to communicate with their children. Feelings get hurt; tempers flare in disagreement. But hurt feelings are a telltale sign of Me, Inc. the haver, angry frustration a sign of Me, Inc. the doer. The problem then is not with truth and communication; it is with falseness and communication. So rather than working on communicating, it is better at such times to examine just what it is we are really trying to express.

The Girl Who Said Kitty

There was once a little girl whose parents were eager for her to learn to talk. They were diligent parents and spent much time trying to teach her the names of things. "Kitty!" they would exclaim—"Cup! Chair!"—trying to get her to repeat the sounds. The child was fascinated with the kitty, cup, and chair and she was entertained by her parents' animated behavior. But she did not learn to talk. Finally, one day the cat walked in and she said it: "Kitty." Great joy showed on the parents' faces. Hugs and kisses were bestowed on the child. She said it again: "Kitty." More hugs and kisses.

A number of days went by and the little girl kept saying *kitty* but did not acquire any new words. The parents' enthusiasm for *kitty* waned noticeably, and suddenly the little girl began calling everything *kitty*, cup and chair included. The parents were dismayed and discouraged. "No," they said. "Not *kitty*. *Doggie.*" Eventually the little girl said "Doggie," and the hugs and kisses were renewed. But the parents were disappointed to find that with the coming of *doggie*, *kitty* disappeared. Now the little girl called everything *doggie*. Even the cat.

As Me, Inc., we find ourselves trying to use our children to have and do truth for our own pleasure and sense of power. The girl who said *kitty* was getting the idea that the word is for pleasure. She thought speech was for getting hugs and kisses. Soon she would come to believe that learning was for praise—not for understanding. And, because she had no idea what speech really is and does, she was not learning to talk.

The Boy Who Said Won't

A father expressed a desire for better communication with his son. Asked what he meant by that he said, "Well, I have to teach him what he should do, right? I want him to do what he should do. So I tell him to wash the dishes and simple things like that, but he ignores me or talks back and says, 'Why should I?' and 'Who gave you the right to tell me what to do?' It's very unpleasant, and he won't do anything he's supposed to do. So I want to know how to communicate better with him."

To Me, Inc. the doer communicating means telling his son what to do. And of course the son is very obedient in a way. He has adopted his father's view that the whole issue in life and the purpose of speech is to exert power. So he communicates with his father by saying "won't." They have a complete and active misunderstanding, and they communicate a lot.

How Many Me, Incs. Does It Take to Change a Light Bulb?

While we all have different emphases at different times, we all behave as Me, Inc., both the haver and the doer of truth. And whether it enters through the ear or leaves by the mouth, whether it takes place between God and self or self and other, we all perceive the word as the junction of idea with effect. So we seek to understand the truth and bring it into experience by means of the word. Through the word we seek to bring to ourselves wanted pleasure and to bring about by ourselves what we will. It seems reasonable, intelligent, a truthful approach. Yet experience conflicts unreasonably with all our expectations. When we try to communicate with others we find them unreasonable and displeasing in their reactions. When we try to live rationally we find ourselves behaving irrationally. Could our premise be mistaken? What premise? Good question!

In the comics when someone has a sudden understanding or gets an idea, this event is depicted by showing a light bulb over his head. Recalling our light-questing clown (pages 19 and 108) to the stage for a moment, if we put a light bulb in his hands he will first use it in one of two ways. If he is Me, Inc. the pleasure seeker he uses the bulb to warm himself. If he is Me, Inc. the power seeker he wields it as a tool or weapon for pushing things around or perhaps hitting people over the head.

As silly as this seems, it is analogous to the way we use words and even *the* word, as long as we think of ourselves as separate material persons, as Me, Inc. In reality, of course, the light bulb is for shedding light and enables the clown to see what is and to discover what he is himself, an intelligent seeing being rather than a groping, bungling, grasping, grappling fool.

In reality the word, too, sheds light. Like the light bulb, it can do this only when it is plugged in to its source of power: truth, God, What Is. The difference between Me, Inc. and the seeing being is in what it perceives to be the source and nature and purpose of the word. As Me, Inc. we misperceive the word as the means whereby we can have our way with reality. But as seeing beings we recognize that the word is the means whereby reality can have its way with us. As seeing beings, we can use simple words again—*I* and *love* and *God*—only now we don't have to, because there isn't anything else to see or be.

When the clown screws the bulb into its socket it becomes one with and expresses its unity with the light as illumination. Now, too, the clown's oneness with the light is made manifest as seeing. This is communication. It is not the coming together of the clown and the light bulb but rather the coming to light of the oneness of both clown and bulb with the force of light. So light expresses itself through both the clown and the light in unique ways, as illumination and as seeing. And through its oneness with the light is each life fulfilled and enhanced and thereby also enhances the life of the other.

> *For with thee is the fountain of life;*
> *in thy light do we see light.*
> —Psalm 36:9

> *Thy word is a lamp to my feet*
> *and a light to my path.*
> —Psalm 119:105

> *My soul cleaves to the dust;*
> *revive me according to thy word!*
> —Psalm 119:25

My soul melts away for sorrow;
strengthen me according to thy word.
—Psalm 119:28

The Child as a Truthful Model

Do not say things. What you are stands over you the while, and thunders
so I cannot hear what you say to the contrary.
—Ralph Waldo Emerson, *Letters and Social Aims*

If there's one thing most children do with astonishing speed and ease it is acquire language. Young children can master as many as three languages simultaneously with perfect accents, very little mixing of them, no text and no teacher, lessons, tests, tapes, or books. Some say that there is something about the young child's brain that makes this possible—that in the entire rest of a human being's life it is never possible to learn languages as easily or well as when he is a young child.

What is it about the young child's brain that gives it this facility for learning languages? I believe it is not what the brain has so much as what it lacks. The child who does not yet think of having a mind (good or bad) or of getting intelligence or doing well or being right or having his way has something else on his mind. What is he primarily concerned with? He is concerned with seeing and being. He is interested in finding out what is and then being that.

That is exactly how children learn language. Like computers they begin on a sort of on/off basis. The child's equivalent is true/false, question/answer, yes/no, in sum: *is* and *isn't.* Children do not successfully learn to talk in order to please or get praise. They do not successfully learn to talk even to exert power. They are motivated to understand and learn to talk with remarkable efficiency in order to *find out what is so that they can be that.* Once they understand the questioning and answering inflection of speech, language develops in a flurry. From "Peek-a-boo—*Where's* Mommy? *There* she is!" to "Is that the bear? No, that is not the bear. Yes, *that* is the bear!" the guiding and facilitating interest of the child is *what is so?* and *what isn't?* It has nothing to do with pleasure or power or self or other. He does not learn speech to please himself or his parent; he does not communicate to exert power or even to make contact with others but to come to conscious oneness with the truth.

That this is the way children learn is demonstrated negatively by both "The Girl Who Said Kitty" and "The Boy Who Said Won't." Both manifest Emerson's idea commonly paraphrased as "the way you are speaks so loudly that I cannot hear what you are saying." In both cases what the parents *said to do* was entirely secondary in the child's mind to what was *expressed (communicated) about being*. Children approach everything with an interest in *what is so*—with the idea of being real through seeing the real.

The fact that this is a valid orientation in life is evidenced by the tremendous efficiency with which they learn and with which their lives are transformed by their learning. Misled by their parents, the girl who said *kitty* and the boy who said *won't* demonstrate this efficiency somewhat sadly. But the vast number of children who, less distracted (or despite distraction), do master highly complex languages in only two or three years provides a positive demonstration of the fact that we are seeing beings and that *seeing what is* (and recognizing *what isn't*) is our best orientation.

Pit Pat

So here comes little Pit Pat
up to us, listening
through those clear blue eyes
with 20/20 hearing
to every word we are.
She may or may not
understand the words we say;
But she listens carefully
to our much louder
pointing of view.
Her seeing hears every word
our being is saying.
She only sees in order to be,
and as far as she knows
the way we are
is telling it like it is. So
(regardless of what else
we are telling her to do
and how to do this

and why not to do that)
pit pat off she trots,
seeing being as we saw it;
saying her self
as we said ours;
being exactly
as she was told.
Poor little spitting image,
apple of my eye,
spitting at the sky.
But try as she may,
even with all our help,
Little Pit Pat can't
put out Old Sun.
Still, still it shines
and dries her face
and warms her hair
and lightens her way
and brightens her day.

* * *

For as the rain and the snow
come down from heaven, and return not
thither but water the earth,
making it bring forth and sprout,
giving seed to the sower and bread
to the eater,
So shall my word be that goes forth
from my mouth;
it shall not return to me empty,
but it shall accomplish that which I purpose
and prosper in the thing for which
I sent it.
—Isaiah 55:10–11

Even a child is known by his doing,
whether his work be pure, and whether it be right
The hearing ear, and the seeing eye,
the Lord hath made even both of them.
—Proverbs 20:11–12

The Articulate Parent

1. The Parent as Word. The parent *is* the strongest statement that the child hears regarding what it means to be alive and real. More than what we say or do, the way we are expresses what we think it means to be alive. So the articulate parent is less a telling than a listening individual. By listening inwardly to what is, we become to the child God's word about God. We are not self-expressive, but God-expressive. We do not rely on what we know or feel, but consider from moment to moment *What is love-intelligent? What of God can be discerned or expressed here? How can the fact of love be evidenced? How can the goodness of order be appreciably manifested?*

2. The Parent as Beholder. The child is God's word to the parent. By viewing the child as a word—for meaning and significance—we get told what we need to hear. Whatever we discern of God in the child enlightens us. Whatever seems not to be of God instructs. The child's way of being "talks back" and explains to us what other idea of self we are expressing to the child. We are thus guided by the idea of "First cast out the beam in thine own eye, and then shalt thou see to cast out the mote that is in thy brother's eye." Rather than defining and insisting on what the child should be, the articulate parent watches to see what God's definition of the child is. Constantly beholding the child as articulated to and by God, we distinguish the truth of the child from the false. As much as possible in thought and word we acknowledge and address ourselves to the true, ever turning the child over to God. We constantly behold the child as a spiritual consciousness and regard him as living and moving and having his being in God.

3. The Parent as Preparer of the Way. The best way to prepare the way is to get out of the way. With regard to communication, primarily this means to cease from "self-saying," abandoning two-way communication and keeping open the channels for one-way communication. Thus we may help to preserve the child's inner hearing of God's still small voice, which occurs in her (in each of us) as the impulse to see and be what is. This voice is always there to guide. It never ceases; it can only be drowned out.

A voice cries;
In the wilderness prepare the way of the Lord,
make straight in the desert a highway for our God.
Every valley shall be lifted up,
and every mountain and hill be made low;
the uneven ground shall become level,
and the rough places a plain.
And the glory of the Lord shall be revealed,
and all flesh shall see it together,
For the mouth of the Lord has spoken.
—Isaiah 40:3–5

4. The Parent as Preparer of the Truth-Centered Environment. Everything in the truth-centered home is oriented to expressing divine qualities. Consideration is constantly given to the question of *what is and what isn't*. What idea is being expressed? The atmosphere is shouldless, nonjudgmental. Space and time are allotted and maintained for quiet listening—both shared and private. Privacy and quiet times are given a high priority. Books, tapes, chairs, and lamps are thoughtfully located for effortless access. Reading, walking, and trips to the library may be frequent.

5. The Parent as Communicator. In the communicative home there is an understanding on the part of the parent that true communication is conscious oneness (communion, communing) with truth. Whenever we use words, the aim is not to control or tell so much as to bring the child to some conscious firsthand encounter with the value of truth. This does not mean giving long explanations or talking about the truth. Nothing so cheapens the truth or so effectively closes the child's mind as preaching. On the contrary, as understanding parents we speak rarely of "the truth" and then only sparely and only when freshly inspired, framing words that our whole being has already made plain to the child.

Children respond much better to positive statements of what is and isn't than to negative ones of what should or shouldn't be. For example, instead of "Don't jump on the sofa," we might say, "The sofa is not for jumping. There is a better place for that. How about the mattress in the basement instead?" Or, "How would this be?"

Conversation is viewed as shared participation in the discovery of truth. Therefore instead of telling, the parent is often asking.

"What do you suppose it means when the dog growls like that?" Not only words, but also things and events are looked at for meaning. Whether or not God is mentioned, from evident blessings the child can learn to see that life is fundamentally ordered in favor of good. From apparent problems the child can learn to seek a lesson.

As communicating parents we may teach our children to pray. Prayer may be presented as "listening to what God has to say" or waiting for a good or wise or loving idea. Or waiting quietly for love to "take place." Before offering quick answers, we may suggest that the child first pray and offer to wait prayerfully with him while he prays.

6. The Parent as Supplier. The articulate parent is guided in selecting and presenting materials and experiences that can help the child grow in her ability to understand meaning and express truth, and to become aware that there is one love-intelligent mind constantly being expressed and that she can discern it directly. Primarily we seek to reinforce three convictions in the child: *(1) that life is good and that she can continue to expect it to be so; (2) that problems can be seen through and transcended; (3) that she is a fully equipped consciousness, not dependent upon us—that she can and will be able to see her way through anything because God will always be with her to give her the needed idea at the needed moment.*

Awareness of these issues provides us with love-intelligent guidelines for selecting good books for our youngest children and, as they grow, helping them learn to deal with so-called bad influences they meet in books, films, television, and in the world at large. (See also pages 299 and 318–326.)

Truth and the Seeing Being

To the seeing being, words are turning points between idea and event. Listening with the single ear and seeing with the single eye *through* the word, the seeing being seeks oneness with the One Mind as conscious awareness of what is. As money signifies, but is not, gold, so to the seeing being, the Word points to, but is not, God.

The seeing being is not getting the word or having it or doing it or using it to express himself (or herself) or fulfill his express wishes. To the seeing being the word is God's way of using him to express God. Paying attention to the still small voice is the seeing being's way of letting God use him.

Being of No Mind—with the Father

The seeing being does not think he has intelligence—either as a receptacle or as a generator. He does not think he has a mind. He knows he *is* a consciousness. He recognizes that all intelligence comes from God as the One Mind. By setting aside all thoughts of future and past, self and other, wanting (pleasure) and not wanting (pain), willing (what should be) and willing not (what shouldn't be), the seeing being seeks to be intelligent through being conscious of God's intelligence. He remains intelligent by being mindful of divine intelligence and receptive to its ceaseless inspiration. Assuming a state of love-intelligent attention is one way the seeing being seeks to be in contact with God.

This attentiveness is the seeing being's way of worshiping, devoting himself to God. It may take the form of contemplative discerning between what is love-intelligent and what isn't, or it may take an active form in which we align our whole being with and stake our life on the idea that love-intelligence really is. When we are so oriented, we recognize the presence of God by the establishment of our love-intelligent attention as a love-intelligent state of mind. The seeing being recognizes a divine idea by the fact that it is both surprisingly loving and surprisingly intelligent at the same time. If it is only "loving" but not intelligent, or if it is only "intelligent" but not loving, the seeing being is rightfully suspicious and on the lookout for Me, Inc. as the inadvertently fraudulent perpetrator of fraud and defrauder of God.

> *For though we walk in the flesh, we do not war after the flesh: For the weapons of our warfare are not carnal, but mighty through God to the pulling down of strong holds; Casting down imaginations, and every high thing that exalteth itself against the knowledge of God, and bringing into captivity every thought to the obedience of Christ.*
> —2 Corinthians 10:3–5

All Life Is a True/False Statement

To the seeing being everything is a word. Like words themselves, the seeing being perceives everything he sees as a symbol, as points where ideas become manifest. All people, all actions, all things, all feelings, all sights and sounds, all events are expressions of ideas and are therefore words or statements. All of these statements are either true or false. All of these statements are self-expressive. All true statements express God. All false statements express Me, Inc. By looking at everything as meaningful words from this spiritual, true/false viewpoint, the seeing being is always growing in consciousness, and everything both true and false is telling him of God.

God's Word as the Seeing Being

The seeing being is himself a word of God—the turning point between divine idea and divine expression, between divine cause and divine effect, between intelligence and love. Becoming as a child, the seeing being understands that the whole point of seeing is not doing or having but being. And so it is that the true seeing being with all his understanding is not after all preeminently knowledgeable but preeminently loving.

> *One word determines the whole world;*
> *One sword pacifies heaven and earth.*
> —Lao Tzu, in *The Gospel According to Zen,* ed. by Sohl and Carr

> *For the word of God is living and active, sharper than any two-edged sword, piercing to the division of soul and spirit, of joints and marrow, and discerning the thoughts and intentions of the heart.*
> —Hebrews 4:12

> *Truth is always truth*
> *untruth always untruth*
> *this is what matters, this is right desire.*
> —Buddha, in *The Dhammapada,* trans. by P. Lal

> *Through faith we understand that the worlds were framed by the word of God, so that things which are seen were not made of the things which do appear.*
> —Hebrews 11:3

You must understand that One exists who is without not only speech but mouth itself, who lacks eyes, the four elements and the six roots of perception [in Buddhism the mind is a sixth sense]. Yet none can call him a void, for it is he alone that brought your body and mind into being.
—Keizan in *Zen: Poems, Prayers, Sermons, Anecdotes, Interviews,* ed. and trans. by Stryk and Ikemoto

Words do not matter; what matters is Dhamma.
What matters is action rightly performed,
after lust, hate, and folly are abandoned
with true knowledge and serene mind,
and complete detachment from the fruit of action.
—Buddha, in *The Dhammapada*, trans. by P. Lal

Practical Information for New Parents

Of all "Practical Information" sections, this one on language, communication, and books is the biggest and broadest in scope. While the long bibliographies of children's books are for very young children, the emphasis on the value of books and reading applies to children of all ages. I would especially hope that parents of older as well as younger children would turn to "Read-Ins" (page 296), "Reference Books" (page 316), and "Influences: Good and Bad, False and True" (page 318), before proceeding to the last chapter (page 321).

Babies, Books, and Learning to Talk

Many are surprised to hear that books can be used with children under a year old. But the right book may be worth a dozen toys even for a child who can't crawl yet. You know the little striver is tired, yet when you try to hold him close, he struggles out of your arms and wriggles away. Just snuggle him into your lap, open a big book around him and see what happens. After hours of looking at nothing but the floor without craning his neck, here suddenly is the world in VistaVision—a whole new view of it on every page, with everything he couldn't get to on his own coming to him instead! Experiment with books early—around five or six months of age. Try different books at different times. No interest? Try again soon. Never insist, but don't give up too quickly either.

What's the hurry? Certainly it is not to push our children or fill them with information or qualify them at three for Harvard at eighteen. Language is the thing. Books are a gateway to the freedom of speech. A common assumption is that books aren't for children until they can talk. But a good picture book can help a child learn to talk. And through learning to talk the child gains the freedom he needs to find out what he needs to know, to orient himself and navigate in the world, and above all, to seek and find meaning in life.

Where's Mommy? *There* she is! As soon as a baby can play peek-a-boo she is ready for her first book. One way to tell if you are starting books soon enough is whether or not the child tries to eat them. If she doesn't already know that a book is not something to eat you are starting right on time. First she will have to give a book the taste and tussle test. A cloth book to chew and an old telephone book to tear will do for a start. (Doctors assure us that no child would be hurt by the amount of telephone book he would care to consume.) The telephone book is a disposable practice book for the child to use by herself. A big urban one will outlast its usefulness no matter how much it gets torn, crumpled, eaten, drooled, scribbled, or painted on. To the child it is a wondrous magic block that turns out to be made of a thousand smooth, flat, thin things that can be flipped over and that sometimes flop back delightfully by themselves.

The first time you show her a picture book she will probably try to pick up the things pictured on the pages. But after a few times she will switch to simply patting the pictures. What a revelation for a six-month-old—those round things are flat! Those flat things look so round! She may also try to grab the book and tear or chew the pages. It isn't that she's too young for books; you just have to be on hand. Once she has explored all its physical properties, learns to turn pages, and understands that a book is for looking at, the tearing will cease.

Learning to Talk

If it is clear that language is primarily a means of finding out what we don't know, rather than showing off what we do, then it is also evident that simply teaching children the names of things is not particularly helpful. To be able to say *fish* won't add anything much to the child's life. To have to repeat it for every relative and friend of the family will do even less. But to have a way of finding out that that bright wiggly thing *is* a *fish*—now that really adds a wonderful dimension to her life.

So by the time our babies are three or four months old, it is most helpful to talk to them in phrases, mostly questions and answers about whatever they are momentarily interested in. "Do you see the fish? *Is* that the fish? Yes, that's a fish." We are helping our children discover the question and answer format. So we hide and say, "Where's Daddy?" We pop up and say, *"There* he is!" Later, as we look at a picture book with many pictures on one page, we say, *"Where's* the bear? Is *that* the bear? Yes, *that's* the bear." And we tap the picture of the bear with a finger (our own or the child's).

Suddenly our question and answer inflection begins to make sense. She knows vaguely what "Where is?" or "What's that?" means: it means seeking. She senses what "There it is" or "Yes, that's a" means: it means finding. The question expresses her urge to understand. The answer celebrates her finding out. A few single words may come first, but the question will come quickly. A whispered "Whassa?" "Where'sa?" "Dassa!" "Deresa!" and she has cracked the code. There's no stopping her now.

But yes, don't correct. *Yes* is useful in helping children learn to talk and enjoy books. If she points to a telephone and says, "Dophone," don't say, "No, that's a *tel*-ephone." Say, "Yes [i.e., I understand what you mean and it's true], that *is* a *tel*-ephone." *No* is not only discouraging, it's misleading. The child may think, "Oh, that's not a telephone?" Children first attempting words of more than one syllable often get the sounds scrambled. For example, one child crouched down behind the bed and jumped up shouting, "B'kee!" His parents recognized that he was trying to say *peek-a-boo.* "Yes, peek-a-boo," they said, joining his game.

"There's Tommy!" *B'kee* grew into *buh-ka-pee* and finally *peek-a-boo*. The parents realized they did not need to correct their son, only to demonstrate the correct pronunciation. Realizing that the main issue was communication, they were able to respond helpfully and enthusiastically to their son's first understandable efforts to talk.

If we can teach our children that speech is the means of formulating their endless questions, and if we can learn from our children to sincerely ask questions, then something really good has taken place. Our children will talk sooner and learn more; we will talk less and learn sooner (and more).

Story Times Shared and Private

An immediate benefit of an early introduction to books is the freedom they bring to child and parent to be together in a truly enjoyable way. Books can be a channel for some of our most inspired and happy times together. It isn't only the truthful and interesting ideas that come through the books, but also what happens between us—the mutual growing awareness, the communication. And certainly in the interest of truth is the way books help us take our minds off each other (off what we want and don't want from each other) and refocus our attention on what is before us. After only a few sessions books become vehicles where child and parent can relax together and still get around.

Odd Times

Sometimes parent and child just wrestle the day away. The parent plans to play with the child "just as soon as the housework is done." But the housework is endless, and the phone keeps ringing, and the child keeps messing up the house and whining, and the more you try to get her to wait the less she can.

Sometimes all she needs is to know where she is on our list of priorities. We don't want to reward demanding behavior, and the child doesn't have to come first all the time. But sometimes there's a legitimate need to know love is available. Sometimes we need to put love first.

Reading a quick story can be helpful—right off the bat at the beginning of the day. Five minutes and you may find that you are both free to go separate ways for a time. While reading you are side by side rather than at or for each other, which is how the struggles get started.

So when she's lying on the floor wrapped around your ankles, before running away from home, try a book. Just take time out. "Now let's read this together. And when we finish the story, what are you going to do while I vacuum?"

That bedtime is story time is obvious. But try some stories at odd times, too, such as when she wakes up or at the end of a meal. Books can be a great way of changing the subject when the subject needs to be changed.

Private Times

"Let's take a little time out for a book." "If I get ready for bed now will I still have time for a book?" "Oh, good, tomorrow it's Saturday and I can stay in bed longer and read." "While you buy the groceries, may I wait in the bookstore?" What is healthier for a child than getting hooked on books early in life? It is well known that good books are an unmatched resource for providing concepts, information, and entertainment. But the book habit itself can be an important mental hygiene practice. Here are some areas in which a good book habit can contribute to a child's mental health.

● *Peace.* In our society many people find even a few moments of peace and quiet uncomfortable. And yet peace is necessary to us as seeing beings. Peace is an opportunity for inspiration, a time to reestablish conscious contact with God. Taking the time to read a book, we find many of Me, Inc.'s concerns first have to be dropped. The child who enjoys a quiet, private book time is cultivating an appreciation of and tolerance for peace.

● *Discipline.* When you tell a misbehaving child to stop, often he is unable to. So we realize a little discipline is in order. Discipline means teaching. When a child is misbehaving he is being disciple to a mistaken idea. Before he can stop, the mistaken idea must be replaced. The old-fashioned tactic of sending him to his room is not bad. But let him choose a book on the way. Losing

himself, even briefly, in a joyful, funny, or lovely book may be all
it takes to put joy, good humor, and love in charge of him again.
For the seeing being this shifting of viewpoint is a preliminary
exercise in prayer.

● *Self-esteem and assurance.* These days much emphasis is placed
on relating to others. This leads to a tendency to feel lonely and
unsure when there are not others around or to be anxious and
attention-seeking when they are. Ease with others is desirable, but
its prerequisite is ease with oneself. Books are a doorway to the
appreciation of solitude. The child who discovers the joy of quiet
book times has a refuge from both loneliness and excessive in-
teraction.

Read-Ins

In our house Friday night is the most shouldless time of the week.
No homework presses and there is plenty of weekend ahead for
chores. Because on this night life seems to make fewer demands
on us, we tend to make fewer demands on each other. So on these
nights we have more time and find it easier to be with each other.

Sometimes instead of movies or television or various individual projects of one sort or another, we have a read-in. Oh, these
are memorable nights indeed! By now the boys are old enough to
get books from the library and read to themselves. When they were
smaller and we had such reading times, they would ask, "Is it a
quiet read or an out-loud one?" Years ago for a "quiet read" they
would get stacks of books—maybe ten apiece—to "read" to themselves, just quietly turning pages and looking at pictures and thinking over the familiar stories. So even before they could read we had
quiet reading times; and even now that they are big we still have
out-loud ones in which one person reads to us all or we take turns.
We don't do it as often as we mean to, but there is no question that
our read-ins are to be counted among our best family memories.

Reading Stories to Preschoolers

Until recently most picture books with real stories were not designed for children under five. But with a little help younger chil-

dren can use certain of these for longer and to better advantage than the older child. A good story book can serve first as a word book, then a concept book, only eventually becoming a connected story adventure. While an older child may toddle off on his own firsthand explorations, the lapsitter, less free to roam, benefits greatly from the discoveries he makes in books about what's what and how it all adds up.

There are a number of simple techniques for reading aloud to pre- or barely verbal children:

● *Read the child more than the book.* Read the pictures more than the text. Initially our reading consists almost entirely of off-the-cuff conversations about the pictures. *Do you see the truck? Yes! Vrmm, vrm —there it goes! Oh, what a nice soft puppy! Yes, we are patting the puppy!* Watch to see what interests her, what she does and does not understand. Speak of these things in whatever terms she can understand and only as long as she remains interested. It's easy to tell when we stray because the child begins to crawl away. Speaking of clear communication!

● *Let your fingers do the talking.* It may not be polite in society, but when reading to little children, always point. Even tap audibly. Even if she is listening, at least half of what we say probably means nothing to her. So if there are twenty-five animals on the page and you are talking about the mouse, point to the mouse. This is both clarifying and fun, a sort of hide and seek with our fingers. "I see a mouse on this page, do you?" The child looks all over and then points to the found mouse. "There's the mouse!" In a sillier version we walked suspensefully on two fingers all over the page looking for the sought detail.

● *Story telling.* Once the child is familiar with basic words and concepts in a book he may be ready to become aware of the story. Unless the text is exceptionally simple you will still not read the words on the page. First boil the story down into a sequence of words he can understand. Sum up key events; gradually bring the child to the discovery that one thing leads to another. Important phrases now are: *and now . . . and then . . . and suddenly . . . and after that . . . and then what do you think happened?*

● *Finger telling.* Again finger dramatics are very helpful when helping the child to discover story continuity. Trace occurrences as you read, pointing to the characters and showing, e.g., who threw the ball and where it went. This is especially useful in explaining the appearance of the same character in several pictures. Small children will not immediately infer that these are of the same character. Unless we show with our fingers that this bear walked out the door with his hat on there and now is taking a walk here, children may think that this is a book full of many bears that look alike.

● *Pantomime.* Don't let your finger steal all the limelight. Simple acting out of words and events can make all the difference in whether or not the child knows what's going on. She may know the word *throw,* but have no recognition of it in the past tense. A simple throwing gesture when you read "He threw the ball" may make it perfectly clear—and much more inviting and fun.

● *Question and answer.* Simple questions encourage the child to verbalize and help him discover that books are means of finding out. Furthermore, through question and answer you can discover where he is—what he understands and doesn't, what does or doesn't interest him. From simple "Where is the—?" questions you can move to unspoken questions, pausing momentarily in your reading and silently inviting the child to fill in the blank. Sometimes children are also amused when you intentionally misread words, leaving it to them to make corrections.

● *Expression.* Speak and read with expression. Animation makes the reading more interesting and provides clues to the meanings of pictures and words.

● *Abbreviation.* Some say never to speak to children in anything but full sentences. This seems silly. Short brief phrases may be clearer. You can fill in more words as she is ready to understand them.

● *Filling in the rest of the story.* Once the tracks have been laid and you are sure the child has a general idea of the story's direction, you can begin to run the whole train over them, adding car after car at whatever pace is appropriate. Eventually you may be able to read the full text. As soon as the child is clear about what is happening in the story, he may happily listen to even the most sophisticated words and details. Even the words you don't explain will eventually become clear. He will guess many from their context, and the rest will be decoded later, perhaps from hearing them used in other situations.

Selecting Books

The books recommended in *Whole Child/Whole Parent* were selected from among six or seven thousand reviewed. I believe they represent the best available. But there are many wonderful books not mentioned here and new ones coming out all the time, which you and your child may like as well or better. And there are books for older children which we haven't even considered. In making your selection (and helping your older child to make hers) and deciding which books to buy and which to borrow from the library, perhaps the following guidelines will be helpful:

● *Truthfulness.* Almost every book makes some sort of a statement about life. The best do so in an unspoken way while telling an entertaining story at the same time. Good questions to ask are: *What is this book saying about life? Will it augment or diminish the child's sense of enthusiasm, competency, assurance, humor, peace of mind, kindness, understanding, and freedom as he goes forth into the world?* For borrowing but perhaps not buying are books that say important things, but not in a sufficiently entertaining way to be reread many times. Sometimes a child chooses books with really awful values. O.K. By reading and talking them over together, we can help him discover healthier ones.

● *Artistic value.* Is this a sound, well-illustrated story that will enhance the child's appreciation of good language, literature, and art? *In both art and text does it foster the child's awareness of beauty by being well crafted and designed, graceful, original, beautiful?* For preschoolers important qualities of beauty are clarity, simplicity, vitality, brightness, joy. Finding real stories that very young children can enjoy is especially difficult. In many books the text is only a flimsy excuse for the pictures, or too sophisticated, or just boring. Children lose interest in such books after only a few readings. Grabbers and holders such as *Goodnight Moon* are rare and priceless.

● *Educational value.* In assessing nonfiction and resource books a good question to ask is: *Does this book offer skills or information the child needs or craves and couldn't pick up more easily, cheaply, or satisfactorily elsewhere?* On this basis I exclude most counting and ABC books, but include "passion books" (e.g., dinosaur, truck, horse books for children with special interests), activity books, and only those concept books with a little something extra, such as Spier's *Fast-Slow High-Low.*

• *Entertainment value. Will the child like it and enjoy it? Will it effectively sustain her interest?* We may think it's good *for* her, but if it doesn't seem good *to* her it's probably a waste to buy it. Is the ratio of text to picture appropriate, or will the child get bored before it's time to turn the page? If it seems especially worthwhile but too long, can it be simplified while reading aloud?

• *Dollar value.* All things considered, *is this a good purchase, a better borrow, or an oh-forget-it?* So many really fine books are available as reasonably priced paperbacks. Especially for preschoolers who don't yet get around much, it is good to have a great many books. Even some mediocre ones are worth buying to give the child maximum freedom of choice. Some books are worth buying in hardcover no matter what. I feel that way about *Little Pear* and *The Poppyseed Cakes.* But you can judge for yourself. Consider probable mileage, long- and short-range value to the child, your and your child's individual preferences, appropriateness of price. When in doubt head for the library to try before you buy.

Books and Buoyancy: Values in Children's Books

It is commonly known that things often happen to us according to our expectancy. The individual with a sunny outlook tends toward a sunny life experience. Free of suspicion and fear, he moves with assurance, friendliness, and good humor, thereby attracting predominantly pleasant responses from the world. Difficulties tend to roll off his back and he moves through adversity with strength and assurance, learning easily from even his bad experiences. The fearful individual, by contrast, is always on guard. He approaches others with suspicion and interprets difficulties very personally as discouragement, failure, or persecution. So each of these approaches to life is self-perpetuating and tends to grow stronger through constant reinforcement.

But don't we have to teach our children to be realistic? Don't they need to learn the hard facts of life? Don't worry, they will. Certainly positive thinking—Pollyanna whitewashing—is no answer. There is no good gained from pretending good. But painting a black picture is also false, and much trouble follows from a falsely fearful perspective. When selecting books for children, we certainly want realistic ones. But the most realistic values are those that will best enable the child to *realize* his potential for a good, happy life.

The child looks to his books for a picture of what life is all about. He may derive from them a picture of what to expect in life and how to respond to what comes.

Many books have been written to teach lessons in living—how to make a friend, how to treat this or that problem (divorce, death). They may have some usefulness, but often they also carry the subtle message that life is a problem which one may or may not be equipped to deal with. Many books overemphasize the issue of how one feels—an emphasis which contributes to a child's self-centeredness and vulnerability. In these ways the most "realistic" books may, in fact, be the least so.

Especially on the preschool level it is best to look for stories —be they "realistic" or "fantastic"—that will increase the child's positive expectancy of life and his confidence in his ability to respond to it. This is less a matter of giving him specific answers to specific situations than of letting him know that he is capable, and that whatever comes along is likely to bring a revelation of some new good. Even when problems arise help will be there—whether it takes the form of a helping hand such as the policeman in *Make Way for Ducklings* or an intelligent idea which the child himself discerns as in *Pippa Mouse.* Let him know that life will support him even when he makes mistakes—as with the duck in *The Story About Ping* who makes choices and survives consequences.

Let your child's books increase his sense of buoyancy—his own buoyancy coupled with the buoyancy of life. Let him know that to weigh anchor does not mean to be adrift. At home or abroad he is not at sea—he is afloat.

Good Books for Children

A good children's book is like an onion, with layers and layers to be discovered. The young child's interest will carry him through endless readings of the same book, not because he likes repetition but because he still finds something new to understand. Once he has understood everything he finds to question, his interest will taper off suddenly. He will ask for his favorite story and, before you have read three pages, begin to wriggle away. It's time to retire that book and find another. Sometimes the retirement is temporary and in a few months he is ready to discover a new layer of meaning. And sometimes, years later, a book he loved as a little child will suddenly come to mind, bearing an important and needed message.

Here, in four groups of increasing sophistication and difficulty, are some of the best story books for preschoolers we know. Not all of these books are in print. They come and go, in and out of print. But we hope you will be able to locate copies in the library if not in the bookstore.

Stage One Stories

These are for the child who has a vocabulary of single words (25 badly pronounced ones will do for a start). At first they can be used as word books, then as connected ideas, and finally most of them as real stories. Use them along with the Mother Goose books. These pre- and first stories introduce connected ideas and lead up to real stories. Most are set close to home. There are not many suitable stories available for this stage, but the few that do work are good for an almost endless number of readings.

> *ABC: An Alphabet Book,* by Thomas Matthiessen. A single word for each letter illustrated with a bright, clear photograph. Useful with children less than a year old. Includes many things that first capture a child's attention. This book was published by Platt & Munk, then by Grosset & Dunlap. Now it's out of print. 5 months–1½ years.
>
> *Best Word Book Ever,* by Richard Scarry. If you had to buy only one book for the first two years, this would be a good one—1400

lively captioned pictures of things, actions, and animal people are grouped helpfully around such topics as getting dressed, airport, etc. Useful from as young as six or seven months as a word book until the child is three or four years old as a story book encyclopedia. One of the first books children "read" to themselves, immersing themselves in the pictures, and coming up only to ask questions. Random House, 6 months–4 years.

Big and Little, by J. P. Miller. This artist portrays animals for tiny tots better than anyone else—bright, bold, friendly ones. In this case his animals present opposites: fat/thin, few/many, tall/short animals of various sorts to talk over with the very young child. Random House, 1–2 years.

The Early Bird, by Richard Scarry. A little bird sets out to find a worm for a friend. A funny idea that captivates children. They just love to see the different ways that Early Bird and his friend do all the same things they do. This was the first book in which Scarry's best-loved Lowly Worm character appeared. Random House, 1–2 years.

Farmer's Alphabet, by Mary Azarian. The letters of the alphabet presented in beautiful woodcuts of traditional American farm life. More than an alphabet. Frame and hang individual pages—all if feasible, or a few to be changed from time to time. Any child who eats oatmeal in front of these prints will see more and more in them and get an early start in appreciating fine art. The publisher performs a service in making such work available in such a quality edition and so inexpensively. Godine, all ages.

500 Words to Grow On, by Harry McNaught. 500 basic words, contextually grouped (e.g., kitchen words, people words) and illustrated with very realistic, beautifully rendered paintings. Perfect for the child who is just breaking forth into speech. Neither confusingly cluttered nor too simple-minded. A gem at a very low cost. Random House, 1–2 years.

Go Dog Go! by P. D. Eastman. A very first book for a two-year-old, a very first reader for the older child. This truly zany book combines the clear presentation of paired concepts (in/out, over/under, up/down) with the purely cuckoo. Random House, 1½–6 years.

The Golden Egg Book, by Margaret Wise Brown. When he can't crack open an egg he finds, little bunny finally falls asleep. Now the duckling hatches, but *he* can't get that bunny to open his eyes. Darling illustrations with a funny story. Golden, ½–4 years.

Good Morning, Chick, by Mirra Ginsburg. The first funny adventures of a chick. How he hatches, meets a huge cat, falls into the puddle of a fat laughing frog, and finds refuge under his huge mother's wing. Perfectly timed to get youngsters to join in; perfectly designed to show that the unexpected isn't the disastrous. Perfect. Greenwillow, 1–3 years.

Goodnight Moon, by Margaret Wise Brown. Just the best, coziest good night ever. The bedtime book of all bedtime books, by the master of the gentle whisper. Harper & Row, 5 months–2½ years.

If I Had a Bus, If I Had a House, If I Had a Farm. Each of these three small books includes 17 thick little pages that fold out into a stand-up panorama. "IF I HAD A BUS . . . I would sleep in it." "IF I HAD A HOUSE . . . there would be a tree inside." "IF I HAD A FARM . . . I would name the goats Billy, Dilly, and Silly." Grosset, 1–3 years.

Is This the House of Mistress Mouse? by Richard Scarry. Well, is it? Put your finger in the hole and see if *you* can guess what that furry thing is. And if it isn't Mistress Mouse, then for goodness' sake, WHO IS IT? Golden, 1½–3 years.

Jamie's Story, by Wendy Watson. "I open my eyes. The sun is up. Mama comes." From waking to dressing, to playing, to eating, Jamie tells and shows it "like it is" when you are more or less one or two years old: colorful, bright, simple, impressive, wonderful. Philomel, 6 months–3 years.

Jump, Frog, Jump! by Robert Kalan. How did the frog catch the fly? How did the frog get away? Let's hear it for the frog! *Jump, Frog, Jump!* And let's hear it for a book during which a really young child will sit still but not keep quiet. Greenwillow, 1½–4 years.

Lois Lenski's Big Book of Mr. Small. Set in sunrise to sunset terms a child can understand, the daily routine of Mr. Small as old-time farmer, cowboy, and policeman is still the perfect introduction to the idea of a story line. Youngsters like the sunny, peaceful mood and identify with the friendly child-faced man. From time to time other single stories about Mr. Small are also available. Walck, 6 months–4 years.

Lowly Worm's Word Book, by Richard Scarry. Of all of Scarry's animal folk, Lowly Worm is the most intriguing. With a shoe on one end and a hat on the other, Lowly Worm hides out in Scarry's big books for children to find. Here he is in his own book of first words: holding a toothbrush, kicking a ball, and doing other things in his extraordinary way. A handy, fist-sized, block-shaped book of heavy cardboard. Random House, 1–2 yrs.

Pat the Bunny, by Dorothy Kunhardt. This old-timer is a uniquely happy introduction to books for the very littlest ones. The children in the book can pat the bunny, play peek-a-boo, look in a mirror—*and so can you!* Golden, 1–2 years.

Pigs Say Oink, by Martha Alexander. Any new talker loves learning animal sounds and meeting the animals that make them. *Pigs Say Oink* is full of animals sounding off and making friends with children. The sounds of each animal and a few things are printed clearly but unobtrusively above each. Alexander's pictures have a lovely sweetness without becoming saccharine. An altogether pleasing, educational, and affordable book. Random House, 1–2 years.

Sam's Car, by Barbro Lindgren, illustrated by Eva Eriksson. When Sam won't let Lisa play with his car, Lisa smacks him. Then Sam smacks Lisa, and now they both feel sad and don't know what to do. This is a real-life drama a really young child can strongly identify with. Simple, absorbing, exciting, and reassuring. A rare one. Morrow, 1–4 years.

Sam's Cookie, by Barbro Lindgren, illustrated by Eva Eriksson. Sam's dog wants Sam's cookie, which makes Sam mad, which makes the dog growl, which makes Sam scared. Another very young real-life predicament presented in an extraordinarily simple and dramatic way. Another rare one! Morrow, 1–4 years.

Sam's Teddy Bear, by Barbro Lindgren, illustrated by Eva Eriksson. Sam loves his teddy bear and plays happily with him in his crib. Sam's dog loves Sam and plays happily on the floor with Sam's slippers. Then Sam's bear falls out of reach and into a terrible predicament. This makes Sam sad and gives his dog a chance to be a big hero. Funny, exciting, wonderfully unpatronizing. Still another rare one by the same Swedish team. Morrow, 1–4 years.

Springtime for Jeanne-Marie, by Françoise. A little girl and her sheep Patapon have a hard time finding their lost friend Madalon, a little white duck. This text of many words can be reduced to a few at first. The story stays interesting to children for several years. Scribner's, 1–3 years.

The Three Birds, by Hilde Heyduck-Huth. "By the river there was a town. In the town there was a garden. In the garden stood a tree. Among the branches was a nest. In the nest there were three blue eggs. From the eggs came three little birds. The three little birds flew over the house. A boy watched the birds from his window. He saw the three birds fly home to the nest." A very sturdy cardboard book with a story that doesn't need to be boiled down. Harcourt Brace Jovanovich, 1–2 years.

The Toolbox, by Anne and Harlow Rockwell. A simple picture and a single sentence about each of fifteen tools. A strikingly lovely little book that presents each tool as a work of art. Also look for the Rockwells' *Machines* at the library. Macmillan, 1–2 years.

Elsewhere in this book see also *Catch Me and Kiss Me and Say It Again* (page 268). And do be sure to have a book of Mother Goose rhymes. Although the stories they tell are often silly or incomprehensible and their values either undetectable or poor, Mother Goose rhymes are part of our culture and offer much of use to the child. A good collection of these rhymes is an unmatched means for simultaneously amusing him and fostering language development. Rhyme, rhythm, and repetition help him master basic speech sounds; and through picture and context he builds a preliminary vocabulary of words and concepts. Best of all, these silly little story/verses offer first experiences in story continuity and some general exposure to the wider world. The most useful Mother Goose anthologies have lots of illustrations for the child to "read" to himself as you read the verse aloud. So look for one in which each rhyme is illustrated with at least one picture. Long before the rhymes are understood, the heavily illustrated Mother Goose can be used as a word book. Find and talk about familiar objects in the pictures and name the unfamiliar ones. Then move on as the child is interested, reciting rhymes and repeating favorite ones at other times without the book. Most enjoyable are the ones that you rehearse over and over as part of your daily doings. Particularly nice are those you can sing and act out, such as "One Misty Moisty Morning" (with its handshaking *"How do you do and how do you do and how do you do again?"*). Some especially nice Mother Goose books include big ones by Briggs, Provensen, Richardson, Wright, and Rojankovsky *(The Tall Book of M.G.),* as well as smaller ones such as Rockwell's *Gray Goose and Gander* and Spier's *To Market, To Market.*

Stage Two Stories

Some of these have a lot of words, but they are all composed of concrete events that can be told in a few words and understood quite young. It doesn't matter if the child does not get the main point; he will nevertheless enjoy the story sequence—seeing that things are connected if not exactly how.

A Boy, a Dog, and a Frog, by Mercer Mayer. After skillfully outwitting the efforts of a boy and dog to catch him, a lonely frog trails his would-be captors to a joyful bathtub reunion. There is no text to overlook here—only delightful pictures for story-telling adventure. Dial, 2–5 years.

Anybody at Home? by H. A. Rey. What do you think is in this hole or hive or tank? Make a guess and then unfold the page to see. Houghton Mifflin, 2–4 years.

Are You My Mother? by P. D. Eastman. If *you* hatched when *your* mother was out, how would you recognize her even if you could find her? Designed for beginning readers, baby bird's quest makes a charming story to chuckle over for new listeners as well. Can be carefully abridged—*Is the kitten his mommy? No! Is the dog his mommy? Naah! Is the boat his mother?*—and gradually developed into a full story. *He meets the cow. Is the cow his mother bird? No, silly, of course not!* And then, before you know it: "Hey, remember how I used to love this book? Well, listen! Now I can read it!" Random House, 2–6 years.

The Country Noisy Book, by Margaret Wise Brown, illustrated by Leonard Weisgard. Muffin the dog goes to the country with his family and hears many new sounds. Children identify happily with the little dog who, traveling in a box, has no idea of where he is going or what will happen next. They love to guess what makes each sound that Muffin hears. Harper & Row, 2–5 years.

Feed the Animals, by H. A. Rey. Another Rey guessing book with fold-out surprise pages. Guess whom the zookeeper is going to feed next? Houghton Mifflin, 2–4 years.

Goodnight, Richard Rabbit, by Robert Kraus, illustrated by N. M. Bodecker. Richard Rabbit can't go to sleep because he is imagining things. But fear by fear (and excuse by excuse) his patient mother shows him what really is and isn't there until at last Richard Rabbit is fast asleep. Cute as can be, with charming illustrations. Windmill, 2–4 years.

The Little Fireman, by Margaret Wise Brown, illustrated by Esphyr Slobodkina. A big and a little fireman respectively put out a big and a little fire in their big and little ways. But falling asleep at last, the big fireman dreams a little dream, while the little fireman dreams a great big one. Scholastic, 2–4 years.

The Little Fur Family, by Margaret Wise Brown, illustrated by Garth Williams. "The fish didn't have any fur and they didn't have any feet and they swam around under the river. The little fur child watched them for a long time." The wonderful simple adventures of a furry fellow who adventures alone in the bright world and finds his way home again just when it's getting too dark. Reassuring and loving—an ideal bedtime story. Harper & Row, 2–5 years.

Little Gorilla, by Ruth Bornstein. "Once there was a little gorilla, and everybody loved him." Just who loved little gorilla and how is this book's charmingly simple story. That he kept on being loved even when he grew into a huge gorilla is its special message. Scholastic, 2–4 years.

The Runaway Bunny, by Margaret Wise Brown. When a little rabbit imagines going away and becoming something else besides his mother's son, Mrs. Rabbit wisely reassures him that love will be there with him in some other form, too. "If you become a bird and fly away from me," she says, "I will be the tree that you come home to." This amazing story reassures children that wherever they go they will find love taking new shape to meet their needs. It is not necessary or wise to explain this to our children in detail, only to be quite clear about it ourselves. Harper & Row, 2–4 years.

Whither shall I go from thy spirit?
Or whither shall I flee from thy presence?
If I ascend up into heaven, thou art there.
If I make my bed in hell, behold, thou art there.
If I take the wings of the morning,
and dwell in the uttermost parts of the sea,
Even there shall thy hand lead me,
and thy right hand shall hold me . . .
—Psalm 139:7–10

See the Circus, by H. A. Rey. Yet another of the Rey fold-out books. Houghton Mifflin, 2–4 years.

The Snowman, by Raymond Briggs. A boy and a snowman share a wonderful night of adventure in each other's worlds. As soundless as snow itself, Briggs' lovely pictures are better than words. A gentle, charming fantasy. Random House, 2–6 years.

The Snowy Day, by Ezra Jack Keats. A city child wakes to find that mountains and mountains of snow have fallen. Striking pictures convey the momentousness of every child's first snowfall. Viking, 2–4 years.

Sunshine, by Jan Ormerod. From the moment the sunshine wakes the little girl to the hilarious departure of the whole family for school and work, the message of this book is that sunshine makes sunshine. A book for parents as well as children to wake up by. A wordless book with lovely, loving, and funny pictures. Lothrop, 2–6 years.

The Winter Bear, by Ruth Craft, illustrated by Erik Blegvad. In these days of television and electronic games it is distressingly possible for a child to grow up without discovering the mystery and beauty of long walks. That's what makes this superbly illustrated book about three country children such a treasure. From pattable cow to a lovable toy bear caught in a tree, this story/ poem is a tempting invitation to the joys of a winter walk. Atheneum, 2–4 years.

Stage Three Stories

Longer than the stories in Stage Two, these range farther from home but are still quite concrete. By now the child is ready for a greater number of stories with somewhat fewer repetitions of each one.

Blueberries for Sal, by Robert McCloskey. A little girl and her mother and a bear cub get all switched around and wind up with the wrong mothers while picking blueberries. A gentle suspense story that resolves itself with reassuring smoothness. Children love the fact that they recognize the mix-up before the book characters do. Viking, 3–5 years.

Caps for Sale, by Esphyr Slobodkina. When a hat peddler angrily tries to make a bunch of monkeys return his stolen caps, they seem to make fun of him. Only when he flings down his own cap in disgust do the mimicking monkeys throw down his wares as well. Absolutely captivating. Funny and wise. Scholastic, 3–5 years.

Chicken Forgets, by Miska Miles. Little chicken is on a mission for blackberries, but will he remember what he is supposed to get? Doubt becomes suspense as one creature after another confuses the suggestible chicken. Any child who's ever been asked, "Are you old enough to . . ." will find this a real cliffhanger— and a big relief. Little, Brown, 3–6 years.

The Christ Child, illustrated by Maud and Miska Petersham. Selections from the Bible tell the story of Jesus from the prophecy of his birth through childhood. The lovely illustrations and traditional text make this an ideal book for Christian children to grow up with. Doubleday, 3 years and up.

Clipper, by Debbie L. Carter. Clipper keeps a lighthouse and wishes for company to share his nice but slightly lonely life. At last a storm brings him a wet, green friend who is only too happy to share shelter, friendship, and hot chocolate with Clipper. Simple and with charming pictures, *Clipper* presents the value of companionship. Harper & Row, 3–5 years.

The Goblin Under the Stairs, by Mary Calhoun, illustrated by Janet McCaffery. To the child who spies him through a knothole in the wall, the boggart is a "wee frisky man," a playmate. To the mother he appears "a good servant elf," and to the father "a house-plaguing goblin." The most violent predictions prevail until the father gives up trying to get rid of the boggart his way, and the mother serves up some of the hospitality a tidy servant elf deserves. Morrow, 3–5 years.

The Happy Lion, by Louise Fatio, illustrated by Roger Duvoisin. The beloved lion of a French zoo is bewildered by the startled and unfriendly response he receives when taking a stroll among friends outside the zoo. Only the zookeeper's son greets him in a kindly way and saves the day. McGraw-Hill, 3–5 years.

Jack Kent's Book of Nursery Tales, illustrated by Jack Kent. Every event in each of seven nursery classics is illustrated with a lively picture, making this the best first nursery tale book. Soon the child can learn to "read" the pictures and tell himself the familiar story. And then you can move on to the wealth of good nursery tale books with more traditional illustrations. Included in Kent's book are "The Three Little Pigs," "The Little Red Hen," "The Three Bears," "Chicken Little," et al. Random House, 3 years and up.

Ladybug and Dog and the Night Walk, by Polly Berrien Berends. One night Dog invited Ladybug and her seven baby cousins for a night walk in the countryside around the farm. Fireflies and insect music and the fascinating life of the night delight the friends until the awful discovery is made that one little ladybug is lost. Finally friendly fireflies come to the rescue by making Dog's nose into a flashlight. "Warm and gentle as a hug" according to *Publishers Weekly.* Random House, 3 years and up.

The Little Engine That Could, by Watty Piper, illustrated by George and Doris Hauman. Adults tend to find this story slightly sugary, but children adore it and are evidently encouraged by the little engine who pulled the broken-down trainful of toys over the mountain, saying, "I think I can, I think I can." Grosset, 3–5 years.

The Little House, by Virginia Lee Burton. Children love to hear again and again the story of the nice little house in the country that became a city house and got rescued. Houghton Mifflin, 3–6 years.

The Little Island, by Golden MacDonald (really Margaret Wise Brown), illustrated by Leonard Weisgard. On the surface this is a pleasant story of an island day by day, season by season, plant by plant, and creature by creature. But tucked away is the amazing thought (which a kitten must take on faith) that the island which seems separately afloat is really a part of the land and, like the kitten himself, at once "a part of the world and a world of its own." Doubleday, 3–5 years.

The Little Red Lighthouse and the Great Gray Bridge, by Hildegarde Swift and Lynd Ward. A small lighthouse is relieved to learn that its usefulness is not over when a towering bridge with a huge beacon is built over it. "Quick, let your light shine again. Each to his own place, little brother." A tremendous favorite with youngsters. (The lighthouse still stands beneath the George Washington Bridge in New York City.) Harcourt Brace Jovanovich, 3–6 years.

Make Way for Ducklings, by Robert McCloskey. Children who are also little and new in a huge strange world love this tale of a duck family in busy Boston. Everything is just right for preschoolers in this exciting yet comprehensible adventure. Tops among the classic McCloskey books. Viking, 3–6 years.

Midnight Moon, by Clyde Watson. In rich yet simple poetry Watson places your hand in the sandman's and sends you to visit the Man in the Moon. He'll play you tunes, show you his trick dog, and tell you stories of the earth, before sending you back—just in time for Mother Sun to wake you up. Collins, 3 years and up.

Pippa Mouse, by Betty Boegehold and Cyndy Szekeres. Six just-right stories about a little girl mouse who wants to try things and does. From making a door to keep out the rain to sleeping out overnight, the results are a 50/50 mixture of success and failure that any child will happily call adventures. Pantheon, 3–6 years.

The Poppyseed Cakes, by Margery Clark, illustrated by Maud and Miska Petersham. Two children always get into trouble when left alone—and they always get forgiven in the end. Any preschooler who ever gets into trouble is filled with suspense when these two do—and vastly relieved when they are rescued. Beautifully written and illustrated. This book and *Little Pear* provide a bridge from picture books to longer classics. A must. Doubleday, 3½–6 years.

The Sailor Dog, by Margaret Wise Brown, illustrated by Garth Williams. When Scuppers the sailor dog got shipwrecked and needed a house, he built one. When he needed tools, he found some. When he needed supplies, he fixed his ship and sailed after some. "And here he is where he wants to be, a sailor sailing the deep green sea." Wonderful pictures, wonderful story. Inspires children with a sense of order, possibility, and self-confidence. Golden, 3–6 years.

The Story of Babar, by Jean de Brunhoff. How Babar the elephant grew up and went to the city and came home in clothes to be crowned king and marry Celeste. The classic beginning of a storybook elephant civilization that has lasted through two authors (father and son), more than a dozen sequels, and thousands upon thousands of enthusiastic children. Also available on record. Random House, 3–6 years.

Wake Up, Bear . . . It's Christmas, by Stephen Gammell. Having set his alarm clock for Christmas, Bear wakes up just in time to trim a tree and spend an amazing evening with a remarkable little stranger in red. (Guess who?) The gentle mood and beautiful pictures cannot fail to carry small listeners right into the starry sky with Bear and his friend. Lothrop, 3–6 years.

Stage Four Stories

Some of these are longer than those in Stage Three. Others are not necessarily longer, but conceptually harder.

Bravo Ernest and Celestine, by Gabrielle Vincent. To earn enough money to fix their leaking roof is a big problem, but Ernest, with little Celestine's help and encouragement, finds a wonderful way. Working together brings many more benefits besides the needed roof. All the books about this improbable pair, a child-like mouse and a fatherly bear, are marvelously illustrated and call to mind the tenderest and funniest moments we share as parents and children. Greenwillow, 3–6 years.

The Camel Who Took a Walk, by Jack Tworkov, illustrated by Roger Duvoisin. A beautiful camel out for a walk on a beautiful day remains oblivious of, yet mysteriously protected from, a lurking hungry tiger. The suspense is terrific and the surprise ending both hilarious and meaningful. Dutton, 4–6 years.

Ernest and Celestine, by Gabrielle Vincent. When Celestine loses her beloved toy bird and it finally turns up wet and ruined in the snow, Ernest tries everything to cheer her up. Greenwillow, 3–6 years.

Ernest and Celestine's Picnic, by Gabrielle Vincent. When it rains on their picnic day, they have a rainy-day picnic; when accused of trespassing, they befriend their accuser. As with each of the other books about these two, this one has a truly lovely, loving atmosphere. Greenwillow, 3–6 years.

The Fire Cat, by Esther Averill. A little bully of an alley cat becomes a skillful important firehouse cat, and then must still learn to be kind. He reflects, "Once I chased a little cat up a tree. Oh me! Oh my! Why did I do that?" Loving, accepting. Dismisses badness as ignorance. Harper & Row, 4–6 years.

The House on East 88th Street. The story of a citified crocodile who terrifies, charms, and wins the love of everyone he meets. Fanciful and entertaining, with just enough "real" world to set a child's imagination perking. There are several other stories about the beloved Lyle Crocodile, all available in both recorded and book form. Houghton Mifflin, 4–6 years.

Katy and the Big Snow, by Virginia Lee Burton. The enthralling tale of a red crawler tractor that plowed out a whole town after a snowstorm. A big bonus in this book is its little picture catalog of many other kinds of road machines. Houghton Mifflin, 4–6 years.

Little Pear, by Eleanor Frances Lattimore. Sooner than you think, the child who has been thoughtfully exposed to books is verbal enough to enjoy a story without seeing many pictures. There are no two better to start with than *Little Pear* and Margery Clark's *Poppyseed Cakes.* In *Little Pear* a Chinese child's curiosity gets him into one scary and hilarious predicament after another. And time and again he is lovingly rescued, scolded, and forgiven. Another must. Harcourt Brace Jovanovich, 4–6 years.

Little Raccoon and the Thing in the Pool, by Lilian Moore, illustrated by Gioia Fiammenghi. On his first solo trip to the pool, Little Raccoon is warned by many animals about the "thing" he will find there. When he arrives, sure enough, the fearful thing stares back at him from the water. After all his efforts to scare the thing fail, he runs home and learns from his mother that the way to tame the "thing" is to smile at it. McGraw-Hill, 4–6 years.

Mike Mulligan and His Steam Shovel, by Virginia Lee Burton. Mike Mulligan and his steam shovel Mary Ann are being put out of business by more modern diggers. Finally they get a job digging the foundation for a town hall, for money if they can do it in a day, for nothing otherwise. They succeed with the job, but in their haste dig themselves into their own deep hole. All problems are solved by converting the steam shovel into a furnace and Mike Mulligan into the superintendant of the new town hall. Houghton Mifflin, 4–6 years.

Moon Mouse, by Adelaide Holl, illustrated by Cyndy Szekeres. A small mouse goes to see what the moon is made of and, at least to his satisfaction, finds out that it is delicious. Lovely illustrations. Random House, 3–5 years.

My Box and String, by Betty Woods. A boy makes something from a box and learns that the real fun is in the making and sharing, not only in the having. Scholastic, 4–6 years.

Our Animal Friends at Maple Hill Farm, by Alice and Martin Provensen. From Max the Cat, who is clever and hates snakes, to Whiney the Sheep, who is dumb and confused and faints from fear when she gets sheared, to Goat Dear, who is very gentle and likes people, all the animals at Maple Hill Farm have personality, and are appreciated—faults and all. Highly original and entertaining. Also a helpful tool for teaching respect and acceptance of others. Random House, 4 years and up.

Smile, Ernest and Celestine, by Gabrielle Vincent. When little Celestine secretly explores the drawers of fatherly Ernest and finds a bundle of photographs, she is overcome with jealousy. But gentle Ernest knows just what to do with her complaint that "there's not a single picture of me." All children who have ever sneaked a peek at their parents' things—and many foster or adopted children—will find this a special book. Greenwillow, 3–6 years.

The Story About Ping, by Marjorie Flack. Rather than receive a spank for being the last on board his Chinese junk home, a yellow duckling chooses to stay behind. After an exciting adventure and a narrow escape he finds his boat again and opts to return, spank or no spank. This story of a daring duckling who disobeys and survives can be helpful to parents and children as they try to deal with freedom and discipline. Viking, 4–6 years.

The Tale of Peter Rabbit, by Beatrix Potter. Every home library needs at least one of the beautifully illustrated books by Beatrix Potter —and if only one, then surely *Peter Rabbit.* His dangerous adventure in Mr. McGregor's garden will snare, scare, delight, and turn out all right. Frederick Warne, 4–6 years.

Three Grimm's Fairy Tales, illustrated by Bernadette. A boxed set of three classic Grimm's tales presented, almost miraculously, in simple enough terms for young children. In "The Fox and the Geese" a gaggle of not-so-silly geese outfox a hungry (and silly) fox. In "The Magic Porridge Pot" a little girl is the only one who can save a whole town from drowning in porridge. In "The Silver Pennies" a poor but generous child gives away all she has on earth and receives more than she needs from heaven. Mysterious, meaningful, and magical. Lays groundwork for reading more fairy tales later. Little, Brown, 4–6 years.

The Tiger in the Teapot, by Betty Yurdin, illustrated by William Pène du Bois. After all the threatening, ordering, bribing, and pleading of the rest of the family fails to induce an unwelcome tiger to leave their teapot, it is the littlest girl, gracious and graceful, who finally succeeds. Holt, Rinehart and Winston, 4–6 years.

A Personal Selection

I wish every child could own:
> *Goodnight Moon*
> *Midnight Moon*
> *Make Way for Ducklings*
> *The Poppyseed Cakes*
> *Little Pear*
> *Jamie's Story*
> *Catch Me and Kiss Me and Say It Again*
> *The Little Fur Family*
> *Good Morning, Chick*
> *Jump, Frog, Jump!*
> *The Sailor Dog*
> *The Country Noisy Book*
> *Father Fox's Pennyrhymes*
> *Our Animal Friends at Maple Hill Farm*
> *The Runaway Bunny*
> *What Do People Do All Day?*
> *Sam's Car*
> *Sam's Cookie*
> *Sam's Teddy Bear*

Toddler-Told Tales

If besides being chief cook and bottle washer, you are willing to be your children's occasional scribe, you can begin to foster their literary and artistic creativity, as well as their appreciation of books. Telling tales is tops for toddlers: making books is even better. By taking time to make little books of a child's ideas, we contribute to her sense of worthiness and freedom of expression. Here are a few suggestions for getting started:

● Offer to write captions for your child's artwork. Don't ask "What is it?" because maybe it isn't a what—maybe it's a feeling or an exploration or some other kind of happening. Just try, "Talk to me about your picture and I'll write down your words." Sometimes the answers are pure poetry.

● Help the child cut out a picture from a magazine and glue it on a piece of paper. Invite her to tell you about it. Write down her "story" below the picture. At first maybe she'll just tell what it is; later maybe she'll want to make up a story about what is taking place in the picture.

● Divide a piece of paper into squares for recording stories in comic book fashion. This can help a child to look at a story in terms of a sequence of events. Depending on the child, either of you may draw the pictures. Or maybe you can work on them together. Good old stick figures are just fine.

● Fold some pieces of paper in half to make a little book with pages that really turn. Maybe the child has a story in mind. Or maybe she hasn't a clue of how or where to begin. Then we can help by asking leading questions. Once there was a ———— who went ———— when suddenly ————. How did it feel? What did it look like?

Reference Books

Children's questions can be so difficult—especially the simple ones, such as "What does *nevertheless* mean?" It's so easy, until you try to explain it in words that your four-year-old can understand. And so the cranky expression comes out instead, "Stop asking me so many questions! Can't you see that I'm busy?"

Of course we wouldn't want them to stop asking questions. Yet dialogue is something we seem to have to learn. A very big stumbling block to dialogue in families is the popular belief that parents are supposed to have all the answers. So, instead of an interest in finding things out together, many of us are overly preoccupied with seeming to be right. We would rather sit at the dinner table and argue over the meaning of a word than take two minutes to look it up in the dictionary. Somehow we equate not knowing with stupidity. But as the old sage said, "My only wisdom consists in knowing that I know not."

As a reminder and as an exercise in this wisdom of ignorance, it is helpful to have a place set aside at home where the dictionary can be kept open. Better than a children's dictionary is a big unabridged one with plenty of illustrations and charts. Keep a list of words and facts that you and your child want to look up; and set aside some time each day to do so. A dictionary also makes a wonderful picture book just to poke around in at random with a child. And how about an atlas, a one-volume encyclopedia, and a Bible?

Besides the obvious intellectual benefits to the child, the look-it-up habit brings long- and short-term benefits to the mental health of the whole family. The family that can find things out together can also talk things over together. And when our children are teenagers, they will more readily turn to us with their more troublesome questions if we *don't* have all the answers than if we think we do. Some good books for family reference are: *What Makes It Go, Work, Fly, Float?* by Joe Kaufman (Golden Press); *The Children's Picture Atlas, The Children's Book of the Earth,* and *The Children's Book of the Seas,* by Jenny Tyler and Lisa Watts (Usborne).

Cassette Recorders

"A gawk! Dassa gawk!" pipes a tiny, remarkably familiar voice.

"Right!" says a fatherly voice. "So then the dog went to sea on a—what did he go on?"

"In da waff."

"Yes. Very good! He went on a raft."

"Is that me?" says the now big boy. "Did I really say 'gawk' for dog?" He seems proud of that somehow. And we are touched. His voice is already so much deeper, but the resemblance to the little pipsqueaking on the tape is unmistakable.

The tape recorder's usefulness and potential contribution to family life is still not widely recognized. With preschoolers the possibilities are vast. You develop a certain style of inflection when you read something repeatedly. To the child that becomes part of the book—the way it's meant to sound. Tapes of such readings can be listened to over and over by the child—not as a substitute for but as a supplement to the shared times. Quite early children can learn to operate cassette recorders alone. Then they can take a book and our recording of it and "read" privately at will. And then there are the songs we sing together, and the stories a child makes up. One of our favorite recordings is of an entire bedtime—the story, some songs, and our one-and-a-half-year-old's gradual acceptance of "Night, night," and his final babblings to himself in the darkness as he drifted off to sleep.

Influences: Good and Bad, False and True

As our children travel in ever wider circles and for longer periods of time away from home, we are inevitably concerned about outside influences. Especially now when travel is so easy, communications so vast, we do not have to wait until our children are very old before such concerns arise. In fact, the so-called "outside influences" do not stay outside, but invade the home like burrs on socks. They arrive by cereal box, by fourth class mail, and by commercial-singing kids brandishing toy weapons. Television sponsors proposition our children with everything from cosmetics to electronic games. Even the educational programs that rely on fascinating sounds and animation not only teach children to read but also foster their dependence on constant entertainment. A child commits a murder, a young man attempts to assassinate the president of the United States—both supposedly "under the influence" of what they have seen on television or in the movies. We are shocked when drugs and alcohol turn up in high school; we are more shocked to hear of their presence in junior high; we would like to withdraw our children from the world altogether when we find these nightmares haunting even the lower grades. To the suggestion that it is only what we as parents cherish, fear, or hate that influences our children (see page 3) our first reaction is fear and an eager denial of blame. But a second look, from a spiritual perspective, makes this after all a hopeful and promising thought. If it is only ideas of great importance to us that capture our children's interest, then they are not at the mercy of the world at large. Because then, if our invalid values can be recognized and replaced with valid ones, our children will be freed as well.

We know we cannot change the world for our children. We know we cannot keep them from the world. But as seeing beings we can learn to keep custody over our thoughts, once the primacy of thought is recognized. Indeed, while all our children are barraged with all the world's mistaken ideas, with each child it is only certain ones that "take"; only a little honesty can show us the presence of parental values in those that do. For example, does the sports hero or beauty queen on the cereal box really exert a direct influence on the child? No, only some children are impressed. And

PRACTICAL INFORMATION FOR NEW PARENTS

even for these is there not also some secret parent factor as well? *If my child is not good at sports, will she be accepted? If he cannot beat others and be a winner, will he be a loser?* And the coveted Darth Vader mask of another child—do we *fear* the evil Darth Vader represents? Do we *cherish* the child's acceptance by others? Do we *hate* to think of our child lacking what others have? Do we secretly equate having things, having what others have, with being worthy and loved? As Me, Inc., we all fall prey to some of these ideas, and there is always some cherishing, hating, or fearing on our part to match any cherishing, hatred, or fear on the part of our children. What is truly nothing, truly holds *no* interest for us, will not capture our children's attention either—at least not for very long.

Sometimes a parental cherishing is reflected in our children as an opposing fear or hatred. For example, if we overvalue success we may sire either a breathless achiever or an individual dogged by lethargy and failure. By constantly fault-finding and correcting our child anxiously, we who overvalue social acceptance may sire a child who is either a charming "operator" or one who is socially insecure.

This desire for acceptance is particularly prevalent and insidious. It is striking that in the addict's language a dose of narcotics is referred to as a "fix." Do all our loving attempts to "fix" our children so that they will be accepted only give them the idea that they are unacceptable and need to be fixed? Are the first experiments with drugs only attempts at being accepted? Is it only when having a "fix" that these youngsters find relief from the nagging sense of personal shortcoming and unacceptability?

Sometimes our fears and hatreds turn up in our children as cherished interests.

> In our son's nursery school carpool there is a boy who is fascinated by guns. The other children can take or leave them. When they go to Billy's they play cowboys or cops and robbers or soldier as he insists. But without him they usually choose other play. Guns are all that Billy wants to play with or talk or read about. Isn't it strange? His father, a psychiatrist, is a pacifist who has done alternative military service as a conscientious objector. Both he and his wife are strenuously opposed to guns!

There is really no such thing as outside influences. While our children will be exposed to many undesirable ideas it is only those we ourselves cherish, fear, or hate that can influence them. In this regard we can say that *the only influences on our children are* inside *influences. Rather than fearing outside influences we can better be mindful of our own inside influences and whether they are true or false.*

When the toddler is small, it is convenient to sit him before the television in order to get a few moments to ourselves. So we give power to the television and use it to influence (by entertaining) or otherwise control the minds of our children. As our children grow we are usually concerned with how to go about influencing them positively. But the belief that we need to influence each other is itself false. As long as we are trying to exert any kind of personal influence on our children we are really making them vulnerable to influence. The desire to exert power, to be successful, to get what others have, to have "clout," to impress, to please, to be in charge, to be accepted—these are all *influencing* ideas. As long as we attempt to influence our children whether for bad or for good we are teaching them that influencing (that is, exerting personal will power over others' minds) is what life is all about. From such a standpoint crime, war, seduction, alcohol, narcotics may all come to seem attractive as means whereby the child can successfully exert influence over others.

So the parent as a seeing being is thankful to discover something better and truer. When we are seeing clearly we not only recognize that there is no such thing as an outside influence, but also that in fact *no personal influence is a good influence.* Since the idea of personal minds exerting power over each other is basically false, it is also basically unhealthy. Instead we come to understand that *the only good influence is truth itself.* So we learn to be less concerned about being a good, strong, or even the right kind of influence on our children than with what it is from moment to moment that is influencing us. Our prayer is likely to be similar to Paul's: "Let that mind be in us which was also in Christ Jesus." When we are thus more concerned with being "in our right mind" than with having the "right" thoughts, many inspired ideas arise as needed to help free our children from the influence of false ideas and to raise them to be uninfluenceable custodians of their own consciousness.

In our town children refer to playing electronic games as "wasting quarters." "Hey," they ask each other, "want to waste some quarters?" While our sons are not encouraged to spend their money this way, one day while waiting for a takeout pizza I offered my son a quarter to play one of the games in the pizza parlor. "No thanks," he said, "I don't waste quarters any more." "That's fine," I said, putting the quarter away. A minute later I took it out and handed it to him. After all, what kind of a statement was I making? Would I only give him money if he was going to "waste" it?

A typical dilemma for our time is the question of television watching. If each of three children in one family is allowed to select one half-hour T.V. program per day and to watch the others' selections, and if they watch together two additional hours on weekends, then in fifteen years each will have spent more than a full year of twenty-four-hour days sitting in front of the television set!

In many homes favorite programs govern activities, determine mealtimes, interrupt responsibilities, and weaken resolve. Some parents feel guilty about the amount of television their children watch, and in some homes T.V. is forbidden. But many children who feel "deprived" of television at home spend as much time as possible watching it in friends' homes.

So what's best? The seeing being realizes that to watch T.V. or not to watch T.V., even the content of the shows, is not of paramount importance. In raising our children the primary issue is mesmerism, addiction, seduction, hypnosis, mind control, brain washing. The real issue is consciousness. How can we raise addiction-free, influence-free, discerning, discriminating children?

Immunization Rather Than Ignorance

Be ye wise as serpents and innocent as doves.
—Matthew 10:16

We cannot spare our children the influence of harmful values by turning off the television any more than we can keep them home forever or revamp the world before they get there. Merely keeping them in the dark is no protection and, in fact, can make them vulnerable and immature. In one family a firm disposing of the television to make room for other things may be the right response, but in another the T.V. may remain as something to reckon with.

The principle of immunization is that an injection of small, harmless doses of a disease rouses the system's defenses and strengthens it against further exposure. Then when a large dose of the disease is encountered, the body is prepared to repel it. With values such immunizing can occur through watching television except that here the immunization process occurs in the mind of the child.

Television mirrors the world's fantasies about itself. Popular shows reveal popular values. However crudely portrayed, it is the public's own secret desires that characterize a successful show. Many popular programs suggest that sex, power, and possessions are the most important things in life. By their very success these shows also reveal what society at large values. Our children will need to be able to move about in a world where such values are worshiped without actually falling prey to them. Thus, with all of its bad influences, T.V. is not to be feared. Used aright, it can be a fairly safe laboratory for confronting, seeing through, and thus being immunized against unhealthy values so as to be "in the world but not of it."

Who's in Charge?

She began to be aware that the T.V. habit had grown too large. Initially, she admitted, she had relied on T.V. as a babysitter for her children. But it had gotten out of hand. She considered imposing restrictions. But then a better idea occurred to her. She knew it was best for the children to learn to choose for themselves. If she forbade them then she would be in control. If she did nothing the T.V. would remain in control. Either way the children would be controlled, passive, gullible, and "under the influence" of one thing or another. She considered carefully what was so objectionable about excessive T.V. watching and presented it simply to the children:

"When you are watching television you only get ideas that the television people want you to get. If you aren't watching T.V. you may get some other ideas—ideas meant just for you. Maybe they will be the best ideas you have ever had in your whole life. And they will come to you firsthand—they won't be somebody else's secondhand ones."

"I'm going to try it now," said one child, walking away from a favorite show.

"Me too," said the other, all excited. "I wonder what ideas I am going to get."

They turned off the set and walked off to their rooms, transported with enthusiasm and scientific curiosity. For several hours they played. Forgotten toys were discovered, new games invented. One child began to write a play. They saw. They really saw something about how you have to be available to good ideas for them to occur to you. They learned something about mental hygiene. They became aware of their own capability to be inspired. They saw that T.V. can interfere with inspiration.

Try It, You'll Hate It

How manufacturers attempt to influence parents by influencing children in television commercials hardly needs to be said. Ad after ad attempts to program our children to plead with us to buy things. We can tell them it's junk, but to them it looks fabulous. Of course, we're in charge and what we say goes, but the problem comes up repeatedly. Wouldn't it be better if they could discern for themselves? Sometimes we just have to be firm, but sometimes we can recognize opportunities for letting our young seeing beings see for themselves.

The Ghastly Green Disappointment

Our children fell for a television commercial for a ridable inchworm. The ad showed children riding through a field on cute green inchworms. You could just imagine yourself riding this friendly creature through a sunlit daisy field, falling into conversation with chipmunks and bunny rabbits. Instead of just saying no, we decided to test market the inchworm. We got into the car and drove to the store. Excitement was high. If it was good maybe we would bring it home! Down rows and rows of toy-laden shelves we quested after the coveted mount. At last in Aisle Six we found it. What a disappointment! Dwarfed by tall metal shelves, there on the drab linoleum floor the plastic—oh, so plastic—inchworm drably stood. Having come this far the kids resigned themselves to a test ride. How had they thought

it would look? How had they thought it would feel? It wasn't clear
—but not like this. Although they had seen it with their own eyes on
T.V., somehow something had been left out. The ride clinched it.
It was so noisy! Even the toddler could tell that it would be tough
if not impossible to ride through a field. "I don't want it, Mommy.
It's awful!" said the first rider. The other couldn't even be bothered
to take a turn.

Now the children are less seducible. Marketing experts can turn
on them all their weapons—animation, music, laughing children,
clever copy—but they are never completely convinced. "Hey," they
say. "Wouldn't it be nice if that was really nice?" And when something looks good, they don't just start in wanting it. Instead they say,
"Do you think we could take a look at that in the store and see if it's
any good?"

Wanting is a kind of pain. Every time a child watches an ad and
believes what he's told he gets this pain of wanting. But even as
children they are already seeing beings who can find out for themselves that there really is not much out there worth wanting.

The Best Thing in Life Is Life

Crummy toys aren't the only things that T.V. peddles. Crummy
values are also proferred. In itself the inclination to watch excessive T.V. expresses a certain erroneous value: the idea that happiness is to be entertained, to sit bloblike and be titillated by fac-
similes of life. Real life, in which we play an active part, is
associated with effort, with work. Passivity comes to be associated
with pleasure, activity with displeasure. Incredibly, we buy it. Then
there's the content of the shows, which suggests that sex, power,
money are happiness. We buy that too. We buy it every time we
trade in our real living for the counterfeit lives on the "tube" Next
to T.V. our own lives look humdrum, so we watch T.V. to get some
vicarious excitement.

Parentally it is easier with toys. Our children can try them and
see that they are crummy. But we'd just as soon not have them test
market all the false values they see. Will they have to become
junkies or get pregnant or wind up on Skid Row to find out what
isn't *the life* after all? Will they have to struggle for years over the
fact that they aren't superstars or superjocks or sexpots before

learning that these weren't such great goals to begin with? There must be a better way.

And that's the secret—finding a better, a truer, a truly fulfilling and happy way. If you have already eaten, you aren't hungry.

Often, disgusted, we say, "Can't you find something better to do than watch that dumb show? Turn it off and find something better to do." Grumbling they turn it off. But while we are racing around to get dinner, because we wasted time watching a flick, we notice our toddler is just hanging around—bored. A roomful of toys and he's bored? In fact he's lying on the dining room floor, rocking back and forth, humming to himself—just waiting for life to happen to him. So turning off the T.V. is not, in itself, the answer, because the problem isn't T.V.; it's the false belief that happiness means being entertained; it's the lack of a truer, better idea of what it means to be alive.

Do we ourselves equate work with being active, and pleasure with being passive? Have we some lively interest? Are we helping our children develop their own interests by providing time, supplies, and help as needed each day?

> Our children went through a Mommy I'm Bored period. This coincided noticeably with a particularly busy time in my life when I didn't think I had much time for anything except work and putting meals on the table. So for a while we began to set aside the last half hour of every day for "something creative." Sometimes we made things with clay. Sometimes we had a puppet show. Sometimes we painted or drew, sometimes we all did different things. We made sure everything else was done first, setting it up as a special creative time. We didn't keep it up, but the idea was planted and its benefits sampled. So now sometimes the children do it on their own, even walking away by themselves from a favorite show to "do something I've really been wanting to do and now's my chance."

Most helpful is a good reading habit. After years of bedtime books most children develop an enthusiasm for reading. It is not uncommon for book-loving children to look to see what's on television and then walk away because of a preference for reading.

"Mom, are you busy? If you are, could I watch T.V.? If you're not, could we do something together?"

Putting "first things first" is the best way to deal with any ignorant values that rise up to capture our attention or seemingly "influence" our children. After all, they are ignorant or false—not bad—values. Putting first things first is the same as what is meant by the first commandment: "Thou shalt love the Lord thy God with all thy heart and with all thy strength and with all thy mind—and thou shalt have no other Gods before me." For seeing beings this worship means valuing and having no priority ahead of love-intelligence. It is not just religious gobbledygook; it is a way of giving truth charge of our lives. When *what is* is in charge, *what isn't* has very little credibility and therefore very little influence. Earlier we considered the principle of discernment and saw that the necessary and practical are points of contact with the essential and spiritual. Here we see it again. In any given moment that we stop to consider and commit ourselves to whatever is love-intelligent, love-intelligence takes over. Homework, practice, clean room, table setting, whatever the mandates in any family—these things need to be put first with only extraordinary exceptions. And if things are put in intelligent order—first things first—T.V. and everything else finds its proper place. Whenever we line ourselves up with what is love-intelligent, the more love-intelligence takes over and leads us along.

Given a healthy set of priorities most children will find that they are too busy to spend much time sitting before the tube and that, in any case, they really do have better things to do. Awareness of having better things to do with their lives is the secret to immunizing our children against false values—whether presented on television or in "real life." The child who finds fulfillment in music or reading or cooking or swimming or writing or drawing is not as easily convinced that he needs recognition or power or some "high" to feel worthwhile and good. T.V. or not T.V., outside or inside, right or wrong, good or bad influences—are not the question. To be or not to be—what is and what isn't—that is the question.

8
Love

L ove. Oh, boy, do we want love! Give me love, we say. Love me because I am nice. Love me because I am smart. Love me because I am beautiful. Love me because I am rich and strong. Love me because I am poor and helpless. Love me because I am sweet and dumb. Love me because I am smart and tough. Love me because I am competent. Love me because I am funny. Love me because I am cute. Love me because I say so.

Love me by approving of me. Love me by accepting me. Love me by touching me. Love me by *not* touching me. Love me by agreeing with me. Love me by liking what I like. Love me by looking up to me. Love me by taking care of me. Love me by letting me take care of you. Love me by giving me gifts. Love me because of the gifts I give you. Love me by doing me favors. Love me by letting me do favors for you. Love me by picking up your socks.

Talk to me. Confide in me. Let me confide in you. Smile at me. At least look at me when I talk to you. Love me because I am a wonderful husband. Love me because I am a wonderful wife. Love me because I am a wonderful parent. Love me because I am such a great kid.

Oh, well, then just notice me. See, I'm over here! Do you see me? Me me me me me me me. Hear that? I *ex-iiiiiiiist!* Don't you love it?

If you don't love me, I'll die. See? I'm dying. I'm not kidding —this time I really mean it! Aren't you worried? It just kills me when you don't love me. . . . At least *say* something. (*"O.K., something."*) That was mean. Oh, well, then go ahead and be mean and rotten. I don't care what you do, just so long as you don't ignore me. *I can't stand that.* When you ignore me I could just scream. Love me or else.

Now then, let's be reasonable. How about this? I'll love you, and then you love me! I'll even go first. See? I did it. I just loved you. Now it's your turn to love me back. What do you mean you don't feel like it? Not in the mood! No fair. You can't quit in the middle. I hate you for not loving me. Do me good, bay-baby, *or I'll die.*

Rock-a-bye baby
on the tree top.

When the wind blows
the cradle will rock.
When the bough breaks
the cradle will fall,
and down will come baby—
cradle and all.
—Traditional nursery rhyme

Ashes ashes
we all fall down.
Ashes ashes
we all . . .
—Traditional nursery rhyme

For he is like a refiner's fire.
But who may abide the day of his coming,
and who shall stand when he appears?
—Malachi 3:2

He that loseth his life for my sake shall find it.
—Matthew 10:39

As Me, Inc. we are desperate for love. Getting love is our whole life, and we will go to any amount of trouble to get it. We grow up, get married, have children—anything to get love. We never doubt that love is something between people, something interpersonal. (*You mean, it isn't? Well, what then? I have a dog—but that's not the same at all.*) Of course love is interpersonal! First it was supposed to come from our parents; now we're supposed to give it to our children. They'll love us in return; we'll all love one another. Maybe we'll even go public and get the world at large to love us. (*"I don't know about you, but personally, I've never loved a president yet."*) (*"Since I'm running for the school board, I'll just pretend I didn't hear that."*) We completely blind ourselves to the fact that even if we succeed in getting love from each other, each other is going away. (*If you don't mind, I'd rather not continue this conversation.*) The children are growing. Soon they'll be going. And they aren't the only ones. (*I said I'd rather not . . .*)

Even with spiritual ideas, the pitfall remains that we will continue to go about life in general, parenthood in particular, with the idea of doing it right. So we can get what we want. We keep deceiving ourselves. (*Now I get it! This book shows how to be loving parents. The spiritual way! This is really going to work.*) As if we were parents to achieve certain results! But that is invalid. Parenthood does not exist so that human adults can turn human children into more human adults, but for turning seemingly human parents into spiritual children. We—parents and children together—are a result that God is achieving. How much easier it would be if we understood that! But we don't. We keep trying to prove ourselves.

See how patient I am? I'm just being good. I'll think good and I'll do good. That'll be good. Now look—I'm being strong and disciplined, and self-sacrificing, and brave, and faithful. And I'm a wonderful parent. Now do they love me? Mom and Dad, do you still love me? See how good I'm doing? Do you love me *yet?* (No answer.)

> Me, Inc.: *God? . . . Are you there?*
> Still Small Voice: *God is . . . but you're not.*
> Me, Inc. [gulp]: *But what about love? Don't we have to love each other?*
> Still Small Voice: *Each other. This message does not compute.*
> Me, Inc. [incredulous]: *Just let me run this through again. I said e-a-c-h-o-t-h-e-r. Me + you = LOVE.*
> Still Small Voice: *Each other me you. Does not compute.*
> Me, Inc.: *I don't feel so good. I'm not doing so good.*
> Still Small Voice: *Don't feel not doing. Does not compute.*
> Me, Inc. [fading]: *. . . what then?*

So Me, Inc. comes to the end of its sleep and the beginning of its life. We used to be just plain old havers/doers. And then we became seeing/doers. But at long last we give up and are ready to be seeing beings, which we are brought to see means being loving. Because now Still Small Voice is whispering to us.

Before Abraham was I am.
—John 8:58

Son, thou art ever before me.
All that I have is thine.
—Luke 15:31

I have loved you with an everlasting love.
—Jeremiah 31:3

We love because he first loved us.
—1 John 4:19

After all, love is not something that we get or do, but something that we are. Always were. Always will be. To himself, the clown of our story is Me, Inc. (pages 19, 108 and 281); everyone (and everything) else is to use to give himself pleasure (*When I'm with you I feel warm inside. When I'm with you I feel warm all over*) or to shed light on his personal importance and power (*You make me feel ten feet tall. When I'm with you I feel on top of the world.*) His version of love is utilitarian. In perceiving himself as an entity he also objectifies everyone else. He regards and approaches everyone else as his private utility, and "loves" the one he deems most useful for warming himself and for spotlighting him.

Each of us struggles in vain to get the other to live on his terms. *I'll be me and you be it. No, you're it. I was it the last time.* So we try to take turns, compromise, swear over and over to "stop playing games," even feign to refuse to play games with each other, boycott each other's games—still pining for love. We have to come to terms. My terms? No, my terms. To terms with each other? Impossible.

Finally we have to come to God's terms, to recognize that we cannot get love from each other, that we *need* not get love from each other, but that we can be loving together.

| Intelligence | Cause | Idea | Truth | Seeing |
| Love | Effect | Expression | Good | Being |

These two sets of ideas are parallel, belong together, are one. So as seeing beings in relation to other seeing beings, we can say the same about expressing love as about communicating truth.

Love is not the coming together of self and other, of clown and light bulb, but rather the coming to light of the oneness of both with the force *and goodness* of light. Love-intelligence expresses itself through clown and bulb, through everyone in unique ways, as seeing and as illumination, as intelligence and love. And through its oneness with the light each life is fulfilled and enhanced and thereby also enhances the life of the other. The awakened clown through seeing sheds light on the value and worth, the goodness and purpose, of the bulb. The bulb through shining sheds light on the value, the worth, the goodness and purpose of the clown. And both express the one great *fact and force and goodness* of the light.

> *And God saw the light and, behold, it was very good.*
> —Genesis 1:4

> *Let your light so shine that men may see your good works and glorify your father which is in heaven.*
> —Matthew 5:16

One Plus One Is One

> *In the higher realm of true Suchness*
> *There is neither "self" nor "other":*
> *When direct identification is sought,*
> *We can only say "not two."*
> —*Buddhist Scriptures,* selected and translated by Edward Conze

So it comes down to the point where Me, Inc. has to let go of itself, and with itself others, in favor of something truer. Most of us do not do this all at once, but over and over until death. But it helps to see that this is necessary. And it helps to know that it has always been so and wasn't just one person's idea of how to get comfortable in or at least used to life. And it helps to hear that this is not only the difficult and hard way, but after all the easiest and best and only way.

> Zen Buddhists tell of a student who could not speak Japanese. Therefore, instead of speaking with him, his master gave him a drawing to meditate on to help enlighten him regarding the truth of being. The drawing was a simple circle with a dot in the center. After a long time the student brought the drawing back to the master to demonstrate his understanding. He had erased the circle. The mas-

ter indicated that while this was a fine beginning, it was not sufficient. So the student went away—again for a long time. This time
when he returned he had erased the dot. He was enlightened. The
dot stood for self. The circle for others. He had discovered that
there was only one mind—one self.

*Jesus said, "Hear, O Israel, the Lord our God is one Lord; and thou shalt
love the Lord thy God with all thy heart, and with all thy soul, and with
all thy mind and with all thy strength. This is the first and great
commandment, and the second is like unto it; thou shalt love thy neighbor
as thy self."*
—Matthew 5:43

The two commandments are the same. There is nothing arbitrary about the first and nothing sentimental about the second.
They are not even commandments, but they form a statement
about what is.

Both the two-commandments-that-are-one and the story of
the Zen student describe the path most of us take toward the
realization of wholeness as oneness. In the early days of parenthood, we try to erase the self to serve the other (the baby). We
can all attest to the benefits of learning in some small measure to
put someone else first. But it isn't enough and, since it isn't really
the truth, in the long run it isn't sufficient. As Jesus' second commandment indicates, the true nature and worth of both self and
other has to be clearly seen. As the Zen story explains, both self
and other as distinct from the One Mind have to be erased. God
is the only I AM.

Before Abraham was I AM
—John 8:58

We are here for what God is. We are here *as* what God is.
We are God's self-expression. This is our life. This is our love.
Some think that erasing the dot and circle, self and other, leaves
nothing. That is what makes it so hard. Will we be nothing?

Will there be no love? But it is not possible to be a loving (or loved) separate self any more than one wave can float a boat or, for that matter, even be a wave by itself. Once self and other are erased (the second commandment), love as conscious oneness with good (God, Love-Intelligence) is left (the first commandment).

Three Sisters

I received a telephone call from a grandmother, a lovely individual concerned about her daughter. "For almost two years I have watched my daughter devote herself with infinite patience to her baby. Nothing has been too much trouble for the sake of that baby —and the baby is as sweet-tempered and alert as can be. But she is a full-time job for the mother because she cannot be left with anyone else. But today my daughter called, finally sounding a little desperate about when she will ever have any time for herself again. She really can't do anything without the baby. The baby has never been left with a sitter. When she is left she becomes unhappy. I know it is really my daughter who has not let go of the baby, not that the baby won't let go of her. I was wondering if there is anything helpful that I might tell her."

"Well," I said. "Often parents and children cannot tell each other anything. Somehow we all have to get over this idea that we are each other's parents and children first. Whether we are thinking of ourselves as parents of our children or children of our parents, eventually we have to come to see that both parent and child are children of God—and that it is God who is raising us and teaching us and bringing us along together."

"Oh!" I could hear recognition in her voice. "Then maybe I have to let go of her! Perhaps *I* need to see that my daughter is God's child and that I don't have to tell her anything!"

A few hours later the wise grandmother called again. "Something wonderful has happened! My daughter just called. For the first time today she was able to leave her baby. She said the child acted as if nothing was happening. She didn't even seem to notice that her mother was gone. It was the very first time she has ever been happy with a sitter!"

When Israel was a child, I loved him, and out of Egypt I called my son. The more I called them, the more they went from me; they kept sacrificing to the Baals, and burning incense to idols. Yet it was I who taught Ephraim to walk, I took him up in my arms; but they did not know that I

healed them as one who eases the yoke on their jaws; and I bent down to them and fed them.
—Hosea 11:1–4

Letting Go

Behold what love the Father hath given us, that we should be called children of God; and so we are. Therefore the world knoweth us not, because it knew him not. Beloved, we are God's children now; it doth not yet appear what we shall be, but we know that when he shall appear we shall be like him, for we shall see him as he is. And every man that hath this hope in him purifieth himself even as he is pure.
—1 John 3:1–3

We are what we think,
having become what we thought.
And joy follows a pure thought,
like a shadow faithfully tailing a man.
—Buddha, in *The Dhammapada,* trans. by P. Lal

As soon as we have conceived, we have to start letting go of our children. In fact, for some people letting go of the idea of *having* children is a prerequisite to conception. So often when couples who have had difficulty conceiving finally give up and turn to adoption, they suddenly discover that the pregnancy they sought to achieve is under way.

Maybe the moment of conception coincides with a shift in our motivation from the desire simply to "have a child of our own" to the desire to become parents regardless. Maybe it is when the parental motive slightly edges out the purely possessive one that the idea of a child (which is conceptually dependent on the idea of a parent) can occur. The child is conceived as the parent is conceived.

But of course this is barely a beginning. We must keep on and on letting go—letting our children be born, letting them sleep, letting them mature. We have to let go of the diapers, let go of the mistakes, and sooner or later we have to let go of the children altogether, let them walk right out of our lives to the care of a sitter, to a first overnight at Grandma's, to nursery school for half a day, to grade school, to college, to marry, to live in another part of the world. It can all be very painful, very hard and sad if we do not understand what all this letting go is for.

Having struggled so hard to learn to love them, we must let them go. But what is the good of the love if the beloved goes away? The fact is that true love, the truth that love *is,* does not come to us until we let go of our beloveds (beloved self, beloved beloved). The real loss in letting go is the loss of two, the two that is you and me, self and other, lover and beloved, revolving around each other in the nothingness, protecting each other from the nothingness, exchanging our nothingness for nothingness. If we *have* each other we *lose* each other, an event so painful that we wonder how we ever could have thought the having would be worthwhile. If we do good to each other, we also do bad to each other; if we help, we also hinder. So what is it all worth? Nothing. As two (not only separate from each other, but separate, two, from *everything*) it is all a fifty/fifty proposition—50 percent of the time you win, 50 percent of the time you lose. It all averages out to nothing. Two cannot become one. So losing this twoness is no loss at all.

When Abraham and Sarah were old and childless, they had to let go of their belief that they were old (persons) and childless (persons) who could not *have* (by personal means) a baby (person). But that wasn't all. Letting go of their sense of personal adequacy/inadequacy (it's the same, of course), they also acknowledged that there was One who could and would fulfill them. Two Me, Inc.'s could not produce a baby, but the One (Mind) could. One did. Sarah conceived and bore a son. When they let go of their sense of personal power and powerlessness they discovered divine power. When they let go of wanting/having a child, they *became* parents. And although they were old before they started, they lived to be—how old? Well, they remained young a long time after they had grown old. So, by giving up a little of their twoness, they discovered that God is intelligence, that God is creative power.

Then they went about the same sublime/ridiculous business of parenting that we are involved in, for of course they were as young as parents as Isaac was young as a child, newborn in the first, most ignorant sense of the word. Isaac must have slept and cried, pleased, perturbed them, worried, and made them proud. They must have struggled to learn to love just as we do. Like us they must have loved their boy—cherished him, wanted to protect him, and hold him close, and dreaded the inevitable, that he must (for his good if not for theirs) move away from them to become a man instead of a child!

Existence having born them
And fitness bred them,
While matter varied their forms
And breath empowered them,
All created things render, to the existence and fitness they depend on,
An obedience
Not commanded but of course.
And since this is the way existence bears issue
And fitness raises, attends,
Shelters, feeds, and protects,
Do you likewise:
Be parent, not possessor,
Attendant, not master,
Be concerned not with obedience but with benefit,
And you are at the core of living.
—*The Way of Life According to Lao Tzu,* trans. by Witter Bynner

Give up what is before, what is behind,
Give up what is now, and cross the stream.
Then will your mind be free,
then will you cross birth and old age.
—Buddha, in *The Dhammapada,* trans. by P. Lal

And he said, Take now thy son, thine only son Isaac, whom thou lovest, and get thee into the land of Moriah, and offer him there for a burnt offering upon one of the mountains which I will tell thee of.
—Genesis 22:2

And so Abraham was called upon to sacrifice Isaac. He loaded Isaac up with the kindling wood for his own sacrificial fire and, knife in hand, climbed the mountain with his son—his cherished, precious, dearest son—prepared to kill him in obedience to God. This time he was prepared to sacrifice the two for the One. In his consenting thought he had already done so. So, of course, such a thing was not necessary. God did not want him to kill his son, only his *own* son, his *having* of a son. But Abraham didn't know that until the last minute.

This time in sacrificing the twoness—his role as a lover (the father person) of the beloved (the son person)—he discovered another aspect of the One. As long as he knew God only as the creator, he was able to imagine (unable not to imagine) God the destroyer. But in surrendering once again his attachment to twoness he discovered this aspect of the One—that God is Love. In the slaughtering of both father and son, neither father nor son is lost, except as insufficient, slaughterable persons. Instead there is revealed infinite love which is no less available to one than to the other. Both father and son are revealed to be *in* love; both are seen to be children of God. Sacrificing *his* child, Abraham discovers that Isaac is God's well-protected child. Sacrificing himself as father (the desire to protect and defend), he discovers that God is father. It is no little thing, but it is no big deal either. The experience of sacrifice may be enormous, but the revelation of truth is that there was never anything to sacrifice, no sacrifice at all, in the first place. There is only love sustaining the only loving.

We all go through this. Each letting go is experienced as a sacrifice—first of ourselves to the child, then the child to the sitter, to other children, to the teacher, to the freedom to make mistakes and be terribly wrong and unhappy. We even supply our children with errors. While we are learning to behold the eternally perfect qualities in our children, we have to teach them the finite. We must teach them worldly, material concepts in what we finally begin to see is a spiritual universe. In the very process of learning ourselves to see with a single inner eye, we teach our son/daughter that he/she has two outer ones. Concepts of quantity, time, space, corporeality—all ultimately false—are necessary for living in the world and become kindling for the fire at which the grown child will ultimately have to sacrifice his own material sense.

> *And Abraham took the wood of the burnt offering, and laid it on Isaac his son; and he took in his hand the fire and the knife. So they went both of them together. And Isaac said to his father Abraham, "My father!" And he said, "Here am I, my son." He said, "Behold, the fire and the wood; but where is the lamb for a burnt offering?" Abraham said, "God will*

provide himself the lamb for a burnt offering, my son." So they went both of them together.
—Genesis 22:6–8

This is such a beautiful detail of the story. Abraham does what he has to do (the laying of the kindling on his son's back), but he *speaks* to him only of God (the spiritual, the true). While doing *as if* for a God who takes away (demands this sacrifice), he speaks of God as the provider. He does not try to carry either his son or his son's burden up the mountain. The son climbs himself, bearing his own burden of error to the summit. But Abraham walks beside him, keeping silent about the sacrifice, the evil, and the error, teaching only that God is good (an idea he is not even sure of himself). At the same time that he supplies his son with the material kindling for material sacrifice, he endeavors wholeheartedly to kindle his son's interest in spiritual reality.

As the son climbs the material mountain, the father ascends the spiritual one. Both child and man are sacrificed upon the mountain. As the child is sacrificed, the man is born; Abraham relinquishes his mental holding of Isaac to childhood. As the man is sacrificed, the child is born; in giving up his aggressive, protective, defensive selfhood, Abraham becomes as innocent, as trusting, and as pure as his son. For Isaac to be born a child, Abraham had to conceive of parenthood. For Isaac to be born a man, Abraham must become a child again.

What really happens in this second birth of Abraham is that, through the loss of both (two) material father and son, the spiritual fatherly/sonly, loving/humble One is born (realized in Abraham's consciousness). There is no loss of individuality, but rather only the fulfillment of individuality. Abraham and Isaac do not become one with each other, but rather each is seen to be individually one with the father.

Thus it can be seen that in losing there is no loss. In sacrificing the material son, Abraham gains and sets free the spiritual one. This son, the perfect, spiritual child of God, eternally in the care of infinite, fathering love, can never be lost to him. Now he and his son share sonship. Having seen the unslaughterable, perfect spiritual identity of his son, Abraham can see it in everyone. And sacrificing his material fatherhood to see the unslaughtering, perfect spiritual identity of the father, he becomes truly fatherly. Thus it is that Abraham sires more children than the stars in the sky. He becomes at one with the father of the eternal, spiritual children of God. He is fatherly with the father and a son with the sons. The twoness of loss is erased when thus the father and son are one. "Son, all that I have is thine."

So it is with us and our children. On the one hand, we *do* for them, and teach them how to get along in the material world, but at the very same time we sacrifice our notion of them as material selves, our notions of our *own* personal responsibilities, and our own personal *having/needing* selves. At the same time that we deal with and seem to be material selves, we behold the spiritual, relinquishing errors, lacks, and problems as nothing (fasting, forgiveness) and maintaining in consciousness the spiritually perfect (prayer, atonement). At the same time that we let our children go from us forth into the world, we acknowledge that there is only one father/mother/parent—infinite, omnipresent love never withheld, only to awaken in.

In letting go of our children it is helpful to know that, although we are releasing them into the world, we are not turning them over to the world. Instead, constantly, consciously, we are turning them over to the one loving father ("Not I, but the father in me," "I and my father are one," "In him we live and move and have our being"). And this is both the secret of our redemption and a vital protection for our children.

There is nothing to be lost but loss. Our loss of a sense of finitude yields awareness of eternity; loss of the sense of power and powerlessness, creative power; loss of the material, awareness of the spiritual; loss of the beloved, awareness of love; loss of personhood, awareness of love-intelligence. In becoming at one with the father instead of striving to become one with each other, both we and our children become channels for and recipients of the infinitely various spiritual qualities of beauty, truth, creativity, and love.

Jesus had no children, yet in recorded history there is no man who ever saw more clearly that each of us is a child of love, born of love, and in essence and consciousness at one with love. It is notable that this most parently of individuals was known above all as God's son, a fact that by itself suggests what parenthood really is.

As the truly parently parent is the childlike parent,
As the truly nourishing parent is the nursing parent,
As the truly teaching parent is the learning parent,
As the truly freeing parent is the obedient parent,
As the truly unifying parent is the unified parent,
As the truly beautifying parent is the truthful parent,
As the truly creative parent is the beholding parent,
As the truly communicating parent is the listening parent,
So is the truly loving parent after all no parent at all, but only the loved child of God.

Seeing is being. Intelligence expresses itself as love. Awareness expresses itself as being. Knowing is loving. Loving is knowing. Intelligence is the only cause, love its only effect. Whether we begin by seeing the truth and become loving, or begin by being loving and then see the truth, one love-intelligent moment leads to another.

The more we realize that seeing is the issue in life,
the more interested we are in seeing.
The more interested we are in seeing,
the more we look at everything for what it has to teach us.
The more we look at everything for what it has to teach us,
the more we see that we are being taught.
The more we see that we are being taught,
the more we know that we are loved.
The more we know that we are loved,
the more we see love.
The more we see love,
the more lovingly we are seeing.
The more lovingly we are seeing,
the more loving we are being.

Afloat

Finally my grandmother died. For more than three years she had
barely been here, hanging on to her old Me, Incorporation and
refusing to take her nap. Somebody said, "Thank God it's over for
her. Now she can rest in peace." I thought, *Rest in peace? I was just
thinking, Thank goodness, now she can finally get on with her life!*

Even before she died, some said my grandmother was gone
already, floating, didn't know what was going on. But I remember
the last thing she said to me, and to me it sounded like a lot was
going on. She had already slipped way back inside, and I had to rub
her hands with my hands and her cheeks with my cheeks to bring her
back to look out of her eyes like windows. "Oh, Nana," I said.
"You're wonderful." "Ha!" she laughed. Slowly, barely, she got out
the words, "I . . . don't . . . see . . . whasso . . . wuful. . . ." But the
laugh was the same old laugh. "Well," said I, "for one thing you
have a great sense of humor." Again the words came very slowly but
this time they were very clear: "A sense of humor helps a lot in a
dreary situation."

Like those oriental pincushions with little satin figures hanging
on, Me, Inc., the would-be complete Me, whole child/whole self,
hangs on to itself for dear life. It is as if we were waves trying to
pull ourselves together, to gather ourselves up under ourselves—
and succeeding only in cutting ourselves off from everything. Me,
Inc. hangs on to this and that and to this one and that one. But
no matter what it gets its hands on and wraps itself around, it is
still simply hanging on to itself. Me, Inc.'s all we come and will
go. The great lesson and art in life is learning to let go gracefully
—at every birth, at every bedtime, at every transition. And each
time Me, Inc. lets go of something it is trying to do or wants
done or of something it has or wants to have, it lets go of a little
bit of itself. And this is when God gets a word in edgewise. And
the word is love. When Me, Inc. has come and when it is gone, I
expect we'll all be shrugging and shaking our whatever is left,
saying: *How funny that I ever fought so hard to hang on.* Because we
will have found that all the love we have been wanting so badly
and doing so hard was all the time what we were and where. Me,
Inc. struggles in vain to last forever, but the seeing being is here
for good.

Further, I say that if the soul is to know God it must forget itself and lose consciousness of itself, for as long as it is self-aware and self-conscious, it will not see or be conscious of God. But when for God's sake, it becomes unselfconscious and lets go of everything it finds itself again in God, for knowing God it therefore knows itself and everything else from which it has been cut asunder in the divine perfection.
—Meister Eckhart, trans. by R. B. Blakney

love is a place
& through this place of
love move
(with brightness of peace)
all places

yes is a world
& in this world of
yes live
(skilfully curled)
all worlds
—e. e. cummings, *Poems, 1923–1954*

Just as a blue, red, or white lotus grows in stagnant water, but rises clear and unpolluted out of it, a truth finder grows up in the world but overcomes it and is not soiled by it.
—*The Dhammapada,* trans. by P. Lal

It isn't something we can do. It is just a point we are brought to, a wonder quietly taking place—like flowers blooming on a pond while the traffic's roaring by. Our strategies are exhausted, agendas thinned, and out of desperation awareness grows and blooms into love. Drifting away is *Why should I? After all he . . .* and *Why shouldn't he? After all I. . . .* Bubbling up is *What is there to lose? What better is there for me? What is more important anyway than love?*

Like the first time we let go of poolside or parent or neck-craning dogpaddle, there comes a moment (no one else sees it) when we let go of everything we think should-be-or-else. Instead, mid-trivia, we rest, stake our very lives, on love—just being loving for goodness' sake. Does one lotus blossom get something from the other? Teach the other? Obey the other? Change for the other? No, the long stems of each run to deep roots, and it is the deep that flowers at the surface. And the whole pond is beautified. And each flower is enhanced by the presence of those nearby. And the roots run deep.

It is so very different from what we imagined. There is no thought of trade or gain. We stop gathering ourselves under ourselves and relax in the presence of infinite love-intelligence as if we already knew that it is and always has been.

And then realization is taking place. Hey, what do you know, it's true. I really don't have to struggle to keep from sinking. I don't have to rely on someone else. I am not on my own. God, love, is. In love I live and move and have my being. Love is and does my being. Loving is it. Now, wantlessly, I can be here for good, can truly love. What quiet, grateful, peaceful, pure joy.

> In thy presence is fullness of joy
> and at thy right hand are pleasures for ever more.
> —Psalm 16:11

As far as I know it doesn't happen all at once. Well, maybe all at once, but not once and for all. Over and over we come to it and it comes over us. But after reaching this point just once, it is forever after easier. From now on we notice differences. Fear and bitterness have somehow shrunk. And as often as they arise, worries subside. Loud accusations drown themselves in silent neverminds. Less gets our goat. More strikes us funny. We are more often moved by gratitude, tenderness, generosity. We are less critical, more compassionate. Less anxious. More peaceful. Forgiving? What's to forgive? We are less nervous. More assured. Sometimes inspired. And more and more we marvel. Afloat in, blooming in, love.

It doesn't happen all at once, but it always happens now and can again anynow. It may not last forever, but now we sense that there's a choice. We may not choose it often yet, but in case we're ever interested, now we know it's there and that now is the acceptable *and possible* time and that one love-intelligent moment really does lead to another.

Bon Voyage

Someone I know is going away.

I was thinking about how I don't want him to go,
and how it is sad to be left behind.

Then I found a card.
There is a beach in the foreground
with huge tracks like a land machine's
going down toward the sea.

At the end of the tracks is no land machine,
but after all a huge turtle
just heading into the sea—
the endless sea that stretches before him.

So this card calls to mind the fact that
where the land ends and the sea begins
the turtle ceases to be a grave, ungainly
plodding creature,
and becomes something graceful and free
that can go on effortlessly forever.

Inside the card said: Bon Voyage
which, it suddenly came to me,
means Good Seeing!*—*
not traveling from this place to that
and leaving anyone behind—just a Good Seeing.

He was going to sea—going to see.
And right here so am I.
And right there so are you.
And everywhere so are our children.

Beneath the greeting the card said:
(And don't forget to write).

Bon Voyage!
Good seeing good!

Index